W9-CBA-540

Madness
Rules
the
Hour

MADNESS RULES *the* HOUR

Charleston, 1860 and the Mania for War

PAUL STAROBIN

PublicAffairs
New York

Copyright © 2017 by Paul Starobin.

Published by PublicAffairs™, an imprint of Perseus Books, LLC, a subsidiary of Hachette Book Group, Inc.

All rights reserved.

Printed in the United States of America.

No part of this book may be reproduced in any manner whatsoever without written permission except in the case of brief quotations embodied in critical articles and reviews. For information, address PublicAffairs, 1290 Avenue of the Americas, New York, NY 10104.

PublicAffairs books are available at special discounts for bulk purchases in the U.S. by corporations, institutions, and other organizations. For more information, please contact the Special Markets Department at Perseus Books, 2300 Chestnut Street, Suite 200, Philadelphia, PA 19103, call (800) 810-4145, ext. 5000, or e-mail special.markets@perseusbooks.com.

Book Design by Jeff Williams

Library of Congress Cataloging-in-Publication Data

Names: Starobin, Paul, author.
Title: Madness rules the hour : Charleston, 1860 and the mania for war / Paul Starobin.
Description: First edition. | New York : PublicAffairs, [2017] | Includes bibliographical references and index.
Identifiers: LCCN 2016045923 (print) | LCCN 2016047572 (ebook) | ISBN 9781610396226 (hardcover) | ISBN 9781610396233 (e-book) | ISBN 9781610396233 (ebook)
Subjects: LCSH: Secession—South Carolina—Charleston. | Charleston (S.C.)—History.
Classification: LCC F279.C457 S63 2017 (print) | LCC F279.C457 (ebook) | DDC 975.7/915—dc23
LC record available at https://lccn.loc.gov/2016045923

First Edition

LSC-C
10 9 8 7 6 5 4 3 2

In Memory of Ruth Rosen Singer

Contents

Author's Note

To grasp prices and values in Charleston, 1860, in today's dollars, multiply by twenty-eight. A $5-a-night hotel room, back then, would cost $140 now. An annual subscription to the *Mercury*, at $10, would cost $280. A field hand sold at a slave mart for $900 would cost $25,200. Real estate valued at $25,000 would be worth about $700,000. The $360,000 in assets of a very wealthy man in Charleston—an oligarch—would be worth about $10 million. A year's cotton production by a prosperous planter of, say, 150 bales, might fetch $36,000 on the market, worth just over $1 million today.

As for pronunciation, the family name of Robert Newman Gourdin and his brother, Henry, sounds like, in the French style, Geh-dine. The surname of Andrew Gordon Magrath is pronounced, in the Scottish style, Ma-graw. Fort Moultrie is pronounced Mool-tree.

Charleston, 1860.

Adapted from Christopher Dickey, Our Man in Charleston, *and the Colton Map of Charleston, courtesy of Special Collections at the College of Charleston.* © *Avalon Travel, Perseus Books.*

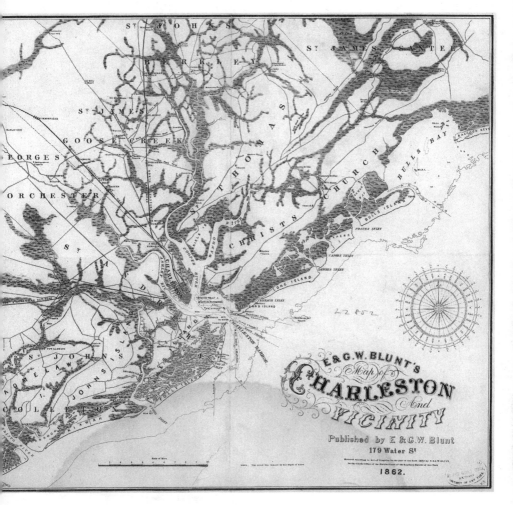

Charleston and Vicinity.

Courtesy of the Library of Congress.

TARGET

Charleston

T he note arrived in Washington on the 14th of February 1862. The war between North and South was still less than a year old. The author was Brigadier General T. W. Sherman, not to be confused with the William Tecumseh Sherman of later, war-making legend. T. W. Sherman, based at Port Royal off the South Carolina seacoast, had a question for his commanding officer in Washington, George B. McClellan, general in chief of the Union Army.

With Confederate forces pressed upon the federal capital, McClellan had much to occupy his anxious mind. The Union had won no important victories, and legions of critics wondered just when he planned to go on attack. What T. W. Sherman wanted to know was this: Should a siege be put to Savannah, the port city some thirty miles to his immediate south in Georgia? Or should he instead train his sights on South Carolina's port of Charleston, some fifty miles to his north?

A look at a map of supply routes and the concentrations of forces suggested no obvious answer. In truth, neither Savannah nor Charleston had much value in strict military terms at that time. The cities' able-bodied men had gone off to battle, leaving behind the women, the children, the elderly, and the slaves. The fighting action in the war was in Northern Virginia and in forts strung along the rivers of Tennessee. But it was not

1

for nothing that McClellan, a native of Pennsylvania and a star graduate of West Point, had acquired the nickname the "Young Napoleon." He fancied himself a grand strategist with an interest in not only the military but also the political and psychological aspects of war. For T. W. Sherman in Port Royal, McClellan had a ready answer: leave Savannah undisturbed. Its capture was not worth "the sacrifices necessary." But as for Charleston, "that is the problem I would be glad to have you study," he told his subordinate. "The greatest moral effect would be produced by the reduction of Charleston."

By "reduction," McClellan meant the levelling, or, in still plainer words, the destruction of Charleston—a city of some forty thousand inhabitants. The city was densely packed with homes, from three-story mansions stuffed with fine European art to backyard slave cottages as well as dozens of churches and a handful of synagogues, schools for children and college students, hospitals, corner groceries, outdoor market stalls, scores of saloons, numerous gambling dens and brothels, a theater, and a few large meeting halls. In theory, the job could be accomplished without a single Union soldier even planting a boot on Charleston's streets by means of the cast-iron Parrott gun, capable of firing ten-pound projectiles from a mile away. The aim might not be great from that distance, but accuracy was not particularly important when the goal was simply to hit something, anything, in the city. The blunt purpose was to induce terror through the indiscriminate nature of the assault. Perhaps a shell would hit the jail on Magazine Street, where the inmates shared quarters with the rats, or, then again, strike the Orphan House on Boundary, America's first public orphanage, where the cornerstone had been laid by President George Washington himself.

As for "the greatest moral effect," McClellan meant an object lesson—of an inspirational and gratifying message to the North and of a cold, brutal warning to the South to lay down its obstinate arms. Charleston, he believed, was fit for a singularly severe punishment—more deserving of payback than anywhere else in the traitorous South was. This, too, McClellan took pains to convey to T. W. Sherman. "There the unnatural hatred of our Government is most intense," he said. "There the rebellion had its birth."

Chapter One

—◆—

"STOMACH FOR THE FIGHT"

Monday, October 17, 1859: The news flash arrived out of Baltimore at Perry O'Bryan's American Telegraph Office on Broad Street in downtown Charleston. As always, O'Bryan's team hustled the dispatch, which they translated from Morse Code, over to the newsroom of the *Mercury* a few blocks away. The item ran in the paper's Tuesday edition, at the top of page three, in the "Latest by Telegraph" feature, dateline Baltimore. "Rumors reached this city," the report said, "of a serious insurrection at Harpers Ferry, Va. The trains were stopped, telegraph wires cut, and the town and all public works were in the possession of the insurgents. . . . All statements concur that the town is in complete possession of the insurgents, together with the Armory, the Arsenal, the Pay Offices and the bridges. The insurgents are composed of whites and blacks, supposed to be led on by abolitionists."

Rumor hardened into fact. The ringleader of the assault on Harpers Ferry was John Brown, a Connecticut-born, militant opponent of slavery who had waged bloody attacks on proslavery settlers in Kansas several years earlier. Brown was quickly captured by US Marines, who killed many of his cohorts, and within thirty-six hours, the "insurgency" was put down. The *Mercury* saw the failed revolt as a signal. "As we anticipated," the paper commented at week's end, "the affair, in its magnitude, was quite exaggerated; but it fully establishes the fact that there are at the North men ready to engage in adventures upon the peace and security of the southern people, however heinously and recklessly, and capable of planning and keeping secret their infernal designs. It is a warning profoundly symptomatic of the future of the Union with our sectional enemies."

After John Brown was on trial for treason and expecting execution, the *Mercury* also turned the episode into a political rallying cry against the North. "The great source of the evil is, that we are under one government with these people," it declared at the start of November. "If we had a separate government of our own, the post office, all the avenues of intercourse, the police and military of the country, would be under our executive control. Abolitionism would die out at the North, or its adherents would have to operate in the South as foreign emissaries, in a country armed and prepared to exclude their intercourse or arrest their designs, and punish their intervention. . . . The South must control her own destinies or perish."

The *Mercury* was the instrument of a Charleston family—a father and his eldest son. The father, Robert Barnwell Rhett—known as Barnwell Rhett, or Rhett, Sr.—put up the money to buy the paper in 1857 with cash raised by mortgaging slaves on a plantation he owned. The son, Rhett, Jr.—or Barny—was the editor in charge of the newsroom. His name was the only one to appear on the paper's masthead, at the top of page four: THE MERCURY, BY R. B. RHETT, JR.

For the Rhetts, a newspaper was a uniquely valuable tool. Despite widespread illiteracy among whites in the South, those who could not read were bound to have their views shaped and influenced by those who could. Although books, magazines, and pamphlets all mattered, nothing was as powerful as a daily newspaper (published every day except Sunday in the case of the *Mercury*) for manufacturing what the Rhetts saw as that most pliable and precious component of democracy: public opinion. "The press—the mightiest instrument of revolution in all enlightened and civilized nations," in Barnwell's estimation, was a kind of god to the Rhetts. Secession—the profound separation of the South from the North—was their message.

For admirers and detractors alike, the paper was impossible to ignore. Radical secessionists like Alabama's William Lowndes Yancey and Virginia's Edmund Ruffin found sustenance in the *Mercury*—and often enough their own speeches and articles were printed therein ("my channel of communication," Ruffin called the paper). Horace Greeley's abolitionist vessel, the *New York Tribune*, America's largest paper by circulation, had great fun ridiculing the *Mercury's* lofty sermons. Newspapers in towns large and small across the South reprinted *Mercury* articles. Members of Congress in Washington quoted from its "authority" in floor debate. In Charleston, the political and business classes debated the paper's arguably reckless zeal, and the British consul clipped pieces to send on to London. The *Mercury* had a devoted reader in Springfield, Illinois, as well, at the law offices of Lincoln & Herndon, which took a subscription at $10 per year. The senior partner, Abraham Lincoln, a former Congressman and failed candidate for the US Senate, was a ravenous consumer of newspapers. Even though he tended to believe that "all this talk about the dissolution of the Union is humbug," he kept a watchful eye on the secession movement through publications like the *Mercury*.

Many newspaper barons of the age sincerely believed the Rhetts' idea that public opinion could be crafted—however cynical that was. For the Rhetts, the great problem was that Charleston, along with the rest of the South, tended toward an alternating cycle of indignation and inertia. A collapse into torpor all too speedily followed its quick-to-rise outrage whenever the North offended Southern sensibilities. One visiting New Yorker noted that Charlestonians, "red pepperish in head," may be "radical in politics" but "seem conservative in almost everything else." A city like Charleston had innumerable pleasures high and low to distract from politics: the theater, banquets, and waltzes; outdoor concerts, sailboat regattas, and fire-engine parades; horse races, saloons, and bordellos. The Rhetts, in this unhappy state of affairs, saw their role as beaters of the drum to rouse public anger that would build and build and at last prove sustaining.

Not long after John Brown dangled at the end of a rope for his deed at Harpers Ferry, Rhett, Jr., complained to William Porcher Miles, Charleston's representative in Congress, of the reluctance of all too many leaders of the South to follow the *Mercury*'s lead toward secession. "My belief is that the weakness is with the public men of the South, who themselves 'have no stomach for the fight,'" Rhett, Jr., told Miles. "Are they men who dare attempt to *make* public opinion? Such men are statesmen," he declared. The assertion was altogether characteristic of Rhett, Jr.—belligerent and categorical, brooking no dissent. Truly, he was his father's son.

Chapter Two

"MEN, WOMEN, AND RHETTS"

For Robert Barnwell Rhett, 1860 appeared to be a last hurrah—if it was to be a hurrah at all. He would be turning sixty years old in December and had spent the balance of his adult life fighting, with no success and at times bitter defeat, for the cause of secession. Yet at the outset of the year, he felt characteristically optimistic. His spirit was buoyed by the approach of a presidential election in November. The Republican Party, an antislavery party founded in 1854, had a genuine opportunity for victory. Here was a welcome opportunity to sharpen the conflict between the sections—and the sharper the better. His election-year message was readymade: if America elects a Republican president, the South must leave the Union.

But it was never only about the cause for the senior Rhett. It also was about the power and the glory he could reap as the leader—the dominant leader, as he aspired to be—of the secession movement. If everything worked out as he dreamed, he would end his long trail of hard labors as the president of a Southern republic.

He was brought up as a country boy, born Robert Barnwell Smith in 1800 in the district of Beaufort, a rural stretch of South Carolina on the Atlantic seacoast well south of Charleston. Robert, who preferred to be called by his middle name, Barnwell, was the eighth child of an often absent and ultimately failed planter, James Smith, and his early education consisted mostly of homeschooling by his grandmother. As a young man, he attended Beaufort College, read law in the office of a private attorney in Charleston, and, with his admission to the bar, launched a law practice with a cousin. He later went on to succeed where his father had failed and established himself as a planter. There was no higher status in Charleston society. Barnwell owned several plantations in lush stretches of the Charleston hinterlands, and by 1850, his holdings had climbed to more than three hundred slaves.

Barnwell's views on race could have been taken from any standard-issue pamphlet of the time. "The history of the Negro Race is simply a page of natural history," he once wrote. "From the Great Desert to the Cape of Good Hope, the true land of the Negro, not a vestige of civilization [is] to be found." He persuaded himself that the slave was not merely "property" of the master but a kind of childlike ward or dependent with "temporal and spiritual" needs only the master could furnish. His militant views on states' rights were inspired by his hero John C. Calhoun, South Carolina's towering politician-philosopher. But his abiding belief in Southern nationalism, in unbridgeable differences between the Northern and Southern ways of life, came viscerally to him. "We are two peoples, essentially different in all that makes a people," was his credo.

Barnwell stood six feet tall and was equipped with a temperament his daughter Elise described as "nervous and mercurial." He was "quick in movement and quick-tempered," she allowed, although insisting, no doubt mindful that others might contest the point, that he was "entirely self-controlled." Politics, then, was his natural vocation. In 1826, at the age of twenty-six, he was elected to represent St. Bartholomew's Parish, a rural district outside of Charleston, in the state House of Representatives in Columbia. In no little time, he attracted attention for a strident address on an issue roiling South Carolina politics: the "Tariff of Abominations." Enacted in 1828 and nicknamed that by Southerners, the tariff further deepened the divide between the North and South. With prodding from the North, Washington had implemented a tariff on imports of manufactured wares from Europe and other foreign sources. The tax on such goods served to protect and nourish America's nascent manufacturing sector, concentrated in New England and the surrounding areas. At the same time, it enabled domestic manufacturers to charge higher prices for their goods. For the South, with an economy built not on manufactured goods but on plantations producing raw agricultural goods like cotton, the tariff was oppressive. Europe had less money to spend on Southern cotton, and Southerners were forced to pay high prices for everyday items like shoes and boots made in the North. As they saw it, they were simply lining the pockets of grasping factory owners in Massachusetts.

Barnwell, true to form, presented the tariff not as a matter of national economic policy possibly amenable to compromise but as a wedge dividing North and South and, even more, as an affront to the Constitution. After all, by what authority granted by the founders could Washington install a tax designed not simply to raise revenue for the Treasury but to favor one section of the country over another? The tariff represented "masked oppression," he told his constituents in 1828. "The day of open opposition to the pretended powers of the Constitution cannot be far off; and it is that it may not go down in blood that we now call upon you to resist."

In Charleston, the junior state representative from the countryside attracted the scorn of sophisticates who mocked his zeal and suggested he might be deranged. In a pamphlet written in a faux biblical style and published anonymously in 1832, he was lampooned as "Robert, the Disunionist," possessed by a demon: "And when Robert had said the word 'Disunion' . . . his brain became dizzy, for he had thereby invoked the evil spirit, and he was given over to the power of its enchantments . . . and he gnashed his teeth, and shouted aloud: 'Tremble not, yet men of the South; Tremble not at the word Disunion.'"

It was no secret that the pamphlet author was a young attorney in town, Christopher Gustavus Memminger, a political moderate. Barnwell took sharp exception, never forgetting and certainly not forgiving the insult. Other detractors branded him a "fire-eater"—their sneering label for orators who used incendiary rhetoric to convince Southerners to break away from the Union. Critics also focused on personal qualities that tainted their opinion of his character. He had "a vast quantity of cranks and a small proportion of common sense," an associate once said. Another described him as "vain, self-conceited, impractical and selfish in the extreme," with "his ridiculous ambition to lead and dictate in everything." That was harsh, but it was true enough: if there was a high horse available to him in a conversation, he was apt to climb on top of it. Those who only read his brash pronouncements might have thought he was apt to fortify himself with alcohol, a common vice in Charleston, but Barnwell was abstemious—completely sober in even his most outlandish utterances.

Despite the disparagements, Barnwell continued to insist on his vision. At a political convention in 1833, he asked, "Sir, if a Confederacy of the Southern States could now be obtained, should we not deem it a happy termination?" By 1837, he had ascended to the US House of Representatives, and he took his seat under the more aristocratic-sounding name of Robert Barnwell Rhett. The surname came from a distant ancestor, and his brothers also adopted the change. In Congress, his radicalism intensified. By then, he had lost most of his hair, and what remained was a scruff at the back and sides of his head, a fitting garnish to his unruly views.

A growing number of Southern politicians also believed in the need to establish an independent Southern nation, and the prevailing opinion was that slaveholding states should join together and secede as a bloc. Barnwell Rhett saw that position as a formula for endless delay and dithering because some Southern states, notably Virginia—by far the most populous state in the South and more than twice as big as South Carolina—seemed hopelessly divided on the question of secession. He argued that South Carolina should prepare to leave the Union on its own, unilaterally, with the aim of sparking a chain reaction, an infectious enthusiasm that would compel all the other Southern states to follow.

But even in South Carolina, with radical ideas in wide circulation, Barnwell Rhett was outnumbered by the so-called Cooperationists, the believers in joint action who viewed unilateral secession as an enormous and unacceptable gamble for the state. Rhett, Sr., derided the Cooperationists as "submissionists" to a Yankee-controlled Union, and in 1849 he resigned his seat in Congress. The following year, the South Carolina legislature elected him a US senator, but the people of South Carolina still were not persuaded to risk all for "separate" secession. In 1851, the Cooperationists triumphed in a hard-fought statewide election for delegates to a South Carolina convention to take up secession. Of the 42,755 votes cast, Rhett, Sr.'s, side won just over 40 percent of them.

In a letter to "My Dear Husband," Elizabeth Barnwell Rhett lashed out at all of those deemed culpable for her spouse's setback. "Has God indeed, forsaken our land?" she wrote. "After all your noble exertions, your generous self-sacrificing devotion to this ungrateful, cowardly, stupid State," she declared, the Cooperationists have "thus disregarded . . . all your warnings & entreaties that they should act like men. . . . My heart actually sickens at the prospect before us—what abject humiliation, what deep degradation is ours. . . . I think death preferable to dishonor."

Barnwell Rhett gave up his Senate seat in May of 1852. His time in Washington was over for good. Seven months later, Elizabeth died after giving birth to the couple's twelfth child. Barnwell Rhett had lost his soulmate, his vision of Southern independence remained unfulfilled, and his rivals abounded. He stopped giving speeches and withdrew from the public eye.

He was hardly, though, a beaten man. He remarried and started a new family with his second wife, Catherine, in a three-story clapboard house in a leafy part of Charleston near the Ashley River. In the front yard were cape jasmines, white flowers prized for their sweet scent, and in the backyard freestanding cottages for the house slaves. The neighborhood, typical for Charleston, mixed rich and poor alike. Chickens squawked and goats bleated in small backyard plots. Workmen toiled at grimy rice- and sawmills, and Bennett's Pond, one block from the Rhetts' home, stank of entrails dumped into the waters by butcher shops nearby. His political duties aside, Rhett, Sr., had something else to worry about: his son Barny had come home from Harvard a few years before and was still in need of a job.

———

Barny was born in Charleston in 1828, just as his father was emerging as a prominent Southern nationalist. It could not have been easy to be raised by an exacting father like Barnwell Rhett, prone to dispensing advice in the form of bromides, such as "Too much pleasure makes boys Stupid," apropos of Barny's unexceptional fondness for riding horses and shooting rabbits. His was the experience of a son always to have it "better" than the father—so of course he would be shipped off to Harvard, in the tradition of Charleston planters and merchants sending their sons to the finest colleges of the North. While in Massachusetts, Barny's politics still tracked closely with his father's. To the faculty's dismay but to the senior Rhett's approval, he had refused to attend services at a campus chapel where slavery was condemned, and he was prepared to leave college altogether should a black student ever be enrolled.

Indeed Barny did not outwardly rebel against his domineering father, but he did take his time deciding what to do with his life. At his father's urging, Barny read law and gained admission to the bar, but a law practice was not in the cards. After a brief stint as a military aide to the governor of South Carolina, he got married, finally, to a lady from Alabama and took on the life of a Charleston planter, studying tracts on "agricultural chemistry" and overseeing his own slaves as well as his father's. In this line of work, too, he had his troubles. He joked to his younger brother that he could surmount his financial problems if "one of you loafers marries a rich girl quick and lends me some money." At last, he received one more piece of advice from his father: "Write for the papers." "It will improve your style and habituate you to think on public affairs."

Ultimately the editorship of the *Mercury* unexpectedly fell to Robert, Jr., as the by-product of a duel. The irony was that dueling was one subject, maybe the only subject, on which father and son had a profound disagreement: the son refused to accept Rhett, Sr.'s, expressed belief in dueling as sinful—and although he would never say such a thing, it is possible he felt inwardly ashamed of his father for refusing to stand by fighting words with a brandished pistol. Dueling was part of the male honor code of the South.

In this case, a duel was fought in 1856 not by Barny but by his cousin, William Robinson Taber, Jr., at that time the *Mercury*'s editor. Taber faced off a Charleston federal judge's brother who sought revenge for personal attacks on the judge in the pages of the *Mercury*. The judge's true offense was being a Cooperationist with an excellent chance of being elected to Congress. As a result of the column, Barny chortled, the judge was a "gone chicken—beyond hope—dead politically." The combatants met at the horse racetrack on the edge of town. The pistols were fired three times, and on the third shot Taber lay dead.

Taber had been a co-owner of the paper. Upon his death, Rhett, Sr., stepped to purchase the paper and install his son Robert as the new editor. Yet the lesson the junior Rhett drew from this grisly episode, which garnered national headlines, assuredly was not that newspaper editors should desist from fighting words. Many years later, while involved in a libel lawsuit that threated to tar his reputation, he engaged in verbal combat with the judge assigned to the case. On being branded by the judge "a thoroughpaced blackguard" and "a deliberate and willful falsifier," Barny issued a challenge to a duel. The weapons of choice were double-barreled shotguns. The first barrel was loaded with buckshot, the other with a large ball. On the second round of firing, from a distance of forty yards, he shot the judge through the heart, fatally.

Anger, then, and a taste—perhaps even a relish—for violence were defining qualities of character in Barny. At times, he could seem angry at everyone: at bloodthirsty John Brown and the fanatic's defenders in the North; at spineless, two-faced, sugar-lipped Northern politicians who vowed to protect slavery in the Union to the letter of the Constitution but did not seem to mean it; and at fellow Charlestonians in his own backyard who seemed maddeningly obtuse, unable or unwilling to grasp the dire political stakes and urgent imperative for action. His great worry in the weeks and months after Harpers Ferry was that the alarm aroused by the raid would be wasted in pointless gestures. Early in December his *Mercury* begged the citizenry to leave the job of guarding against the threat of a slave uprising to the professional police. The focus needed to be on revolution.

As this episode showed, Barny's ire did not prevent him from having a clear-eyed grasp of the strategy and tactics of advancing the secession cause. This aspect of his nature could be seen not so much in the *Mercury*, which he generally wielded as a bludgeon, but in his nuanced private correspondence with savvy men of politics like his friend William Porcher Miles, also a radical on the secession question. Barny did not possess his father's gift for theatrical speechmaking, but, unlike the senior Rhett, he was adept at building alliances with like-minded men in Charleston and across the South.

And he was capable of a laugh at his expense. When the editor of a Florida paper wrote up a caricature of him as a sort of monster bestride a commercial thoroughfare of Charleston, he good-naturedly reprinted the sketch for the *Mercury's* readers to savor: "We doubt not that many persons South, as well as North, have formed an idea that the editor of the *Mercury* is a sort of Captain Kidd, or Blue Beard, or gigantic Ogre, whose supreme delight consists in treason, stratagem and spoils. . . . According to some people's ideas—particularly the Union-saving portion, we suppose Mr. Rhett must stand at least 7 feet 11½ in his shoes, with a head the size of a Georgia pumpkin . . . blood-shot eyes . . . claws, of course, adorn his digits, and that tail of his, as he stalks along King Street, belching forth sulphurous flames."

The *Mercury's* editor in real life stood five feet, nine inches tall, ceding three inches to his father. He was slight of build, at 140 pounds, and he had a cocksure look about him, with a luxuriant handlebar mustache, bushy muttonchops running the length of his cheeks, and a full head of slicked-down, neatly parted hair. Business attire was a full-frock coat and a white-collar shirt with a cravat of black silk tied in a flat horizontal bow. A small cross dangled from a chain fastened to his vest. Such was the Ogre.

———

The *Mercury* came out first thing in the morning, with a deadline that could run past midnight for important breaking news and a press run that typically started at 3:30 a.m. At just about any time of the day or evening, Rhett, Jr., could be found at the paper's offices at 4 Broad Street in the heart of downtown Charleston—just one block south of the slave-trading district centered on Chalmers Street. The trade was conducted largely out of walk-in parlors like Ryan's Mart, named for the city council-man who had founded the establishment. Ryan's included a holding pen for slaves pending sale and a morgue for those who had died from disease or exhaustion before making it to auction. The *Mercury* made money on classified advertisements for the slave trade.

From his command post, Rhett, Jr., presided over an operation that included correspondents in New Orleans, Washington, New York, London, Key West, and Havana. The *Mercury* was not only about sectional politics and the Southern resistance movement. It supplied readers the time and place for the day's meetings of charitable societies and militias; the prices of watermelon, shrimp, and sweet potatoes in the local market and cotton bales on the exchanges; the crime report; steamer shipping schedules; and dispatches on the fashion scene in New York. Its doors were open to townspeople eager to display their achievements—like the giant cauliflower, a spectacular twenty-three inches across the head, shown off by a proud visitor to the office. Barny often placed a poem on page four, just below his name—as often a piece on politics as a sentimental ode to nature. Charlestonians were urged to read newly published novels like *Adam Bede,* the first offering of George Eliot, adept at "picturesque development and fine characterization," for pleasure and moral uplift.

This sort of fare also could be found in the *Courier,* Charleston's other daily. The *Courier,* though, was of a mild disposition on national and Southern politics. It was without a discernable agenda to press, absent the spark that could be found in virtually every edition of the *Mercury.* In a sense, the *Mercury* was a pamphlet disguised as a newspaper. Like the most effective of pamphlets, the *Mercury* had a register, a variation of tone that could range from high dungeon to withering sarcasm. The point, always, was to keep the reader emotionally engaged. This was how "public opinion" was made, and Rhett, Jr., just shy of thirty years old when he took the helm, proved to have an adept feel for how to excite his audience. He was akin to the conductor of an orchestra, the junior editors and the reporters and typesetters assembled below faithful to his direction—or so he believed.

One of his most effective tactics was to bait readers with material reprinted from the *New York Tribune* that he knew they would find outrageous. The *Tribune*'s usual dig was to spoof Charleston as "all talk, no action" on secession. So it was when a *Tribune* scribe, at the end of 1859, reported on the annual dinner of the New England Society of Charleston, a benevolent association for "gentlemen" of the city who were natives of that region. The *Tribune* man found that "the gloom of Destiny hung over the banquet," made evident by toasts to the South as "the foundation of a great and self-sustaining empire." And, "The Union, we need not say, was the *piece de resistance,* a chief dish, of the occasion. It was carved like a dish fit for the gods. Everybody stuck his knife into it. It was made minced meat of. It may be regarded as slaughtered, roasted, hashed, devoured, and forever dispatched." Rhett, Jr., printed the item on page four, under his name. "This editorial is from the pen of a brilliant writer, whose special department in the *Tribune* is to satirize and ridicule the South in every shape and form," he wrote, just in case anyone missed the point.

However his *Mercury* would lecture readers, the South was in some ways deserving of this ridicule. A staple theme was the humiliating dependence of the South on Northern manufacturers of all types. Even a church built in Charleston was apt to have its doors, windows, and even pulpit made to order in the North, the *Mercury* claimed. "We thus starve our own artisan-laborers and send our money away to strengthen, enrich and fatten those who are ready to draw the sword of extermination on us." Worrisome national population trends were another *Mercury* staple. In 1850, there were some 13.5 million Northerners to 9.6 million Southerners, and the gap was steadily widening, with the North growing at nearly twice the rate of the South. Cities like New York, Boston, and bustling Cincinnati were several times larger than Charleston and still rapidly expanding, whereas the population of Charleston, at 40,522 in 1860 (23,376 whites, 13,909 slaves, and 3,237 free persons of color) had plateaued. Indeed, the South Carolina city now had considerably fewer people than both Baltimore and New Orleans. Charleston, a visitor from Maine snorted, was a "little, antique commercial metropolis." Barny printed that comment on his front page. Because of the population disparities, he pointed out, the slave states were expected to have eighty-two fewer representatives in the U.S. Congress than the free states. Thus overwhelmed, the *Mercury* cried, how could the South sit still? "So long as the Union lasts," a predecessor of Barny once said, "Charleston and Savannah will be mere suburbs of New York and Boston." The South and Charleston could be conquered not by force of arms but by demography. That stark fact was all the more reason to get on with secession.

Short of leaving Charleston altogether, Barny could not escape his father's large and imposing shadow. So much in his life—his Harvard education, the editorship of the *Mercury*—had come to him through his formidable, omnipresent parent. In 1860, Rhett, Sr., would indeed return to the public stage to make his first speech in eight years. There he warned of the Republican threat to the Southern way of life and bade the citizenry to prepare for secession. Even in his old age, he was energetic and fit—ready to lead them to independence. His only stubborn ailment was a highly unattractive pimple on the right side of his nose. On a trip to Paris, he had consulted a doctor who told him it was an ordinary lesion, nothing to worry about.

In 1860, his son would be turning thirty-two years old. Even if Barny was something of a late starter in life, unsure of how he could make his mark, the revolution he hoped to enact afforded an opportunity for anyone of talent and drive. In a time of turbulence—uncongenial to cautious temperaments—Barny's recklessness of spirit could be his most valuable asset. Even to a female relative, the Rhett clan could seem like a law unto themselves: "The world, you know, is composed of men, women, and Rhetts."

Chapter Three

"I MISTRUST OUR OWN PEOPLE"

For the best view of Charleston, a newcomer was advised to climb the steeple of St. Michael's Episcopal Church at the southeast corner of the intersection of Broad and Meeting Streets. From this vantage point, the city showed itself to be a smallish-size, blue-water-bound, densely built up, flat peninsula of land. Or, as occurred to a traveler from Massachusetts, Charleston spread out like a fan, bordered on the west by the Ashley River and on the east by the Cooper. The two wide rivers met at the base of the fan, the southernmost part of the city, known as the Battery, and spilled into the harbor. The open Atlantic Ocean was in the distance. The Battery, named for earthworks constructed there during the Revolutionary War, was Charleston's place to be seen and admired. Ladies dressed in the latest fashions from New York or Paris might be spied strolling along the promenade with their gentlemen or ambling by in horse-drawn carriages steered by liveried drivers. A visitor would be apt to notice that many of Charleston's houses were set at right angles to the street—perpendicular—allowing the porches to get a seaside breeze from the south. In springtime, the view from the steeple was a riot of color: the deep purple, golden yellow, creamy white, and flaming red of high-walled, private-home gardens, blossoming with jessamine, wisteria, Cherokee rose, and azalea and alive with hummingbirds. A blue sky, sunlight glinting off the waters, sailboats in the harbor—all of this allowed Charleston to claim to be the most beautiful city of the South and perhaps in America. Many visitors, including those from the North, were disposed to agree.

From this lofty perch, with the aid of a spyglass, nearly everything that mattered to the political geography of Charleston, 1860, could be seen. On St. Michael's Alley just behind the church was the law office of James Louis Petigru. His home was several blocks down Broad toward the Ashley. Petigru, a vestryman at St. Michael's, was an esteemed town elder and Charleston's liveliest wit, possessed of the gift of an unblinking eye. The city not infrequently exasperated him, but this was a lover's quarrel, as he cared deeply for Charleston and its people. He was the boyhood tutor of Rhett, Sr., and one of the man's few defenders in town, but their political views could not have been more different. Petigru was an outspoken Unionist with a caustic disregard for the secessionist cause, which he viewed as overheated and captive to a "narrow patriotism." Cool reason, he believed, was needed to subdue zeal. As the radicals rightly feared, there remained a reservoir of tender feelings for the Union in Charleston—and Petigru was the sharpest, most visible exponent of the sentiment.

A brisk ten minutes' walk west from St. Michael's was the home of Christopher Memminger, the archrival of Barnwell Rhett. He no longer outright ridiculed "Robert, the Disunionist" as he did decades earlier, but as a leading member of the South Carolina House of Representatives, he was among the most powerful of the state's camp of Cooperationists. Less bold than his rival but far superior in intellect, he thought deeply and constantly on what it took to preserve civic order in Charleston. He had unwavering support for free blacks as a stabilizing buffer class and an opposition to breaking up families in slave auctions. For mid-January he was planning a trip to Richmond to try to persuade Virginia's political elite to agree to a conference of Southern states to consider "measures for united action." Barny and his father, convinced as ever that "cooperation" was a barren path, prayed for his failure.

A short block up from the church, on cobblestoned Chalmers Street, in the heart of the slave-trading district and a block north of the *Mercury*'s offices, was the federal courthouse. There presided a man of large but thwarted ambition, Judge Andrew Gordon Magrath. There was bad blood between the Rhetts and the Magraths, one of Charleston's great feuds: Magrath had been the target of the vicious *Mercury* column four years earlier that had prompted the former editor's duel with his brother. The event obliterated his hope to fill the seat representing Charleston in the US Congress. Underneath his black robe was a heart that beat with passion for the South. He had a reputation for taking politically charged cases and deciding them with obvious favor to his native section and its "rights." He was well versed in the case against slavery from his studies at Harvard Law School and rejected every part of it. But he was still a Cooperationist. He had not joined hands with the radicals in the camp of the Rhetts, and to do so, as a federally appointed magistrate, surely would have been seen as treason in Washington.

As the son of an Irish immigrant, Magrath had a base of political support in the outer neighborhood of Charleston known as the Neck. This section of town, well north of St. Michael's, contained factories and railroad yards, mansions of rich gentry, and slums teeming with white workingmen and their families, many fresh from Ireland. Few of these men owned slaves, and their great issue was not the Union's oppression of the South but the need for a decent-paying job. Their resentment focused on free blacks performing work the workmen thought belonged exclusively to them. They wanted slaves to remain slaves.

The same could be said of the pastors of Charleston's dozens of churches. The men of the cloth habitually railed against lust and drunkenness, greed and sloth, but virtually never against the brutal ownership of captive human beings. Indeed, some were slave owners themselves. At the same time, they were reluctant to get directly involved in politics. The delicate balance between religion and politics could be seen in the dean of the Charleston clergy, the Reverend John Bachman of St. John's Lutheran Church on Archdale Street, a few minutes' walk from St. Michael's. Born into a German family in upstate New York, Rev. Bachman enjoyed great standing with Charleston's large community of immigrants from lands like Saxony and Bavaria. He was a renowned naturalist, a collaborator with John Jay Audubon, but his adamant defense of slavery strained ties with his Northern comrades in science. Excitable by nature, he violently loathed the abolitionists, many of whom were ministers, but had managed to keep his feelings confined to private exchanges with like-minded friends.

Several blocks to the rear of St. Michael's, at the foot of Meeting, by the Battery, was the home of the Gourdin brothers. Both lifelong bachelors, they were among Charleston's most prominent merchants. Robert, the younger of the two, was an ardent secessionist who had craved Southern independence just about all of his adult life yet doubted his dream ever would be fulfilled. His brother did not share his enthusiasm. But Robert had a far-flung network of sympathetic friends, men like Representative Miles and D. H. Hamilton, the US marshal in Charleston and a secret secessionist. Hamilton believed that faced with the option of "abolition or war," ordinary Southerners were apt to quail at war: "I mistrust our own people more than I fear all of the efforts of the Abolitionists," he said. Robert was not quite so pessimistic, and the question he often asked himself in his seemingly perpetual angst was what he could do, personally, to realize his vision.

He understood how hard that task would be, for even his planter friends tended to be skeptical of the cause. Few among them were radicals; most still believed secession had to be done collectively by the slave states. Their plantations ran to the north and south of Charleston, most too far away to be glimpsed from St. Michael's. The masters of these estates typically had second homes in Charleston, and they were intimately involved in the city's and state's politics.

By 1860 the question of secession was also talked about endlessly over glasses of madeira in the parlors of Charleston's finest homes. It tended to be a conversation both earnest and abstract, unmindful of realities like the US Army garrison stationed at Fort Moultrie by the harbor and armed with cannon. In the end the issue stood to be settled by "the people" so distrusted by D. H. Hamilton—the throngs that filled the churches; paraded through the streets in militia regiments and brass bands; manned the firehouses; tended the bakeries and pubs, the clothing shops and cigar stores; and gathered at fairgrounds, assembly halls, and the theater for Shakespeare and magic and minstrel shows. Nowhere could their voices be heard in greater volume than at Institute Hall, two-and-a-half blocks up from St. Michael's on Meeting. It was one of the largest indoor public gathering places in the South, capable of jamming together some three thousand souls.

In April Charleston would be hosting the Democratic National Convention. Delegates from every state in the Union, including the entire party establishment, would be assembling at Institute Hall to pick the party's nominee to go up against the Republican candidate in November. Familiar with the town's reputation for belligerence, some Northern Democrats worried of the threat of "personal violence" at the proceedings. They were right to be concerned. Even though the Democratic Party was generally committed to the protection of slavery, the radicals on secession thought their cause might be advanced with the ascension of a Republican to the White House. They believed the upcoming convention might be an opportunity to keep Democrats from uniting and force the people of the South to choose, finally, between the promise of an independent, slavery-upholding republic and the continued pain of existence in a Union on the march to abolition. It was a formula that depended on wreaking havoc in Charleston.

Charleston would be in the national spotlight in 1860, and for impatient secessionists across the South, from Virginia to Mississippi, the city was the great hope. No town better embodied the combative and combustible spirit of the region—not Richmond or Savannah, not Montgomery or New Orleans. But for Charleston to fulfill its promise to make history by lighting the fuse that at last blew up the Union, the town had to come together to find the transcendent unity of purpose and determination that had always eluded it.

———

If he could look past this picturesque and seemingly placid panorama from St. Michael's steeple—the flower gardens and the sailboats and the oddly aligned homes—a discerning viewer might notice a less charming aspect of the city, which would be unmistakable once his feet were back on ground. There were constant patrols of dark-blue uniformed police armed with swords and pistols, some mounted on horseback, everywhere, at all hours of the day and night, as if trouble might be expected at any moment. And indeed that was the case. City authorities might be inattentive to the foul refuse of Bennett's Pond or to the horse manure that piled up on the streets, but they were ever alive to the whiff of unrest. A drumbeat began at ten minutes to nine every night, the signal by the police force for every person of color to get off the streets and get home by the stroke of the hour. Invariably, cheeky young boys baited the patrolmen with a favorite game. "Buzzard!" they would shout in the face of their would-be captors before retreating to Charleston's warren of backstreets, alleys, and footways. It was their fun to liken the police to the city's most famous bird, especially abundant at the market district a few blocks up from the *Mercury*. The boys danced, they turned somersaults, and they usually eluded the slower-footed patrolmen, sometimes with a leg up and over a garden wall, perhaps snatching from a tree a peach or an apricot, a fig or a pomegranate, as they scampered away. But the police would always nab some people too tired or perhaps too tipsy to make curfew, and these folks would be taken to the Guard House at Broad and Meeting, across the street from St. Michael's, to be detained until morning. The punishment for violation of the curfew was a flogging—which accounted for the "cries and shrieks" that might be heard in the still night air of Charleston. A visitor from Britain once asked a city guard the reason for security measures that seemed suited for wartime. For "keeping down the niggers," came the reply.

Chapter Four

"PROWLING ABOUT US"

Bitter cold and an icy rain greeted the New Year of 1860. Charlestonians shivered awake to find the milk congealed and the water frozen in pantry jugs. Carriages skidded along rutted roads, and steamships shuddered across the harbor. On January 3, male citizens of St. John's Berkley, a wealthy planters' district just north of Charleston along the Cooper, trudged into Black Oak Church for a public meeting. Black Oak, an Episcopalian church, was the most prominent house of worship in St. John's Berkley and was attended not only by English but also French Huguenot and Scottish old-line families of the district. This was a group that prided itself on its learning and cultural refinement. Among those present on this occasion was Henry William Ravenel, a planter and a botanist of some repute, known for his devoted study of mushrooms.

The meeting began with a declaration of its purpose: "concert of action and strict vigilance for the protection of our property and our institutions against the increasing encroachments of our northern enemies, who are prowling about us in every imaginable device and garb." With that, the assembly moved to break into committees to craft a response. The result was a set of resolutions denouncing the current security forces in the area with a preamble that read, "Whereas . . . we deem the present police system of our Parishes insufficient for the exigencies of the times . . . " It was a slap not only to the police but to civic leaders like Rhett, Jr., who pled for the citizenry to leave law enforcement in the hands of professionals. By deeming the police "insufficient," members of the planter class announced that they were not so easily instructed as that.

John Brown's raid at Harpers Ferry—indicated by the oblique reference to "the exigencies of the times"—was nearly three months past, but still such fear abided that, as a letter writer to the *Mercury* wrote, "our negroes are constantly tempted to cut our throats." And the fear of the slave owner was not only for his family's skin but for his wallet as well. Insurance policies on his chattel, such as written by the Charleston Southern Mutual Life Insurance Company, typically would not pay out "in the consequence of . . . an insurrection."

The preamble went on to call particular attention to "emissaries" of the "Abolition party" of the North, meaning the Republicans, who "come among us in various disguises and under manifold pretexts. They combine the subtlety with the wickedness of the serpent." So it might be that "the school-master, warmly welcomed to the family hearth, and the book or map agent, hospitably entertained, may leave the germ of insubordination and insurrection among the domestics." As for a specific example of a schoolmaster or book or map agent found out to be a secret agent of abolitionism, none was offered.

The recommended resolutions called for the citizens of St. John's Berkley to organize into a Vigilance Association to be divided into five beats. Each of the standing beat committees would be "vested with power to enforce whatever Police regulations may, in their opinion, be deemed advisable or necessary." As for the possibility that innocent people might get caught by this dragnet, "if indiscretions or unnecessary violence has been, or should be committed against a few unoffending Northerners, they had to look to their homes for the cause, the South acting on one of the first laws of nature—self-protection." The resolutions were debated and adopted with nearly unanimous support.

In Charleston proper, the popular demand for vigilance likewise took the form of a new, citizen-run Committee of Safety, with branches in the city wards and a mandate to "ferret out and hand over all guilty and suspected persons to the proper authorities for examination and punishment." Notwithstanding the protest of Mayor Charles Macbeth that the committee intruded on the proper procedure of law or the *Mercury*'s worry that "irresponsible and disorganized bodies" could do injustice to innocents, the committee assumed a wide-ranging set of investigative tasks, from keeping an eye on Northern salesmen in town to reviewing possibly subversive books and newspapers read by blacks. The committee was to look into Negroes congregating illegally in grog shops serving alcohol and was even to ask "as to whether strangers ought not to be prevented from publicly expressing their peculiar opinions." In a note sent to London, the British consul in Charleston—a secret admirer of John Brown—likened the Committee of Safety to the *Comite de Salut Publique,* the tribunal of the French Revolution that had near dictatorial powers during the Reign of Terror.

That was not quite right: Charleston's Committee of Safety had more limited powers. Still, a full-blown panic unquestionably was under way. The enemy was a specter: there was no large-scale abolitionist invasion of Charleston or neighboring districts after Harpers Ferry. Still, even the irrational tends to follow a kind of logic. A familiar pattern was reasserting itself: a perceived threat to the established slave order, a frantic counterreaction, and the prospect of mob "justice."

———

"Negroes are to this country what raw materials are to another country," the Charleston planter Charles Cotesworth Pinckney—an aide to George Washington during the Revolutionary War who served as a delegate to the Constitutional Convention at Philadelphia in 1787—once said. To protect their investment, Charleston's representatives at that conclave had insisted "some provision should be included in favor of property in slaves." The result was the fugitive-slave clause in Article IV, Section 2: "No person held to Service or Labour in one State . . . escaping into another . . . but shall be delivered up on Claim of the Party to whom such Service or Labour may be due." The provision meant that a Charleston slave in flight to Boston had to be sent back to his or her owner in Charleston. With slavery as old as Charleston, founded in 1670, this clause was sacred writ. South Carolina ratified the Constitution at a convention of elected delegates gathered at the newly built Customs House, at the end of Broad Street by the Cooper River, in the spring of 1788.

Charleston had so many slaves that a visiting Scotsman said the town might be mistaken for "solely a black settlement." The fear of a slave uprising, ever present in the city's psychology, had a rational grounding. In 1860, many men and women of the Charleston gentry were old enough to remember the Vesey rebellion of thirty-eight years earlier—the most comprehensive attempt at revolt in the city's history. Denmark Vesey was a former slave who had won his freedom in a lottery and worked as a carpenter. He could read and paid close attention to the creation of the Republic of Haiti by slaves in a bloody uprising against their French colonial masters. He took to heart his bible and especially its tale of how the Jews, as slaves in Egypt, fought for their deliverance and obtained it with God's own hand. Why not in Charleston? And so he began plotting.

The scheme, though, was betrayed by a household slave who confessed to his master. Vesey was captured, tried, and sentenced to death. In the end, thirty-five people were convicted of conspiracy and executed, twenty-two of them in a mass hanging and several by pistol when the noose failed to work. White Charleston was inflamed, imaginations feverishly at work. With the last of the executions performed, the chief prosecutor noted, "There can be no harm in the salutary inculcation of one lesson, among a certain portion of our population, that there is nothing they are bad enough to do, that we are not powerful enough to punish." The state then established near the center of Charleston an academy known as the Citadel to train and equip a specialized cadre of teenage boys, mostly from the countryside, to guard against and, if need be, put down a future slave uprising.

Three days after the hangings, a Charleston widow wrote to her sister in Philadelphia, "Ah! Slavery is a hard business, and I am afraid that in this country we shall know it to our bitter cost some day or other."

Panic, then, was familiar to white Charleston, and there seemed to be no brake in the civic mechanism to stop it. Harpers Ferry seemed to unmoor the Reverend John Bachman of St. John's Lutheran, who was entering his seventieth year with a full head of white hair. The abolitionists will "rob and plunder and bully us in the Union until they [have] their feet on our necks and their daggers in our throats," Rev. Bachman wrote shortly after the start of the New Year to his friend from Virginia, the secessionist Edmund Ruffin. That sounded like an endorsement for secession—but still, this was not a subject on which Bachman expressed himself at the pulpit. "My religion bids me forgive," Rev. Bachman confided to Ruffin on the matter of abolitionists, but "God help me I would rather have them hanged first and forgive them afterwards." So spoke this native of New York who had once met Charles Darwin and accompanied Audubon on outings to the Lowcountry in pursuit of South Carolina's native birds.

For the radicals, the hopeful news was that Harpers Ferry was stirring not just a familiar panic but renewed thoughts of secession. "You are aware that I have always been a great lover of the Union, and have clung to it, with a sincere devotion," James McCarter, a Charleston bookseller, wrote to Rep. Miles in mid-January. "And even now," McCarter continued, "I do not give up any hope that some fortunate person may find out some way of escape from the evils of dissolution! But my fears are now greatly in advance of my hopes."

Chapter Five

"THE CHARLESTON BOY"

On a Wednesday, the 11th of January, two days after his fifty-seventh birthday, Christopher Memminger set out from Charleston, bound for Richmond by overnight train. His fifteen-year-old daughter, Lucy, sat beside him. They made for an agreeable pair. Lucy, though not yet a debutante, was accomplished in the social graces and comfortable engaging in conversation with people three and four times her age. In Richmond she could look forward to a procession of parties held in her father's honor. He was a handsome, distinguished-looking man. His steely gray hair tumbled just over his ears, and he had a prominent nose and deeply set, mild, bluish-grey eyes. He was somewhat stiff and formal in bearing, not one for idle chatter, and at times frosty to the point of being curt. His truly distinctive quality, though, could be seen in those eyes, "at perfect rest when he was speaking to you," a friend once said.

Memminger had the gift of composure. Nervous excitement seemed foreign to his being, and he was not known to lose himself in anger. In his calm manner, he was the temperamental opposite of all that Charleston, justly, was thought to be—excitable and quick to take umbrage, the qualities that made the city an incubator for firebrands like the Rhetts. "Red pepperish in head" he was not. And yet Memminger was thoroughly of Charleston, an integral and esteemed member of its elite.

The idea had been his to go to Virginia to persuade its leading politicians to join with South Carolina and all of the slave states in securing a "common defense" in the wake of Harpers Ferry. He would request that Virginia participate in a conference of the Southern states to consider a plan of united action—to go as far, hard-liners hoped, as departing from the Union in a bloc. His fellow legislators in Columbia blessed this initiative, as did the governor, and so he was off to the Old Dominion as a kind of ambassador, South Carolina's "special commissioner" to Virginia. Yet radical secessionists feared Memminger's efforts would only delay—or worse, smother—the revolution they were seeking. That might have suited Memminger fine, for he abhorred the idea of revolt.

Christopher Memminger was born in 1803 in the duchy of Wurttemberg in southwestern Germany. His father, a quartermaster in a rifleman's battalion of a prince, was killed on duty just five weeks after Christopher's birth. It was the time of the Napoleonic Wars in Europe, and the continent was in a seemingly permanent state of upheaval, with large tracts in ruins. Like many others, Christopher's mother and grandparents left their home in Wurttemberg in search of a better life, or at least a refuge, in America. Yet shortly after their arrival, his mother died, and just after his fourth birthday, Christopher's grandmother deposited him in the Orphan's House on Boundary Street. He was to spend the next seven years of his life there, under the care of the matrons.

He could have landed in a much worse place. Charleston's civic elite took pride in its orphanage, seeing it as a place not simply to warehouse the waifs and keep them from starving but to tend to the education of their minds, spirits, and bodies. Success might be for the child to learn a trade and gain an apprenticeship with an artisan. Rarely did a child leave the Orphan House on a track to enter the gentry, but Christopher was that child. Alexander Hamilton–like, here was one who might rise up. He attracted the eye of a wealthy commissioner of the institution, Thomas Bennett, who made Christopher a foster son and welcomed him to the Bennett family at the age of eleven. A man of political and business prominence in Charleston—a state representative, a banker, an architect, and an operator of lumber and rice mills—his new father was in a position to ensure Christopher's future.

At the age of twelve, Christopher's father and tutors took the measure of his gifted mind and found him ready for South Carolina College in Columbia. His classmates, all of whom were at least several years older, were astonished to find him in their midst. "You would have thought him to have been one of the children of Columbia who had wandered into the campus," a fellow student recalled. Yet the judgment soon enough became that the "Charleston boy," as he was called, belonged there. If Christopher found it terrifying to be cast into these novel and intimidating surroundings or felt homesick for Charleston, he did not show it. He displayed a quality of dutifulness—never late with his work, always in attendance at chapel services, ever in accord with the rules of the college. "There were others in our class who were thought to possess more brilliant intellects, but none who were more earnest in their labors or more direct in their methods," a classmate recalled. Proficient in algebra and English grammar, at the study of Virgil's *Aeneid* in Latin and the Gospel of St. John in Greek, he graduated second in his class. To the senior class, at the age of sixteen, he delivered an oration on the "Influence of Popular Opinion," characteristically stern in tone. "So accustomed is the human mind to the pursuit of vice, that none but the most powerful inducements can stop its impetuous career," he warned.

On Christopher's return to Charleston, Bennett again smoothed his way. Christopher was immersed in his legal studies at the age of nineteen in 1822 when the Vesey plot for a slave rebellion was discovered. He had an intimate view of the effort to squelch the uprising because his foster father, at this time, was serving as the governor of South Carolina. Two of Bennett's own slaves were put to death as leaders of the supposed conspiracy. Bennett himself believed the threat had been exaggerated, as "the public mind had been raised to a pitch of excitement" over rumors of a revolt. The lesson Christopher drew from this experience was not, as some in the gentry felt, that the free blacks had to be obliterated as a class to eliminate their subversive potential. Rather, he arrived at his deeply held conviction that free persons of color, despite this episode, were part of the glue that held Charleston together—and in the years to come he established himself as their foremost advocate in Charleston. He did not see the city, as some did, as ever on the brink of a rebellion.

As he became a pillar of the Charleston elite in his own right—solicitor to a bank, a city councilman, head of the school board, a state representative, a director of the Charleston Gas Company, an officer of the Carolina Art Association—Christopher developed a sophisticated idea of how to promote civic order. The point was not to preserve the town in amber, to keep things as they always were. Reforms, carefully applied, could accommodate change and position Charleston for the future. His hero was the planter-philosopher Thomas Jefferson, a fellow man of the Enlightenment. At dinner parties at his home on the corner of Wentworth and Smith, guests including the Reverend John Bachman chewed over elevated topics like the "social systems most conducive to human happiness." He married the daughter of a physician and practiced the Episcopalian faith of the Bennett family while accumulating a small fortune from his law practice. He was active in church councils, and his piety was such that he was well known not to work on Sundays. He owned fifteen slaves.

Christopher's initial perspective on the Union was akin to his view of Charleston as a mosaic that must accommodate stresses and strains. One Revolution was enough. If the republic was good enough for a slaveholder like Jefferson, it was good enough for him. He looked for ways to tie North and South together and specifically to hitch Charleston to the rest of industrializing, modernizing America. He created the city's first public school system to cultivate an industrial working class, and he was an advocate for building a railroad line through the Blue Ridge Mountains to link Charleston to the Ohio and Mississippi River valleys. He did not think the Union could be easily sundered; he thought secession might well mean war, with the Carolina Lowcountry wide open to attack.

Christopher's antirevolutionary mind-set made him a natural antagonist to men like Barnwell Rhett, with his muscular form of Southern nationalism. But as the secessionist urge in South Carolina persisted, Christopher sought not to try to block secession outright but to show how the radical idea of "separate secession" was fatally flawed. He penned a treatise arguing that if one State seceded alone, then "patronage and power" would tend to accumulate in the legislative and executive branches of the state because a "consolidated government" would be responsible for both domestic and foreign policy. As a result, the citizens of a new Republic of

South Carolina in time would have the same complaint against overweening government as South Carolinians presently had against Washington.
The "check" between states and the federal government, so wisely put in
place by the founders, would be gone and liberty at risk.

This was his stance at the outset of the 1850s, and it remained his position throughout the decade. No one in Charleston, and perhaps in all
of South Carolina, was as rooted in the moderate ground on secession
as Christopher. And his views were well known in the political class
throughout the South, including Virginia, a state chronically ambivalent
on the question of secession. He and Lucy arrived in Richmond early in
the evening of Thursday, January 12, and were met at Union Station by a
delegation of legislators who anointed Christopher a "guest of the State"
and provided an escort to the Ballard House, a five-story hotel built in
the Italian style. Certainly Virginians were glad for his arrival if only because he was understood not to be among the "many fire-eaters" of his
homeland, as a correspondent for a Petersburg paper wrote. Memminger
is "mild as a lamb, meek as a Christian, which he really is, and would
sooner pour oil on the troubled waters than add fuel to the flame," the
reporter said.

Dovish Virginians pressed on Memminger ideas that would fall far
short of secession, such as a united Southern action to cut off trade with
the North and thereby induce Yankee capitalists to use their influence
to pressure the Republican Party to back off its antislavery crusade. At
the same time, he faced demands from the Charleston radicals to accept
nothing less than Virginia's acquiescence to a path leading to the establishment of a Southern confederacy. "The South can never know peace
and security again in the Union," William Porcher Miles told him in a
letter. His own view was equivocal; he still thought it possible, he wrote
Miles, that "new terms, fresh constitutional guarantees" might preserve
the Union. A conference of Southern states could conceivably demand
a national constitutional convention, Philadelphia-like, at which a new
generation of "founders" could craft a pact that would grant permanent
safety to the South's slave institution.

But how to get Virginia to agree even to the idea of a conference?
Christopher did have one good card to play—what might be called the

"just dare us" card. If Virginia refused to sit down with the other slave states to devise a joint plan of action, then impulsive, hotheaded South Carolina might just leave the Union on her own, no matter the chaos to follow. Virginia's former governor raised just this concern, warning that if the Southern states would not get together to confer, then South Carolina "would go on, act alone, and drag them along" in her wake. "Probably a true prophecy," Christopher agreed in his clipped way.

Seven days after Christopher's arrival in Richmond, the sitting governor invited him to speak to the General Assembly, made up of the House of Delegates and the Senate. A military escort guided father and daughter from the Ballard to the Capitol Building, and their route was lined with cheering, flag-waving spectators. Ladies packed the galleries inside the hall. Memminger spoke for nearly four hours, paying homage to Virginia in every conceivable fashion—her "hallow" soil the resting place of George Washington, of Patrick Henry, of Jefferson, of Madison. He expressed sympathy for Harpers Ferry, "the attempt to involve her in the horrors of servile and civil war." Today, he said, "we have before us the North and the South, standing face to face, not yet as avowed and open enemies, but with deep-seated feelings of enmity rankling in their bosoms." As these feelings would not abate and as no Southern state could escape the conflict, "shall we act in concert? That is the great question." He assured the audience that secession need not be the foregone result of a Southern conference—and that even admittedly impatient South Carolina would be "willing to respect and abide by the united judgement of the whole. If our pace be too fast for some, we are content to walk slower."

Ten thousand copies of his peroration were printed for distribution to the people of Virginia. But the state could not be flattered, or frightened, into decision. The people and the politicians could not make up their minds on a course of action, and Virginia could not bring itself to commit to a conference that might lead to secession. It could not commit to anything at all, it seemed. Christopher and Lucy cooled their heels for three weeks. On the 7th of February, with the state still mute, he told the governor he was going back to Charleston: "Dear Sir . . . Having discharged the duties of my mission . . . I have been waiting in expectation of bearing back the answer of the General Assembly. But as that honorable body is not yet prepared to respond, and may desire still further time for deliberation, I have concluded to return home."

"What a farce Memminger's expedition to Virginia has ended in," US marshal Hamilton told Miles. "Nothing has come of it—he who possesses neither moral nor physical courage is but a poor advisor; and we who know him best are aware of his sad short-comings." Rhett, Jr., though, saw the bright side: at least South Carolina could not be accused of failing to make an honest effort to bring Virginia into the secessionist fold. The Cotton States of Mississippi, Alabama, and South Carolina on their own could seize the initiative on secession. "The election of a Black Republican"—an abolitionist—would be "quite enough," Barny told Miles, "to dissolve the Union." And if Mississippi and Alabama hesitated, South Carolina still reserved the option to act on its own.

The *Mercury*, choosing tact for once, praised Memminger for his effort. Still, he was a diminished presence as the men of Charleston debated how to proceed. Compromise and conciliation had failed, and with no fresh idea of his own what to do next, he reluctantly conceded that the radical path might have to be followed after all. With the upper states of the South in seeming paralysis, he acknowledged to Miles, "we further South will be compelled to act and drag after us these divided states." The born leader, as a college classmate considered him, was being overtaken by events on the ground and by those with more passionate conviction than he possessed. He would spend the rest of year laboring, dutifully, to catch up.

Chapter Six

"BUILD HIGH THE SHAFT!"

The Ladies' Calhoun Monument Association met on the first Tuesday in March. The idea behind the group was to raise money to erect in Charleston a marble shrine to the venerated John C. Calhoun, and for a dollar anyone could be a member. The group thought the considerable sum of $50,000 was necessary to have the work done. Calhoun already was just about everywhere on display in Charleston: in framed copies printed on satin of his last Senate speech in 1850; on bank notes; in icon-like daguerreotypes of his visage with his familiar hard stare and fierce shock of hair, available for 75 cents; even in the form of a life-sized wax model. A statue of Calhoun by Vermont-born sculptor Hiram Powers stood in City Hall. Commissioned in the 1840s, it depicted Calhoun as a robe-clad, Roman-style orator of antiquity. But the Ladies Association had in mind the grandest tribute of all: an outdoor monument of a colossal scale. The organizers undoubtedly did not need a reminder, but one woman wrote to say, "It seems to me that it would make Calhoun stir in his grave if he were sculptured by a Northern chisel."

In the pages of the *Mercury*, the ladies were presented as an undifferentiated mass, only rarely mentioned by name. They were collectively cast as patrons of the arts, supporters of charities for the poor and orphans, diligent hand sewers of patriotic flags and, often enough, adornments, looking "quite fresh and charming" in their "little kid gloves and per-fumes and plumes" as they filled the Jockey Club Stand at Race Week in February. "There is no rubbing it out: Women are the charm, blessing, beauty and bliss of life—men's life, we mean, of course." As for the proper role of the Charleston wife, the paper supplied a jest: "Somebody says: A wife should be like a roasted lamb—'tender and nicely dressed.' A scamp adds: 'And without sauce.'"

Nevertheless, Charleston's ladies had plenty of sauce. They helped cre-ate the combative political character of the city and could be withering critics of men seen as deficient in the belligerent spirit required to defend the South. And Calhoun was their idol. This might have seemed an odd choice. Born and raised in the South Carolina Upcountry, he had once condemned Charleston for its chronic "intemperance and debaucheries." He lay buried in the city, by St. Philip's, probably against his own wishes. Still, for the feminine mind in particular, Calhoun appeared to embody a rare purity in his elevated ideas. Charleston embraced two religions— the spiritual religion of the bible and the civic religion, which could be called the gospel of states' rights. Calhoun's philosophy, "Calhounism," was a muscular version of states' rights. The doctrine of Nullification, for which he was best known, held that a state, any state, could legally void— nullify—a federal law that the state deemed unconstitutional. The test of this principle came while Calhoun was serving as vice president under An-drew "Old Hickory" Jackson. A former military commander, Jackson did not think much of nullification and sent the US Navy to Charleston Har-bor to keep South Carolina from making good on its bid, as demanded by "nullifiers," to invalidate payment of the "Tariff of Abominations" within its borders. He also privately threatened to hang Calhoun. South Carolina was humbled, and Calhoun resigned, but the state remained nevertheless convinced of the rightness of its hero's convictions.

When Charleston got word of Calhoun's death in Washington on the last day of March in 1850, the ships in the harbor lowered their flags to half-staff and the bells of St. Michael's tolled for hours. For his funeral, public buildings and private homes were draped in black. Charlestonians in black armbands wept while his casket passed by. Among the mourners was Mary Amarinthia Yates, a Charleston lady from a wealthy family and an acquaintance of political figures like Calhoun and Judge Magrath. Yates founded the Ladies' Calhoun Monument Association four years after his death, and the cornerstone was laid in 1858. The monument would reside on the Citadel Green, between King and Meeting Streets on Calhoun Street, as Boundary Street already had been renamed. By 1860, work was well under way at the Charleston marble yard of William T. White. The design called for an edifice of about ninety-five feet in height. From the marble base, a flight of stairs would lead first to a set of four statues representing Liberty, Justice, Eloquence, and the Constitution, and then to a platform with a colonnade of Corinthian columns. There would be carved emblems of both South Carolina and the United States. The monument would be topped by an immense, twelve-foot-high statue of Calhoun with his right arm extended upward and his hand pointed toward heaven. "The entire design is chaste, yet elaborate, and bespeaks the appreciation of culture and refinement," the *Mercury*, whose offices featured an obligatory bust of Calhoun, declared on a viewing. The designer inclined toward Italian marble, but the Ladies Association had still to decide on the material.

The work in progress was the object of a song composed for the occasion of a concert in Charleston sponsored by the ladies' group:

> *Build high the shaft! till it reach the skies*
> *And glows in the setting sun. . . .*
> *In Calhoun's name, the great truth proclaim,*
> *"Let Sovereign States be free." . . .*
> *Build high the shaft! for 'tis woman's power*
> *That hath laid its marble base.*

True enough, the women of Charleston were not universally rapturous for such "truths." On occasion, the town produced a heretic treacherously opposed to the mind-set represented by Calhoun, including his glorification of slavery as "a positive good." But the apostates seldom lasted long in Charleston, as the notorious Grimke sisters proved. The daughters of a state supreme court justice, Sarah and Angelina Grimke defied custom by teaching the house slaves to read (also a crime) and questioning why a slave should be made to "fetch us a cup of tea." They ended up exiles in Massachusetts, outspoken abolitionists banned from Charleston on pain of arrest. Neither set foot there again.

The usual pattern for Northern-born women was for the city to make "good Charlestonians" of the Yankee migrants. Boston-born Caroline Howard Gilman, a published poet and the daughter of a participant in the Boston Tea Party, arrived in Charleston in 1819 at the age of twenty-five, newly wed to a Harvard divinity student. Her husband took over as the pastor of the Unitarian Church on Archdale, and she presided over a household attended to by "faithful" slaves. She even set forth her careful parsing of "the religious privileges of the negroes in Charleston" in her 1838 book, *Recollections of a Southern Matron*. A niece back North was an abolitionist.

For the Charleston radicals who aimed to break the South from the Union, the ladies served as a reserve corps of psychological support. Ladies were not allowed to vote or hold political office, but they could attend political gatherings and planned to be out in large numbers for the Democratic Convention soon to come to Charleston. Their spirit, not to mention their lungs, might supply gusto to the secession cause. Popular mythology held that the sainted Calhoun, ten years dead, was naturally on the side of rebellion. The truth was more complex. In 1838, Calhoun had told his daughter in regard to members of the disunionist camp, "Those who make it up, do not think of the difficulty involved in the word; how many bleeding [pores] must be taken up on passing the knife of separation through a body politic. . . . We must remember, it is the most difficult process in the world to make two people of one." By 1860, his words were lost as secessionists claimed his memory for their movement. Cold mute in his grave at St. Philip's, he was in no position to object.

Chapter Seven

TO CHARLESTON, "WITH THREE HUNDRED KEGS OF BEER"

I t would be the largest gathering in the 190 years of Charleston's history, and the Charleston Hotel aimed to be fully provisioned. In March, the hotel put in an order to New York for three thousand common quilts and hair pillows, one thousand mattresses of twisted palm leaf, five hundred curled maple bedsteads, and one hundred large-sized toothbrushes with matching combs. The Charleston was the city's largest hotel, and it was planning to accommodate four thousand guests for one week at $10 per night for an anticipated gross of $280,000, not including the proceeds from the innumerable bowls of green turtle soup and dishes of canvasback duck that diners could be expected to order from the restaurant. As it turned out, many guests would stay longer.

In choosing Charleston as the site for April's Democratic National Convention in 1860, party leaders intended to promote unity in the ranks by mollifying the Southern Democrats who were feeling increasingly misrepresented by a body they viewed as under the sway of an imperious Northern faction. In 1856, the Democrats had met in Cincinnati. Surely, the thinking went, cantankerous Southerners would appreciate the conciliatory gesture of setting the 1860 convention in the cradle of the Old

South. Somehow they managed to forget that Charleston, when given the inch, was apt to take the mile.

The Democratic Party was the only remaining truly national party in America, with a base in both the North and South. It was the big-tent, ever-fractious party of Andrew Jackson and John C. Calhoun, of those believing in a muscular federal union as well as those insisting on states' rights. The Whig Party, led by Henry Clay of Kentucky, had enjoyed broad backing from both sections until the 1850s, when opponents of slavery bolted to form the new Republican Party. The Republicans—who held their first convention in 1856 in Philadelphia—faced unremitting hostility from the South, where a vote for a Republican was generally seen as a form of treason.

Pennsylvania's James Buchanan—the Democrats' weak, ineffectual incumbent in the White House—was expected to be passed over for a second term, and the clear front-runner for the party's nomination in 1860 was Stephen Douglas, the senator from Illinois. The "Little Giant," a short man possessed of an immense head, was best known as the advocate of popular sovereignty—sometimes called squatter sovereignty—to settle the question of whether to allow slavery in the Union's territories. The idea was to let the territories themselves decide whether to be "slave" or "free." In 1857, the US Supreme Court, in its *Dred Scott* decision, struck a blow against Douglas's scheme—and in favor of the slaveholder position—by ruling that territorial legislatures had no authority to ban slavery within their borders. However, Douglas maintained that the territories could still effectively exclude slavery by refusing to enact rules for the protection of a slaveholder's property. He anticipated that he would face stiff opposition in Charleston from Southern delegates determined to resist any effort to roll back *Dred Scott* and to prevent slaveholders from colonizing the territories—but he still thought he would have enough votes to win the nomination.

The Charleston radicals had other ideas for the gathering. The "demolition of the party" was the first step, and a necessary step, toward the ultimate annihilation of the Union, Rhett, Jr., told William Porcher Miles.

It required more than toothbrushes to stage a convention. The Pennsylvania delegation clambered aboard its steamship, the *Keystone State,* with five hundred barrels of hard spirits and three hundred kegs of beer, "enough liquor," the *Philadelphia Bulletin* hazarded, "to flood the vessel clear into the streets of Charleston, and up to the very doors of the Convention Hall." As New York's steamer, the *Nashville,* made ready to depart, "a number of the ladies leaning against the taffrail of the steamer exchanged smiles and signs with the people on the shore," the *New York Herald* reported. The ladies "appeared to be quite well known to everyone except the reporter of the *Herald.* The names of the fair ones did not appear on the list of passengers, but attached to the names of many gentlemen were the words 'and friend.'" Just before the *Nashville* got under way, "mysterious packages," presumably of spirits, were slipped onboard. Massachusetts brought along on the *S.R. Spaulding* the thirty-member Brass Band of Boston, over which Patrick Sarsfield Gilmore, a flamboyant, mustachioed Irish immigrant and a virtuoso cornetist, presided. "Yankee Doodle Dandy" was a standard.

Charleston was most easily gained by sea. At the mouth of the harbor, a ship encountered the first ring of federal fortifications built by the US Army Corps of Engineers to protect the city from a foreign invader, the British Navy in particular. To the right, on Sullivan's Island, was Fort Moultrie, with its federal garrison; to the left, on James Island, was Fort Johnson, largely in ruins; and between them, on a small manmade island of New England quarried granite only partially completed, was Fort Sumter. Charleston beckoned five miles distant, "rising, like another Venice, from the ocean," *Harper's Weekly* mused in its issue timed to the convention. Three-quarters of a mile from Charleston, at the entrance to the Cooper River, was the fourth and last federal fortification, Castle Pinckney, a small, round, brick structure occupying a sandy spit and all but abandoned. Passengers disembarked at the river's wharves to the sight of muscle-bound slaves loading three-hundred-pound cotton bales onto ships bound for Europe. Black female vendors bid them to buy oysters and fresh fruit and spoke amongst themselves in Gullah. It felt to some like a foreign country. "The negroes here speak a lingo incomprehensible to the Northerner on a first visit," a baffled visitor from the North found.

"The voice is excessively shrill, and their conversation resembles more the chattering of parrots than human beings."

By land, the trip required six changes of train just from Washington. On entering South Carolina, the rail passenger looked out at a wilderness of dank, black-water swamp and sweet-scented pine and spruce forest. Woodpeckers hammered at old tree trunks while flocks of larks, quails, and doves flitted about. Deer, turkey, and wild hogs rambled through the brush. Lone, log-cabin homes spaced miles apart were one of the few signs of human habitation. At the occasional plantation might be seen teams of slaves, men and women, spreading manure on fields with their bare hands. Nearer to Charleston, the landscape transformed into fine country homes, magnificent long-limbed oaks draped with Spanish moss, and gardens in glorious April bloom. A group of convention-goers from Wisconsin, having begun their trek in snowshoes, happily looked out at bushes of red roses.

Finally, arrival at the Charleston rail depot was a "miserable affair," as one visitor to the convention described his experience of being "pounced on" by "eleven Irishmen and one nigger," all bidding for the baggage and touting hotels, just $3 a day, stocked with rum and the "best of fare." Whether arrival was at the depot or the pier, the welcoming crew was the same "ferocious-looking policemen, mounted on rickety nags" and equipped with "old-fashioned pistols." The city police force had added seventy-five men to its usual number to beef up security for the convention. Also awaiting the visitors of course was the greeting party of the buzzards, Charleston's most famous bird. The guests were informed it was a $5 fine to harm one.

As Charleston swelled with thousands of visitors, the three-hundred-and-three delegates representing thirty-two states split up into separate encampments. The Alabama, Mississippi, Texas, Virginia, and North Carolina delegations settled in at the Charleston. In a private parlor, William Lowndes Yancey of Alabama set up court. As the leader of the Southern delegates determined to oppose Douglas and his squatter sovereignty, Yancey was a key ally of the Rhetts, neither of whom was a delegate to the convention. The Douglas crew, led by Colonel William A. Richardson of Illinois, took over Hibernian Hall, several blocks down Meeting

Street from the Charleston. The Douglas team put the first floor into use for strategy sessions, armed with ample supplies of whiskey, and lined the chandeliered second floor with hundreds of cots, dormitory style, for sleeping quarters for the delegates from Illinois and other northwestern states. Douglas himself stayed away from the convention, as was the custom for presidential candidates in those times, and awaited the result in Washington.

Maine and Rhode Island were just up from Hibernian Hall at Mills House, and so was the mayor of New York, Fernando Wood, or as the New York press called him, "Lord Mayor." His professed Southern sympathies made him a Charleston favorite, and although not officially a delegate, he nevertheless harbored hopes of gaining the vice-presidential nomination. Massachusetts moved into a boardinghouse at 6 Broad Street, next door to the *Mercury*. California and Oregon, opting to go "frontier style," pitched tents on a vacant lot near the Battery. Snug among its libations, Pennsylvania made the *Keystone State* its home. The waterside was a good choice because the weather greeting conventioneers was hot and humid. The temperature was approaching a sweltering one-hundred degrees. For favorite delegates, mainly Southerners of a sufficiently radical persuasion, Charleston's ladies threw open the doors of their homes and offered the most luxurious accommodation in town—a flower-scented guest bedroom, a full larder and bar, a cushioned lounge chair on a moonlit piazza.

The press, anticipating an epic clash between the Douglas and Yancey forces, invaded Charleston with a small army of its own: editors, correspondents, illustrators, and proprietors representing hundreds of news organizations, from big outfits like the *Philadelphia Inquirer* to small ones like the *Rock* of Plymouth, Massachusetts; the *Patriot* of Jackson, Michigan; and the *Avalanche* of Memphis, Tennessee. Few were neutral observers. Then there were the numerous hangers-on, everyone from the female "friends" of the delegates to the professional pickpockets and card sharks in pursuit of easy marks. Their prey could be found in the lobbies of the hotels swarming with "great portly fellows, with protuberant stomachs and puffy cheeks, red foreheads, hair thin and grizzly, dressed in glossy black and fine linen, with the latest style of stove-pipe hats, and ponderous gold-headed canes," as Murat Halstead, a reporter for the

Cincinnati Commercial, a Republican paper, depicted them. The thirty-year-old Halstead did not hide his dim regard for the "ultras," as he called the Yancey crowd, but he kept a diary of the convention with a perceptive feel for the mood of the delegates and the city.

The conventioneers arrived cash flush. Notwithstanding its habitual railing against the grasping Yankee—"You can get a Yankee to do anything for money," the saying went—Charleston had its own hard and conniving mercenary aspect. The *Mercury* was stuffed with ads for dubious products like McLean's Volcanic Oil Liniment, "the ONLY safe and certain cure for Cancers, Piles, Tumors, Swellings." Much like New York, Charleston had long experience in catering to visitors in town for business or pleasure or both. The convention was a happy opportunity not just for the hotels and boardinghouses, the baggage handlers and the shoeshine boys, but also for the cigar peddlers with their stocks of fat Havanas and for the black matrons hawking fresh-cooked shrimp at the marketplace. Profits beckoned for Charleston's innumerable taverns—which offered cheap beer and snacks like boiled peanuts, pickled pigs' feet, and dried fish—and for the brothels. The highest class among them was the Brick House, on Beresford off of King, which offered women of "all shades." Prostitution was legal in Charleston, and the proprietor of the Brick House, Grace Piexotto, was so secure in her position that she once petitioned the City Council to pave the heavily trafficked area outside her establishment with flagstones. Profits beckoned, too, for the peddlers in the Chalmers Street slave-trading district. A Northern delegate made careful inspection of a bejeweled mulatto girl available for $1,500 but walked off without closing the deal.

Charleston also aimed to educate visitors, especially those from the North, on its history and on the people and places closest to its heart. Conventioneers were guided to Calhoun's grave at St. Philip's and ferried across the harbor to Sullivan's Island. There they were told of Sergeant William Jasper's legendary exploit during the Revolutionary War, when, in the midst of an intense battle with a British warship, he left the safety of his position to rescue a sheared-off South Carolina flag and plant the colors on the wall of a fort. The fort was fashioned from the palmetto tree—the fan palm native to the Lowcountry whose tough fibrous trunk proved capable of absorbing a British cannonball without shattering. The palmetto also could withstand a gale without being uprooted from its sandy soil. As all visitors to Charleston would be given to understand, if they did not know it already, the palmetto was no mere tree but a metaphor for the spirit of the city, the stuff of songs and poems and emblems.

Slavery, above all, was the issue on which Charleston felt its visitors were in need of instruction. White Charleston earnestly believed that those who lived in the free states did not have an informed understanding of the actual situation of a slave in a refined Southern city like Charleston. Now was the time, with a captive audience before them, to expose the malicious lies of the abolitionists. Charleston would show that the slave life was in fact an improvement on the life of a black person in the North who might be legally free but who often suffered from want of a decently paying job and clean, safe shelter. In their resolve to paint a picture of Charleston's contented lot of slaves, and to show themselves as generously spirited, some masters went to absurd lengths. After a dinner party "at which slavery had been demonstrated, from Scripture and nature alike, to be wholly right, and just at the point when our eloquent host was asserting that his negroes were treated like his own children," an invited guest from New York recounted, "an apparently accidental drawing aside of the cloth revealed his little son and a black boy, each about six years of age, fast asleep in one another's arms, under the table."

The myth of the happy Charleston slave was easily enough dispelled for the New Yorker. One evening, around 10:00 p.m., the band brought along by the guest's delegation struck up a tune on the streets of the convention district. In haste appeared Charleston's captain of police. "Play any music you like," he begged the startled musicians, "if you can dispense with your drums." After the nightly curfew had fallen, drums were the signal of a slave disturbance in need of urgent attention. The New Yorker grasped "the ever-present dread of a revolt" in the veins of Charleston's white community.

But Charleston yearned most to see the South, its South, take a decisive stand at the convention—to resist the Douglas forces of the North and, even if outnumbered, to accept no compromise. This was not only a matter of cold, calculating strategy. It was also a matter of warm sentiment, of simmering, pent-up resentment at the Yankees who were finally in the city's midst in appreciable numbers. "If the South sustains Douglas in any circumstance she abandons all she has struggled and contended for, for years past" and "abandons herself to the contempt and to the spoliation of the relentless enemies," merchant Robert Newman Gourdin told Miles. "If we falter now and compromise our principles for party we seal our fate," and "a bloody revolution will be our only hope of redemption," Gourdin said. "The result of the Charleston Convention will tell the future of the South for weal or woe."

Chapter Eight

"SCREAMING LIKE PANTHERS"

The gavel hammered down at noon on Monday, April 23. The host venue, Institute Hall, a few blocks down from the Charleston Hotel on Meeting Street, was unaccustomed to such excitable proceedings. A two-story Italianate brick building, the hall had been constructed in 1854 principally to advance the commercial prospects of the city. Typically it was used for expositions of the latest in mechanical equipment and for cash-award competitions for the best specimens of cotton and rice, tobacco and potatoes. The wall behind the stage was freshly decorated with paintings of the symbols of South Carolina produce and industry along with, improbably, a rendering of a voluptuous maiden with a dagger in hand, the blade pointed toward a globe. The main floor could seat one thousand people in rows of wooden chairs screwed into pine planks. Another two thousand squeezed onto the benches of the galleries overhanging the floor. The press worked out of the basement in space set aside by Dodge's Machinery Depot. For those with a thirst, McDowall's saloon was across the street; for those in search of a more wholesome experience, the Teetotal Restaurant was next door.

Caleb Cushing, a sixty-year-old, veteran politician, and diplomat from Massachusetts, was elected president. Critics in the North scorned him as a "doughface Democrat" unfaithful to his section as proven by his publicly stated support for *Dred Scott*. Just for this reason, Charleston, with its temperamental inability to be indifferent about anyone or anything, adopted him as a favorite son and provided deluxe lodgings at the Meeting mansion of former South Carolina governor R. F. W. Allston. He was a pet of the ladies, who placed fresh flowers on his desk at the hall every day. From there he ruled, spectacles dangling from a ribbon draped around his neck.

The first important piece of business to be accomplished was the party platform. At the entrance to Institute Hall, Barnwell Rhett met with Stephen Douglas's man, Colonel William Richardson, and made Charleston's demand: the Southern Democrats required the delegates' explicit endorsement of *Dred Scott* to preserve the possibility of slavery in the territories. The senior Rhett well understood he was asking for too much. *Dred Scott* was about as unpopular in the North as it was popular in the South. If the party supported *Dred Scott*, it would likely seal the defeat of Douglas or any other Democratic nominee in the November election. "Col. Richardson only smiled," according to Rhett, Sr.—a smile that to him conveyed Richardson's belief that the South was bluffing in its demand for *Dred Scott* and that, before long, "the South would divide and succumb."

A political convention can easily enough be seen as dreary business with its droning speeches and motions on arcane points of procedure. But Charleston had a love of performance—from the theater to the church services—and this event was no exception. Spectators clutched their tickets, and ladies dressed as if attending a play in long, formal gowns and wide-brimmed hats, with their fans and parasols in hand. The speeches and exchanges between dueling parties were all carefully attended to. Here the line between spectator and participant blurred as the Charlestonians who packed the galleries generated an enormous number of competing jeers and cheers. They outnumbered the delegates and set the emotional tone and pace for the proceedings to the consternation of the Douglas camp.

As quickly became apparent, there were, in effect, two conventions taking place in Charleston: one inside the hall and the other on the jammed street outside of it. The street convention operated throughout the day and well into the evening, a soapbox affair of impromptu speeches, often more like tirades, as the combatants exchanged rhetorical volleys to the delight or ire of their listeners. It was North versus South, "fire-eater" versus "submissionist," and also an argument between those who earnestly believed the destiny of the Union was at stake and others who found all such talk overheated political "humbug." Rumors ricocheted around Charleston, such as the one about General John Schnierle—a former mayor, leader of a state militia regiment, and an ardent secessionist—threatening to beat with a stick the editor of the *Richmond Enquirer* in objection to a speech he had made in front of Mills House. The report reached the ear of Schnierle's neighbor, James M. Johnson, a free person of color and a popular King Street tailor. "Allowance must be made for them that after imbibing hot punches, inhaling fresh air will confuse one's ideas," Johnson wrote to a friend outside of Charleston.

Thousands of visitors in town for the convention gathered on the Citadel Green to watch cadets from that academy perform a dazzling array of military marching maneuvers. The martial air was stirred, too, by a parade down King of the German Rifle Club, a leading social group of Charleston's immigrant community. The highlight of these pageants was the Firemen's Parade, a procession of companies with names like Vigilant, Axmen, and Eagle. Their engines were garlanded with flower bouquets and palmetto branches, the men outfitted in colorful uniforms—as in the red jackets and black pantaloons of the Palmetto Company. As ladies cheered from their piazzas, the procession passed through streets packed with spectators. Gen. Schnierle led the Old German Engine Company, with its engine drawn by four bays.

Around 10:00 p.m. on the second day of the convention, a large crowd accompanied by the Palmetto Band assembled in front of the Mills House to call out Mayor Wood of New York. The Mayor was known as an opportunist and seemed an unlikely object of ardor, but Charleston had a tendency to open its arms to just about any Northern politician willing to flatter Southern vanities. Wood appeared on the balcony, made of cast iron in a Philadelphia foundry, to salute his well-wishers and, when the music stopped, paid homage to Charleston as "the empire city, as it were, of the South." The South must "stand up manfully on this great question of slavery," he said, and help the North "defend ourselves against Black Republican traitors." For the crowd gathered below, he commiserated that "aggression upon aggression has been committed on your rights, your interests, and upon everything near and dear to you"—but in the end, he promised, these "evils" would be rectified. He then retired "to long and long-continued applause," according to the *Mercury*, which wrote up Wood's speech for the morning paper.

—·—

Inside the hall, the suspense was all for Alabama's Yancey, a man known for his "sweet voice," violent temper, and ego, which just possibly equaled Barnwell Rhett's. (He once joked about himself as standing "twenty-seven feet high.") Yancey had been a Unionist and a Jackson man in his twenties, opposed to Calhoun and Nullification in the crisis over the tariff in the early 1830s. But by the mid-1840s, while living in Montgomery, Alabama, with a miserable record as a planter, Yancey had become a strong states' rights man, at odds with the national Democratic Party. Fourteen years younger than Barnwell Rhett, he looked to the older, more seasoned man as a mentor and to the *Mercury* for guidance on policy and politics. In 1850, the two had appeared together at a public rally in Macon, Georgia, to pitch for secession. "The godlike Rhett and his adjutant Yancey preached most eloquently on behalf of treason," a disgusted Unionist commented. Charleston's radical secessionists were delighted and came to adopt Yancey as one of their own. One could be a Charlestonian in spirit, after all.

In 1860, Yancey was a member of the Alabama delegation, which, before setting foot in Charleston, had committed to a *Dred Scott* platform, or else. A fastidious man, he offered a resolution on the convention's first day to ask the city to cover cobblestoned Meeting with sawdust or straw, so great was the racket created by the carriages rumbling by outside the hall. Five days later, the Douglas forces were impatient to move to a vote on a party platform—a vote they expected to win—when Yancey rose to speak. He was greeted with applause that lasted several minutes and asked for an hour and a half's time. His stem-winder took the form of a lecture on the historical and non-negotiable rights of the white Southerner to take slaves into the territories and to live untrammeled upon by the Yankee. If there was to be disunion, it would only be because of the North's failure to honor these rights. A thunderous cheer from both the floor and galleries greeted his invocation of Calhoun on the doctrine of the state as sovereign. He now praised as "the country's greatest and purest statesman" the same Calhoun he had opposed decades before as wrong on nullification. He then spoke of the divine prerogatives of the "master race." Even a poor white man, he said, should never be lowered to the menial task of cleaning and polishing a boot, as it was for the "negro race to do this dirty work which God designed they should do." At this, the applause was so loud that a delegate from Indiana asked for the galleries to be cleared, but Cushing declined. To his "countrymen of the South," Yancey continued with a demand: "Throttle anti-slavery" by insisting on "the constitutional right of the slave holder to constitutional protection" and "go to the wall upon this issue if events demand it."

Following Yancey's incendiary speech, George E. Pugh of Ohio—a first-term US senator and a captain in the Mexican-American War—rose to plead for a middle way: "This great government of ours is a government of compromise. . . . The slaveholding States cannot have everything; the non-slaveholding States cannot have everything." After a recess, Pugh resumed his speech. It was late in the night, and he was undisguised in his exasperation: "I want the people of the United States," he declared, "to discuss and canvass some other question than this everlasting one of slavery. When nothing is to be gained by it except ill-blood, agitation, disturbance and disruption of political organizations, it seems to me that gentlemen of the Southern States were never more called upon to rise above passion and prejudice than now."

William Darius Bishop of Connecticut, a former Congressman who had served as commissioner of patents, declared there was nothing more to be said, not even if the delegates stayed in Charleston a week longer to jaw over the slavery question. It was time for the convention to vote. To the Yancey camp, this looked like a demand for a gag. "In an instant the house was in an uproar—a hundred delegates upon the floor, and upon chairs, screaming like panthers, and gesticulating like monkeys," Halstead of the *Cincinnati Commercial* reported. "The reporters climbed upon their tables" while "the people in the galleries stretched their necks and hung over the balustrade. . . . A crowd gathered about Bishop, and some seemed to menace him. The delegates gathered in groups and grappled with each other, and surged about like waves of the sea." At last Cushing was able to gain sufficient control to accept a motion to adjourn, and the delegates and gallery throngs spilled out into the gas-lit streets of Charleston, slick from rain.

Chapter Nine

"FOURTH OF JULY"

T he downpour that had started on Friday, with a plunge in temperature and a burst of winds, continued through Saturday and into Sunday morning. Charleston's dirt streets caked into mud. Throughout the soggy weekend, the Douglas men, droopy umbrellas in anxious grip, tried to find some way to keep the party from splitting. The mood among Northern Democrats soured as expense accounts and whiskey stocks ran down and gambling losses mounted. Some of those who had come to Charleston to cheer on Douglas's expected triumph left the city altogether. With momentum breaking their way, Southern radicals felt rewarded for their refusal to buckle. Yancey was the toast of the *Mercury,* and the spectacle of disorder transfixed everyone in America with a taste for the drama of politics.

Yet surprising as this might seem, the South Carolina delegation was not all radical secessionists threatening revolt and creating chaos. In fact, the sixteen members had been assembled by a crafty Upcountry politician and committed national Democrat, James Lawrence Orr. With the death of Calhoun in 1850 and with Barnwell Rhett's humiliating defeat by the Cooperationists in 1851, Orr, a lawyer and a merchant's son, had filled the vacuum to become South Carolina's single most important powerbroker. Rotund, fond of cigars, and supported by a cane, he was a classic backroom pol, with a spoils network extending deep into Charleston's brackish political waters. His influence infuriated the Rhetts, who rightly sized up Orr as moderate and flexible by temperament, opposed to unilateral secession as well as to Southern Democrats' uncompromising stand on *Dred Scott*. Most maddeningly, Orr still believed in trying to save the Union and viewed the Democratic Party as the best guarantor of the South's rights. "No man now living in this Union," he declared in 1858, "has power to accomplish any great measure or policy without the aid of party."

In short, all that Orr stood for, the Rhetts aimed to destroy. Orr was not himself a delegate, but he was in Charleston for the convention, cigar in mouth and troops seemingly in line. And after Yancey drew the line for secessionists, the boss's men were hounded by Charlestonians appalled that their home-state delegates were letting others take the battle to the foe. Any South Carolina delegate brave enough to be seen on the street was beset with a salvo of denunciations. "You are a Southern traitor," was one rebuke. "You are a South Carolina disgrace," was another. "Our patriots have quit the stable, and you prefer to wallow in manure."

The head of the delegation, James Simons, was a state legislator, a militia general, and a Charleston native with a three-story home on Broad Street. Back in February at a public meeting in Hibernian Hall, Simons had said that, in his judgment, "the power, the grandeur, and the happiness of the country, were best promoted by the preservation of the Union." He had argued, Orr-like, that the differences between the North and South, as painful as they might be, were best fought out under the roof of the Democratic Party. The *Mercury* snorted in disgust. By April, Alabama was primed to lead a walkout of the slave-state delegations, and Orr still believed that the "secession" of any Southern delegates from the convention was "unwise and impolitic." If he followed Orr's lead, Simons would have to hear his own townspeople calling him a gutless apostate.

On Monday morning, the galleries, mostly emptied of Northerners, were crammed with residents of the city who had grabbed unused tickets tossed onto the street. Gentlemen spectators were asked not to spit on the heads of delegates below. The Douglas forces had the majority, and they proved it by winning a test vote on a platform by nearly thirty votes. The issue was joined: whatever the Southern delegates threatened, the North was not going to take *Dred Scott* as the platform. Willard Saulsbury of Delaware, a freshman US senator, pleaded with delegates on all sides not to "stir up the bitter waters of contention." A "true Democrat," he said, "knows no North, no South, no East, no West."

Leroy Pope Walker, chairman of the Alabama contingent and a former circuit court judge, addressed Cushing: "Mr. President, I am instructed by the Alabama delegation to submit to this Convention a communication, and, with your permission, I will read it." The hall hushed. The "communication" enumerated all of the reasons for Alabama's dissatisfaction with a convention that had "refused, by the platform adopted" to settle disputed slavery issues "in favor of the South." Therefore, he said, "it becomes our duty to withdraw from this convention." With that, Alabama's twenty-six delegates got up from their chairs and moved toward the aisles. Mississippi followed close behind. The gallery showered applause on both delegations, and the breakaway delegates met with "nods and glances of approval, a delighted fluttering of fans and parasols" from the ladies. A spirit if not of an unbounded anger, then of a proud defiance, took hold of the rebels and their encouraging supporters. David C. Glenn of Mississippi, a former state attorney general, climbed atop his chair and, with his gaze fixed on the Ohio delegation, said, "It is right that we should part. Go your way, and we will go ours." Louisiana, the third delegation to withdraw, was no less forthright. "We wish to meet the Black Republicans with their abominable doctrines boldly; and if our friends, the Democrats from the free States, cannot join us and fight with us, we must fight our own battle," Alexandre Mouton, a former governor of that state, declared.

When Simons rose, it was plain he did not have it in him to buck Charleston. Most of his colleagues in South Carolina's delegation felt the same way. Before an increasingly anxious audience, Simons read aloud a letter to Cushing signed by all but three of the state's delegates, with his name at the top. As he finally announced their withdrawal from the convention, the gallery exploded with a lusty roar of approval. Traitors one day, heroes the next.

Next, Florida and Arkansas joined in the walkout. "Mr. President and gentlemen of the convention, we are in the midst of a crisis," Charles W. Russell of Virginia declared. "We may be on the eve of a revolution. If this convention should prove a failure, there is reason to fear that it will prove also to be the last national convention of any party that will be assembled in the United States." Among delegates still seated on their chairs, gloom sunk in. "Down many a manly cheek did I see flow tears of heartfelt sorrow," wrote a Democratic newspaper correspondent at the scene. But on the streets, the tears were of joy. As Simons and his rene-gade crew exited Institute Hall, they were greeted with kisses from ladies gathered on Meeting. Revolution was finally within reach. Revolution! For its believers, the word summoned not destruction but rebirth, the founding of something new and heroic, a Declaration of Independence for the South.

Trailed by their lady admirers and a gaggle of reporters and cheered at every street corner, the delegates made their way down Meeting, took a right at Broad, and, just past T. G. Trott's druggist shop, strode into St. Andrew's Hall. Built in 1815 by Charleston's Scots, St. Andrew's was best known as the site for the balls of the Jockey Club and St. Cecilia Society attended by the cream of the Charleston planter world. In 1847, Daniel Webster had been the honored guest at a dinner of the New England Soci-ety. The main room featured a portrait of the young Queen Victoria, and it was there Yancey and his cohorts considered their next move, which was not at all obvious. They had made good on their threat to bolt the convention—and now what? Yancey spoke of the need for "dignity" in moving forward, and he was met with a cry of "three cheers for Yancey!" from Charlestonians who had followed him and his allies into the hall. He then asked everyone who was not a delegate to leave. A colleague chimed in, "It does not become men who are engaged in the grave purpose of maintaining, or pulling down, or changing empires, to permit the angry passions of a mob to influence them in their action." He was in earnest: the bystanders crowded into St. Andrew's, a collection of rouged cheeks and polished boots, certainly did not have the look of a typical mob, and yet they seemed to be able to bend the wills of men in charge of this busi-ness of "changing empires." The "Seceding Convention," as the *Mercury* at first called this spontaneous assemblage of the Southern delegates, decided to adjourn until the following day.

Rhett, Jr., later learned, to his dismay, of a meeting that evening between Yancey and party leaders on the possibility of the Southerners returning to the convention. There seemed to be, he told William Porcher Miles, "some want of nerve in the management of the seceders" by Yancey. But Charleston treated the walkout as a decisive act of defiance. At about 11:00 p.m., Halstead took a walk along Meeting in the direction of City Hall. "The night was beautiful with moonlight," he wrote in his diary, "and made the plastered fronts of the old houses gleam like marble." The music of a brass band filled the air, and "a stranger, unacquainted with the condition of affairs, would not have been long in discovering that something extraordinary was afloat. People hurried by, looking excited and solicitous." A crowd numbering in the thousands was gathered to hear Yancey and other rebellious delegates speak from the steps of City Hall. "Every ultra sentiment was applauded with mad enthusiasm," Halstead observed. And when Yancey declaimed that "perhaps even now, the pen of the historian was nibbed to write the story of a new Revolution," a voice from the throng responded, "Three cheers for the independent Southern Republic!" and the cheers were given.

With the Charleston Brass Band leading the way, the crowd marched to the offices of the *Mercury*, and Rhett, Jr., and his newsroom crew were treated to a serenade. By then the front page of the next day's paper had likely already been composed. In its comment hailing "The Convention Breaking Up," the *Mercury* declared, "The events of yesterday will probably be the most important which have taken place since the Revolution of 1776. The last party, pretending to be a National party, has broken up; and the antagonism of the two sections of the Union has nothing to arrest its fierce collisions."

By the light of dawn, Halstead completed his recording of Charleston's nocturnal excitement. "There was a Fourth of July feeling in Charleston last night—a jubilee," he wrote. "There was no mistaking the public sentiment of the city. It was overwhelmingly and enthusiastically in favor of the seceders. In all her history, Charleston had never enjoyed herself so hugely."

Of course, the cheers for an "independent Southern Republic" came only from the white community. Black Charleston regarded the goings on in the convention district with an instinctive wariness. The tailor James M. Johnson took care not to loiter on the streets, telling his friend that on the first day of the convention the police twice had passed his shop "making arrests of suspicious and rowdy characters" lurking. In this atmosphere, the free blacks felt even more vulnerable than usual. "If you have lost the Rights you ought to find solace in making a Retreat from the Heat," Johnson observed. He did, however, closely follow the convention through reports in the newspapers and from scraps of information obtained from customers visiting his shop. And with other black Charlestonians, he attended the Firemen's Parade through downtown Charleston.

Among at least some members of the white community, there were misgivings about the "Fourth of July" mood as well. "There seems to be a disturbance in the political elements," mused Henry William Ravenel, the botanist who back in January attended the meeting at St. John's Berkley to organize a Vigilance Association. "Our people do not reflect enough upon these things for themselves, but are led on by politicians, and made to think that safety, honour, self-respect and our very existence depend upon these issues." Ravenel inscribed this rebuke of his people in his diary—pages intended for his eyes only. Few in Charleston were unafraid to challenge publically the "disturbance in the political elements."

Chapter Ten

"I FORESEE NOTHING BUT DISASTER"

J ames Louis Petigru was the last Unionist in Charleston—the last, that is, willing to proclaim the Unionist creed for all to hear, and he did so unapologetically with a generous measure of relish. He was a scalding critic of secession as well as of the radical secessionist mind in its impulse toward uncompromising and reckless action. During the convention, visitors from the North beat a path to his door to hear him expound thusly, and—as a man with a theatrical spark and a love of audience—he did not disappoint his listeners. He sat on a bench in the gallery at Institute Hall and fumed at the spectators' browbeating of anyone against Yancey. Yet such was his stature in town that he maintained his standing even with those who vehemently disagreed with him. Despite his dissent, Petigru was obviously devoted to Charleston. As long as he stopped short of abolitionism—and he did because he was a slaveholder—a heresy of one was tolerable.

He was born with the family name of Pettigrew in 1789 in the South Carolina Upcountry, near Abbeville, the son of a Scots-Irish farmer who gambled and drank and lost all of the family's land. His mother home-schooled him and managed to scrounge the money to pay his way through South Carolina College in Columbia. In his early twenties, he changed the spelling of his last name to Petigru to reflect his Huguenot descent,

a mark of social prestige in the state. After finishing his studies in Columbia, he joined Beaufort College and there operated as a private tutor
to young boys in the area including the eleven-year-old Robert Barnwell
Smith. The tutor played games of marbles with his charges and formed
a friendship with Robert that endured even as Robert, by then Barnwell
Rhett, matured into a leader of the secessionist movement. In the financial panic of 1837, with Robert at risk of losing everything, Petigru offered
his former student his credit "to the last dollar" of his property. (The offer
was declined.) "You know how much regard I have always had for Mr.
Barnwell Rhett," Petigru once told his daughter Susan.

In addition to his generous heart and talent for friendship, his inquis-
itive mind and biting wit, Petigru possessed a hungry ambition for social
status and professional accomplishment. After admission to the bar in
1815, and with the help of a well-connected mentor, he swiftly became a
partner in a Charleston law firm. By 1822, he was attorney general of the
state. His contrarian political sensibility seems to have been formed early.
As attorney general, he took the unpopular view that the state's Negro
Seaman Law, the statute that allowed free black seamen from Northern
states to be locked up if they came ashore in ports like Charleston, was
unconstitutional. He resigned from his post in 1830, after eight years in
the job, to muster opposition to nullification. But his state's failure to invalidate the tariff through nullification did not soothe him. He sensed
that "nullification has done its work; it has prepared the minds of men for
a separation of the States."

Petigru was a Henry Clay Whig, not a Jackson or Calhoun Democrat,
and he saw himself as "a disciple of Locke and Montesquieu." He revered
the Federalist founders of America, men like Alexander Hamilton. He was
not opposed to popular democracy in principle, but he felt that an aristocracy of learned, farsighted, cool-minded political thinkers and actors—an
upper class made up of men such as himself—generally possessed the best
wisdom on the questions of the moment. He was a "free-soiler," opposed
to the expansion of slavery in the territories. Although he owned slaves
himself, he supported manumission, the practice by which a slaveholder
could free his own slaves, and he often advocated in court for the legal

rights of free persons of color. The threat of mob violence against blacks repulsed him. In 1849, when white Charleston panicked at the escape of several dozen black inmates from the Charleston workhouse, Petigru restored calm by facing down a white rabble threatening to set ablaze a "nigger church" in town: "How can you be such damned fools, as to attempt to destroy this church, even if you have to set fire to the town? Have you not seen enough of fire here to be afraid of it? It is the only thing that decent men are afraid of! Men, let us call a meeting; if you are right, I will go with you; if you are wrong, you will carry out your proposal over my dead body."

He invited as guests into his home US Army officers stationed in the Charleston area, among them a young lieutenant from Ohio, William Tecumseh Sherman, who was posted to Fort Moultrie in the 1840s. In 1858, many years after Petigru had established himself as a pillar of Charleston society, he delivered an address at Hibernian Hall on the third anniversary of the South Carolina Historical Society, an organization he helped found. His theme was the history of his state and in particular "the bitterness of civil strife" that had marked so much of the life and times of South Carolina. "Zeal in behalf of our country and our country's friends is commendable, and patriotism deservedly ranks amongst the highest virtues," he told the assemblage. "But even virtue may be pushed to excess, and the narrow patriotism that fosters an overweening vanity and is blind to all merit except its own, stands in need of the correction of reason."

Petigru was consumed by his faith in reason and opposition to secession, and his blunt message was always the same. 'My unhappy fellow-citizens talk of seceding from the Union," he told a group from New York who visited his law office on St. Michael's Alley during the convention. "It is impossible, but they will not hear reason. I foresee nothing but disaster and ruin for them." Years later, one of his guests on that occasion reminisced about the encounter. "A venerable figure, with a noble face, his snowy hair falling on his shoulders, with something ancient in the fashion of his dress, he seemed like one of the Revolutionary fathers returned to earth," the visitor wrote. It was an idealized portrait—even at the age of seventy, Petigru had dark hair—but nonetheless accurately portrayed the presence he possessed.

Petigru's fellow Charlestonians enjoyed Sunday dinner parties at his home on Broad Street, just down from St. Andrew's Hall, and he was equally a popular guest at their tables. He served as a director at the College of Charleston and contributed to the upkeep of the Orphan House. He belonged to an informal literary club that met in the rear of Russell's Bookstore on King Street and included the *Mercury* editor, William Robinson Taber, Jr. He was a mentor to many young Charlestonians aspiring to a career in the law, including Andrew Gordon Magrath and also, before he took over for Taber, Rhett, Jr.

Yet none of Charleston's esteem for Petigru made his political views any more palatable. Those in agreement with him, and there were some, tended to keep quiet, whereas others treated his opinions with light, sometimes patronizing humor. His daughter Caroline, who lived in New York, shared his Unionist convictions, and he had a sympathetic ear in his sister Jane. But he did not find an ally in his wife, the daughter of a planter from the Beaufort area, who had brought to the marriage ten slaves, a wedding gift from her father. Jane Amelia had been educated at Mademoiselle Julia Darry's finishing school in Charleston. She was a Charleston lady—and an ardent secessionist.

Chapter Eleven

"THEY WOULD HAVE BEEN MOBBED"

O n the morning after Charleston's "Independence" revelries, the national convention's remaining delegates plodded into Institute Hall. Charlestonians piled in along with them with their spirits still high; the Douglas men looked whipped. Twenty-six of the thirty-four members of the delegation from Georgia announced their departure from the convention, to the cheers of the galley. Ladies placed bouquets of fresh flowers on the empty chairs of renegade delegates.

The South Carolina delegation was down to two members, and one of them, Benjamin Franklin Perry of Greenville, was set on speaking his mind. Perry rose from his chair only to meet with the fury of the gallery. He was called a submissionist and a traitor and mercilessly jeered. Petigru, at his perch in the gallery, was incensed at the heckling of a spectator seated at the next bench over and "longed to pull his nose," he later told Perry. "I really think I would have done it, or at least have told [the fellow] he was a scoundrel, but I was with ladies and with friends I would not compromise and let the miscreant alone," Petigru said. Bedford Brown of North Carolina, a former US senator and an opponent of the Southern radicals, asked Cushing to clear the gallery so Perry could proceed. "Let them remain," Perry said to Cushing. "I wish them to hear what I have to say." At last, the gallery quieted.

B. F. Perry, as he was often called, cut an impressive figure at six-feet, two-inches tall and with an erect military-type bearing. Like his old friend Petigru, he was an unreconstructed Unionist. He was born in South Carolina in 1805, and his father was a Massachusetts man who had fought in the Revolutionary War and later resettled in South Carolina to start up a store. In his late twenties, Perry fought—and won—a duel with a political opponent who supported Nullification. As a lawyer, he mentored the young William Lowndes Yancey in the early 1830s, when Yancey was still a Unionist living in Greenville. In 1837, at the age of thirty-one, he married seventeen-year-old Elizabeth Frances McCall of Legaré Street in Charleston. "By nature I am passionate and high tempered," he wrote in his journal, shortly after his marriage, "and there is no one more tenacious of his rights and honor." But even though "Lizzy," as Perry called her, was a Charleston lady, she shared her husband's political views and was proud of his defiant opposition of her city and state's secessionists. In 1851, Perry launched the *Southern Patriot* as a Unionist newspaper to counter the secession movement, but the paper lasted only four years.

"I stand before you, Mr. President," Perry began, addressing Cushing, "an old-fashioned Union Democrat, born and bred such, and such I have continued, consistently, without faltering or wavering in my faith, amidst the storms of secession and nullification which have swept over South Carolina. I am a Southern man in heart and feeling," he continued, "and identified with the South, my birth-place, by every tie that is sacred on earth and every interest that can bind a man to his own native soil. I love the South, and it is because I love her, and would guard her against evils which no one can foresee or foretell, that I am a Union man."

"I love to think of him standing alone," an admirer in attendance wrote years later, "reviled and hissed, like some great rock standing grand and immovable out of the sea, with the maddened waves hissing and beating against its base." Alone he was. With a broken Democratic Party, it was hard to see how any Democrat could beat the Republican nominee, who would soon be selected at their upcoming convention in Chicago. "The President will be nominated at Chicago" was the glum talk on the floor at Institute Hall, even as the Brass Band of Boston tried to lift spirits with

a medley of patriotic tunes. The remaining delegates could not even produce enough votes to grant Douglas, or any other candidate, the nomination. Party rules required that a nominee win the ballots of at least
two-thirds of the delegates. With Cushing ruling, crucially, that the two-
thirds threshold included all of the delegates who had walked out, even
if they had no intention of coming back, the convention was stalemated.

Charleston's attention shifted to the parallel Seceding Convention—or
as its members called it, the Constitutional Convention. The "delegates"
were largely men of advanced years, cigar-stained professional politicians,
and yet the gathering had an allure of glamour, especially for young people in Charleston who may have felt a naive and visceral attraction to the
new and daring. Some merchants embraced the trend. "The People of the
South Know Their Rights and Will Maintain Them," Cohen, Willis & Co.,
a clothing store on King Street, declared in an ad in the *Mercury*. Proprietor Aaron Nathan Cohen might have felt especially disposed at that time
to assert Southern "rights." In March, a female slave accompanying him
on a business trip to New York had run away, lured to do so, apparently,
by abolitionists.

On Tuesday, after their initial caucus at St. Andrew's Hall the night
before, the "seceders" met at Military Hall on Wentworth Street, a fortress
with castle-like towers built in the late 1840s as a place for militia bands
to meet and drill. They elected US Senator James A. Bayard of Delaware
as president and the repentant James Simons of Charleston as his vice.
Mayor Wood of New York, so outspoken in his sympathies for the South
from the balcony of Mills House just a week earlier, now showed up to express his doubts about the "propriety" of participating in this proceeding
and departed.

On Wednesday, the crew was at yet a third location—the Charleston
Theater on Meeting Street. Hundreds of ladies filled seats in the dress
circle, and the pit was set aside for the delegates. Behind President Bayard, who was seated on the stage near the footlights, was a drop-curtain
painting of a medieval palace used for a performance of the Italian opera
Lucrezia Borgia. The premises were patrolled by a pair of Irish policemen
with eighteen-inch spiked maces in hand. As this was exclusively a Southern assemblage organized by his friend Yancey, Barnwell Rhett agreed

to join. There, the Southerners decided to hold their own convention in Richmond in June, where they would nominate their own Southern rights man for the presidency. Any such figure had virtually no chance of winning a general election but nonetheless could advance the goals of the radicals by siphoning off votes from the Northern Democrats. A Republican triumph, and a further sharpening of the sectional conflict, would thus be more likely.

Unable to surmount their impasse even after fifty-seven ballots, the exhausted delegates at Institute Hall opted to flee Charleston and to reconvene in June on the more hospitable ground of Baltimore. Perhaps there the rules could be reworked to secure the prize for Douglas. Had Baltimore been the first place of meeting, maybe the convention would not have foundered. It was impossible to say. What could be said was that the Democratic Party establishment had gambled on Charleston— and lost. The city had staged the most raucous convention in the party's history—in the history of America, in fact. The Douglas men were understandably bitter: Cushing snuggled in feather pillows at an opulent Charleston home while they broiled on cots at airless Hibernian Hall and was praised by the likes of the *Mercury* for rulings that always seem to cut against their man. He had proved unable—or worse, unwilling— to prevent the proceedings' disruption and upstaging by exhilarated or wrathful Charlestonians in the gallery. A Douglas partisan composed a doggerel branding him "a poisonous reptile, many-scaled, and with most subtle fang."

Soon there was a mad rush to get out of town—"the calls for baggage and bills, the hurried cramming of carpet-bags, valises and trunks, the headlong races up and plunges down stairs, the yelling after coaches, the shaking hands and taking parting drinks." The *Cincinnati Commercial's* Halstead hopped on a train bound north for Washington. "There were many 'distinguished' passengers—there being about an equal number of United States Senators and keepers of faro tables," he observed, "the latter wearing decidedly the most costly apparel, having made the most money during their sojourn in the Palmetto City; one gambling house realized twenty-four thousand dollars clear profit, I am told. The moon was up and the night beautiful, but there was nothing to see from the windows of the car but swamps and pine forests." The *S.R. Spaulding* sailed back to Boston with the Gilmore Brass Band—and a Charleston slave hiding in a coal bunker. He was found roasting away without food or water and, to the unhappiness of some of the passengers, was transferred at sea to a vessel bound for Baltimore. Soon the "fugitive" was returned to Charleston.

Charleston's radicals had won a nearly total victory on their home court. Especially sweet was the crushing of party boss Orr. Just about all that rankled was Virginia's refusal to leave the convention with other slave-state delegations. In a letter to his secessionist friend Edmund Ruffin, Rev. Bachman teased, "Will Old Virginia nestle under the wing of that black buzzard? Will it swallow Black Republicanism, tariff, nigger and all?"

In the aftermath of the convention, B. F. Perry wrote a series of letters published in various South Carolina newspapers including the *Mercury* that attributed the secession of Southern delegates to the "outside pressure in Charleston"—to the "public speeches at hotels" and the "inflammatory speeches in caucuses," to the newspapers that whipped up the public, to the galleries that "hissed" at the members "who dared do their duty conscientiously on the floor." All of this together was "pretty strong outside pressure, producing a pretty strong excitement," he said. "We all know how contagious political excitements are," Perry wrote. "It is hard to resist such a contagion, and the boldest and the most conscientious fall victims to it before they are aware of its influence, and sometimes they never are conscious of it."

In a letter to Miles that recounted the glorious walkout of the South Carolina delegation, Rhett, Jr., confirmed Perry's observations: "Their spirit rose from the time they got to Charleston until they went out of the Convention. When they came, they had no more idea of going out than of flying." But as the pressure on the delegates mounted, the *Mercury*'s editor told Miles, "If they had not retired, they would have been mobbed, I believe."

Barny's privately delivered, frank analysis contradicted the *Mercury*'s front-page report of the "perfect order" prevailing in Charleston leading up to and immediately after the revolt led by Yancey. The public fiction of a peaceful Charleston was apparently vital for him to maintain, for he clung to it throughout the year and might have even started to believe it. Barny could not stop himself, it seemed, from gloating. His dream, his father's dream, of Southern nationhood—who could say it was out of reach? He ran a poem composed by an unnamed Missouri Democrat titled "New Nursery Ballad for Democrats":

> *Sing a song of Charleston!*
> *Bottle full of Rye!*
> *All the Douglas delegates*
> *Knocked into pie!*
> *For when the vote was opened*
> *The South began to sing*
> *"Your little Squatter Sovereignty*
> *Shan't be our King!"*

Chapter Twelve

"BLACK AS A CHARCOAL"

On Saturday, May 19, Charleston jolted awake to a startling newsflash on the third page of the *Mercury*: at the top of the "Latest by Telegraph" column was a dispatch from Chicago sent the day before that read, "It is reported that Hon. ABRAHAM LINCOLN, of Illinois, has been nominated at the Republican Convention."

Charleston craved a foil, something or someone to which to set itself in opposition. The friction created a pleasing blaze, as the city had just shown in the bonfire it lit to roast the Douglas Democrats. Lincoln, though, posed a challenge, for he was not well known to Charleston. In fact, he was nearly a blank slate. Charleston's expectation was for another man entirely: William Henry Seward, a sitting US senator representing New York and a former governor.

Charleston's horror of a future President Seward was easily manufactured out of bountiful raw material. He was a committed moral opponent of slavery who with his wife, Frances, contributed funds to support the abolitionist newspaper of Frederick Douglass, the former slave. He opposed the Fugitive Slave Law, which compelled Northerners to help capture and return runaway slaves, and, at grave risk to his political prospects, he secretly sheltered runaways at his own home to speed their journey along the Underground Railroad. In a landmark speech in 1858, he cast in fatalistic terms the "collision" between the "antagonistic systems" of slavery and free labor. "It is an irrepressible conflict between opposing and enduring forces, and it means that the United States must and will, sooner or later, become either entirely a slaveholding nation, or entirely a free-labor nation," he said. "Either the cotton and rice fields of South Carolina and the sugar plantations of Louisiana will ultimately be tilled by free labor, and Charleston and New Orleans become marts of legitimate merchandise alone, or else the rye-fields and wheat-fields of Massachusetts and New York must again be surrendered by their farmers to slave culture."

The Charleston radicals embraced Seward's notion of an "irrepressible conflict" as helpfully polarizing the political climate. Barny ran a poem in the *Mercury*: "Then welcome be it, if indeed it be/The Irrepressible Conflict! Let it come." In the spring of 1860, with Seward still uppermost in mind, the *Mercury* launched "Glimpses of the Future," a series, based on an unpublished book manuscript written by Virginia's Ruffin, intended to predict the miserable fate for a South that stayed in the Union. The first installment was a letter posted from Washington, DC, on November 11, 1864, "reporting" that President Seward had just been returned to office by a landslide vote to serve a second term. His first term, the letter allowed, had been surprisingly uneventful, but "the power of the President's party and section is now almost supreme in every department of the government," with "the great object of the abolition of slavery" awaiting the South. A later installment had Seward appointing Horace Greeley to federal office.

But the Seward of 1860 had managed to lose the Republican nomination to "a little Illinois lawyer," in his words. When the delegates met in Chicago, the party bosses had come to believe that Seward was perhaps too hot, a possible liability at the head of the ticket. On the first ballot, he drew more votes than Lincoln but not nearly enough to win the nomination. On the second ballot, New England deserted Seward for Lincoln. On the third ballot, the prize was in Lincoln's hands. He won by being the most acceptable contender whose name was not Seward. To complete the ticket, the party selected Hannibal Hamlin for vice president, an antislavery US senator from Maine.

Rev. Bachman suggested in a letter to Ruffin that Republicans, in sub-
stituting for the polarizing New Yorker, might be attempting to "lull us
asleep a little while longer." "They will probably get an ass into the presidential chair & get Seward to lead or drive him," Bachman predicted. But
not even Bachman foresaw that the "ass" would be Lincoln. Flummoxed
by the turn of events in Chicago, the *Mercury* at first conveyed the news
in an uncharacteristically straight fashion. "Mr. Lincoln is a native of Kentucky, having been born in Hardin County, on the 12th day of February,
1809," the paper wrote. "His early education was limited, and he is still a
rough, uncultivated lawyer." The paper described Lincoln accurately as
opposed to the extension of slavery to the territories but also noted, accurately, that he was "not an out-and-out Abolitionist."

This neutral approach could not stand. The stakes were too high. If
Seward could no longer serve as a foil, then Lincoln would have to do,
even though he was not at first glance an obvious demon. So began a sys-
tematic campaign by the Charleston radicals, led by the *Mercury*, to make
over Lincoln—to turn him into a sinister figure capable of arousing the
visceral hatred of Charleston and of the towns and villages and dirt farms
spread across the South.

It was in its own way a brilliant effort, calling upon the *Mercury* to
exercise all of the dark arts in which it was so proficient—rhetorical in-
citement, sly insinuation, the adept use of caricature, the hammer-like
repetition of the most resonant themes. Two personal qualities—neither
of which Lincoln could possibly alter—featured as fodder for this sketch.
The first was Lincoln's Southern heritage and family relations. He had
spent the first seven years of his life in Kentucky, a slave state where his
father served on slave patrols, and both of his parents were from Virginia.
Moreover, his wife, Mary Todd, whom he married in 1842, was also from
Kentucky. Her father, Robert Smith Todd, was the president of a bank and
a cotton merchant with a house serviced by slaves. That made her, in the
Mercury's estimation, "a refined, intelligent and accomplished lady" from
one of the "first families of Kentucky." She was said to be "a lively conver-
sationalist," and her oldest son, Robert, a sixteen-year-old preparing to
enter Harvard, was described as "a bright young man." But her husband,
in becoming a Republican, had betrayed his "native section."

This was no small charge. A Southern nationalist could easily enough understand a man like Seward possessing a personal conviction—like opposition to slavery—consistent with his section. "He is a Northern man—true to Northern interests and Northern feelings," the *Mercury* said of Seward. But a man like Lincoln—born in the South, married to a Southern belle—could not be explained. A Southern Republican was a contradiction in terms, a species not supposed to exist. There had to be something grotesquely wrong with him.

Following this ripe line of thinking, Lincoln's enemies dwelt on their target's physical appearance. True enough, Lincoln was a sight to behold even to his friends. His head seemed much too small for his lanky, six-feet-four-inch frame, and he had a wrinkled, sometimes sad-looking face that seemed old before its time. "He was not a pretty man by any means," Billy Herndon, his law partner in Springfield, once said. Still, for those sympathetically disposed toward Lincoln, there was a charm in his wide smile "lighting up every homely feature" on his face, as a journalist from New England described Lincoln on a visit to Springfield the day after the Republicans had crowned him their nominee.

But for those aiming to denigrate Lincoln, his homeliness became proof, somehow, of his awfulness. With an illustrated portrait of Lincoln from an edition of *Harper's Weekly* in its hands, the *Mercury* recoiled in seeming revulsion—"and a horrid-looking wretch he is!"—and planted the idea that the candidate of the "Black Republicans" might not even be of pure white blood. He was "sooty and scoundrelly in aspect; a cross between the nutmeg dealer, the horse swapper, and the night man," the *Mercury* wrote. "Faugh! after him, what decent white man would be President!"

A writer identified only as "Southerner" passed on a secondhand Lincoln anecdote to the newspaper while on vacation in Saratoga Springs, a favorite rest spot for the Charleston gentry. A friend of "Southerner," the story went, played a trick on an acquaintance known to be an admirer of Lincoln. The prank involved showing the Lincoln enthusiast a portrait said to be of the son of a "notorious buccaneer" from the Gulf of Mexico. The Lincoln fan "exclaimed, with indignant feelings, that all men could see in the lineaments of that face low cunning, deep and damnable treachery and piracy, most distinctly marked." And with those remarks,

"Southerner's" friend pounced, revealing the portrait to be of Lincoln. His acquaintance was supposedly left "speechless."

Lincoln's bravery also came under assault, even though it was not apparently in question. When he was in his early twenties and new to Illinois, a local band of boys known for their rough ways dared him to take on their best fighter in a wrestling match. Lincoln held his own, and, as one version had it, he offered to fight the rest as well, one at a time. After he had proven his mettle, he and the local boys became good friends. Lincoln was not, however, a military man. In an item labelled "Old Abe on the Battle Field," the *Mercury* offered the "story of the first and last military exploit of Abe Lincoln." In Lincoln's own telling, the saga of his involvement in the Black Hawk War against the Sauk and Fox Indians in the early 1830s was mostly material for his self-deprecating sense of humor. He voluntarily enlisted in the campaign and to his pride was elected a militia captain, but the company saw virtually no action. Years later, Lincoln quipped, "I had a good many bloody struggles with the musquetoes; and although I never fainted from loss of blood, I can truly say I was often very hungry." There was one episode of consequence, however. An elderly Indian wandered into camp and was set upon by the men, who threatened to kill him. Lincoln ended that talk with a promise to fight any man who harmed the Indian.

But the *Mercury* mentioned none of this. Instead, the paper reprinted a doubtful tale from the Toledo *Times* of how Lincoln, late one night while the company was sleeping, mistakenly thought the camp was surrounded by Indians about to spring an ambush. He set spurs to his horse only to fall off "headlong," according to this telling. On getting back on his feet, Lincoln shouted, "Gentleman Indians, I surrender without a word. I have not a word to offer. All I want is quarter."

Then there was the "Spot Lincoln" episode, dating to a complaint against Lincoln during his one term as a member of the House at the end of the 1840s. Drawing on his experience as a trial lawyer, Lincoln, elected as a Whig, maneuvered to put a Democratic president, James Polk, on the defensive over Polk's conduct of the Mexican War, then nearing its conclusion. Lincoln introduced a set of resolutions requiring the White House to produce evidence proving, as Polk had asserted, that Mexico had started the war by attacking US citizens "on our own soil" in the state of Texas. Was this "particular spot of soil," Lincoln demanded to know, indisputably part of Texas? Although there was a partisan element to Lincoln's challenge of Polk, the question was not unreasonable. The first blows of the conflict had been exchanged on territory north of the Rio Grande claimed by both the US and Mexican governments. Lincoln's resolutions, though, made no headway, and a Democratic paper in Illinois said the freshman Congressman could henceforth be known as "Ranchero Spotty." For the *Mercury*, this nickname represented a sharp questioning of Lincoln's patriotism: the paper ran an item from the New Hampshire *Patriot* saying that the name "Spot Lincoln" was "given him as a 'brand of shame,' for quibbling about the precise spot where American citizens had been ruthlessly butchered, and that too with a way to embarrass his own country in a just and unavoidable war, and to encourage the enemy to welcome our soldiers 'with bloody hands to hospital graves.'"

In addition to all of these disparagements of Lincoln's appearance and character, Charleston's radical secessionists strained to prove that Lincoln—the same Lincoln who once accepted a legal fee by arguing for the return of supposedly "fugitive" slaves to their owner—was in cahoots with the North's most militant abolitionists. Lincoln was said to be tightly connected to Joshua Reed Giddings, a founder of the Republican Party and a former Congressman from Ohio once censured by the House for championing the mutiny of slaves aboard a slave ship. "A. Lincoln appears to be a man after Joshua R. Giddings' own heart—vile and brutal Abolitionist as he is," the *Mercury*'s readers were told in an item taken from the *Washington Constitution*. "The old fanatic has made a speech at Oberlin warmly commending Lincoln to the support of the Abolitionists of that neighborhood, and has also written a letter to the nominee expressing his pleasure at the nomination." The truth was that Lincoln, in his time in Congress, reached out to Giddings for help on finding a compromise on slavery in the District of Columbia. Giddings felt Lincoln was on the right track—but in no way considered Lincoln a fellow abolitionist. In his letter to Lincoln, which the *Mercury* also ran, Giddings spoke fondly of their time together in Congress, but he offered no particular comment on Lincoln's views on the slave question. "Dear Lincoln: You're nominated,"

the note began. "You will be elected. . . . I have not worked for your nomination, not for that of any other man. I have labored for the establishment
of principles; and when men came to me asking my opinion of you, I only
told them, 'Lincoln is an honest man.' . . . Yours, Giddings."

The *Mercury* even managed to find fodder for its character attack on
Lincoln—this devil with "the soul of a tarantula"—in the antislavery press
of the North. Some Northern papers tended to exaggerate Lincoln's opposition to slavery in order to rally Yankee voters to his side. The *Republican*
of Springfield, Massachusetts, insisted, "We have as a candidate for President a man whose antislavery record is as unimpeachable as Seward's." The
Mercury reprinted the story on its own pages, declaring that the *Republican* "thinks 'Abe' is a full blown Abolitionist—black as a charcoal."

———

So was etched a portrait of Lincoln in the mind of Charleston. Lincoln
himself, with his subscription to the *Mercury*, understood completely what
the paper was all about, in its beat-the-drum campaigns of this sort. "Try,"
he once told Kentucky senator John J. Crittenden, "to circulate W. L. Garrison's *Liberator* where most men are salivated by the excessive use of the
Charleston *Mercury*." As crude as the newspaper's caricature was, it stuck,
not only because it catered to popular prejudices but also because there
was nothing to counter it. Lincoln had never set foot in Charleston. Except for his short time in Washington as a Congressman, his entire career
in law and politics had been spent in Illinois. The lawyers and judges in
and around Springfield who could have attested to his reputation—in the
courtroom, he was known for being diligent and methodical, crafty but not
devious, always good for his word—were nearly one thousand miles away.

Of course, there were sophisticated Charlestonians who made it their
business to follow the national political currents and knew something of
Lincoln's career, including his losing campaign against Stephen Douglas
in the election in 1858 for an Illinois seat in the US Senate. Such people
were undoubtedly aware of Lincoln's speech back in February at Cooper Union in Manhattan—the speech that established him as a plausible
moderate alternative to Seward. As if facing an audience of *Mercury* readers, Lincoln offered "a few words to the Southern people" in his casual

style. "You consider yourselves a reasonable and a just people; and I consider that in the general qualities of reason and justice you are not inferior to any other people," he said. "Still, when you speak of us Republicans, you do so only to denounce us as reptiles, or, at the best, as no better than outlaws. You will grant a hearing to pirates or murderers, but nothing like it to 'Black Republicans.'"

Turning to his fellow Republicans, Lincoln said, "It is exceedingly desirable that all parts of this great [Union] shall be at peace, and in harmony, one with another. Let us Republicans do our part to have it so. Even though much provoked, let us do nothing through passion and ill temper. Even though the southern people will not so much as listen to us, let us calmly consider their demands, and yield to them if, in our deliberate view of our duty, we possibly can." He added, "The question recurs, what will satisfy them? Simply this: We must not only let them alone, but we must somehow, convince them that we do let them alone."

To be "let alone" was a recurrent demand from the South. But despite its solicitous appeal to the South, the Cooper Union speech went unreported in the *Mercury*. Nor was Charleston made aware that Lincoln's political hero was not any founder of the Republican Party but Henry Clay of Kentucky, the Whig leader known as the "Great Compromiser." Clay, who died in 1852, had helped resolve the crisis in the 1830s over South Carolina's bid to nullify the federal tariff by persuading the White House and Congress to agree to a deal that gradually reduced the tariff while authorizing federal military enforcement, if necessary, of the levy. He had been a friend of Lincoln's father-in-law, and the young Lincoln had called him "my beau ideal of a statesman."

In fact, there was one man in Charleston who had direct experience with Lincoln—who had been in the House of Representatives with him, who knew what he looked and sounded like, who understood his political style and sensibility, indeed who was there when he was branded with that abolitionist epitaph "slave hound from Illinois." But a less sympathetic source of information hardly could be imagined, for that man was the senior Rhett.

Lincoln had watched the Charleston Democratic Convention with amazement—"Charleston hangs fire," he wrote a Springfield acquaintance at the end of April, in the midst of the party's agonies. But after he was nominated, he was determined to say as little as possible on how he might deal with a breakaway South. Perhaps he did not know himself.

Chapter Thirteen

"DO NOT BLINK"

T he presidential election was not for six months. For how long could fervor be maintained against the villainous Republican whose triumph loomed? Into the breach stepped planter John Ferrars Townsend of Edisto Island. His long-standing reputation was as a softener of the more radical, sharper-edged impulses of neighboring plantation owners. On occasion he had even ridiculed their beliefs. But as Lincoln's presidency neared, he found his views gravitating toward theirs. The threat to the South and to his way of life was urgent, and he was ready to go public with his newfound convictions.

Every revolution needs its rank and file—boots to march the streets, voices to chant the anthems, and hands to beat the drums, raise the banners, and light the bonfires. Every revolution also needs its storytellers to make sense of the seeming chaos of the moment, to cobble together the strands of a resonant narrative, and to supply the stirring or the cutting phrase at the most opportune moment. This was inevitably a job for the aristocrat, the master naturally fit, at least in his own estimation, to dispense words worth heeding.

With his gold spectacles, leonine mane of white hair, and a touch of arrogance lurking about his thin lips, "our grand old man," as a neighbor called Townsend, fit the part. He was without peer among his planters' fraternity in his gift with words—his ability to give invigorating expression to the issue of the moment. He had the gift, too, if indeed it was a gift, of psychological intuition: he grasped that a man might not consider his life complete without a cause that was worth dying for.

———

Hephzibah Jenkins, Townsend's mother, was born in the cellar of a townhouse on Boundary Street in Charleston in April 1780, the month the British began to lay siege to the city in the midst of the Revolutionary War. While her mother lay sick, close to death, and her father, a captain for the Revolutionary troops, was held captive by the British, a plan was hatched to spirit the infant out of Charleston. According to family lore, the baby was entrusted to the care of two elderly family slaves, old Jack and his wife, Jean. After Hephzibah's mother died and with her but four weeks old, the journey began. In a small paddleboat, Jack and Jean made their way with their cargo south along the coastline, rowing at night and hiding in marshes and woods by day to keep from being spotted by British patrol boats. It took them six days to reach their destination, the family plantation of Bleak Hall on Edisto Island, part of the Sea Islands chain. The property took its name from its exposure to the fierce winds of the open Atlantic.

John was born at Bleak Hall in 1799 and, like any white male in these parts, learned at an early age how to ride horseback, hunt, and shoot. The family's nearly four-thousand-acre tract afforded wide scope for these enjoyments. At the age of fifteen, he went off to South Carolina College, accompanied by his nearly lifelong body servant, "Daddy Sam," who looked after him and his belongings. Illness forced him to leave the college, but he left for Princeton, then known as the College of New Jersey, soon after he recovered. A classmate from Virginia lauded John for his impeccable manners: "That stars might fall, moons fail to give their light, ere Townsend ceased to be polite." After graduating, he at first studied law in Charleston but soon decided he would rather become a planter like his father.

Upon his father's death in 1842, Townsend became the master of Bleak Hall. By then, he had a wife, Mary Caroline Jenkins, the daughter of a planter on nearby Wadmalaw Island. She called him the "Knight of the Golden Crest," and the legend of his wooing saw him galloping on horseback "through all weathers to visit his 'Lady Love.'" Hephzibah died five years later. John and Mary Caroline had four children together, and the family lived in the plantation's namesake three-story mansion on the southeast corner of the island. He was a member of the Quadrille Association, which sponsored formal, stylized dances for Charleston high society.

The privileges and entitlements of life at Bleak Hall were prominently displayed at the Oyster Roast the Townsends held each year around Christmastime. The guests were his neighbors—fellow planters and their wives. The setting was Botany Bay, a small island owned by Townsend and connected to Bleak Hall by a causeway. The island was a tropical jungle of oaks and palmettos, teeming with deer and wild hogs. Partygoers arrived in the afternoon on carriages and stationed themselves at tables set on the beach. The air was perfumed by burning oak, hickory, and cedar. First the oysters were served, just an appetizer, a guest recalled, as "a dozen little picaninnies rushed from the fire with platters filled with hot, sputtering oysters and placed one before each person." Guests washed down the oysters with hot punch poured by a butler from a silver pitcher, a concoction of "lemons, hot water, sugar, and double-proof, imported Irish peat whiskey." After a rest, dinner arrived, a feast including terrapin and a dish known as palmetto cabbage, taken from the heart of the tree, which tasted akin to cauliflower or artichoke. Champagne was uncorked, and the guests stayed at the table for hours, lulled by the soft sounds of the surf and the wind rustling through palmetto fronds. Finally, at sunset, the carriages carted them away.

The most rarified feature of Bleak Hall was a vast, exotic garden. It was a special pride of the Townsends and had been praised for its "taste and skill" by *De Bow's Review*, the New Orleans–based publication run by a Charleston native promoting Southern nationalism. The garden was the masterwork of a Chinese botanist, Oqui, who had come to America in the early 1850s with Commodore Matthew Perry on his return home from his mission to Japan. Through an acquaintance, John Townsend met Oqui in Washington and convinced him to come live at Bleak Hall, where a house was built for him and slaves put under his management. Oqui planted white poppies and olive, orange, and spice trees and also the yellow-blossomed Chinese tobacco plant, brought back with him from Asia, with a flower shaped like a trumpet that was an irresistible lure for hummingbirds. In June 1858, Mary Caroline wrote to her daughter, away at school, "We go out every morning when the sun is not too warm and walk in the garden. The spring flowers have disappeared. We have now gardenias, myrtles, and mimosa in bloom, with pomegranates, and golden coreopsis."

It was a life made possible by the business of the plantation: cotton. Growing cotton on the Sea Islands began in the 1790s. Through experimentation, planters developed a special strain of the plant producing silky and especially long fibers of a creamy hue. Sea Islands cotton, made exclusively for export, became a brand name and was the finest cotton available in America and par to anything produced in the world. At this practice, too, John Townsend excelled. He was as meticulous with his cotton as he was with his garden. Bleak Hall cotton was a household name for the most discerning cotton buyers in Europe.

Cotton production was labor intensive and required large numbers of slaves. The Sea Island planters were well known for their willingness to pay top dollar for field hands in the South's slave markets. Virtually everything that was not outright wilderness was carved up into plantation land. The first census of Edisto, taken in 1790, counted 223 whites and 1,692 blacks, all slaves. By 1860, the number of whites had nudged up to 329, but the slave population had spiked to 5,082 as planters reinvested profits of their cotton harvest back into the purchase of additional laborers. The slaves lived in wooden cabins, some with little more than a dirt floor, and they were organized into work teams managed by a driver, whip in hand, who was himself a slave.

The annual growing cycle began in February, when slaves set forth in flat-bottomed bateau boats to dig marsh mud out of the sides of creeks, and cotton was picked in stages extending from August to December. Even small boys and girls were given quotas, and fully grown adults were expected to pick on the order of eighty pounds in one day. Escape to the mainland was nearly impossible. On occasion slaves protested their condition by breaking a tool.

In 1860, Townsend brought to market 150 bales of cotton, the harvest of his 1859 growing season. Of Edisto's forty-six planters, only thirteen produced more than 60 bales, and only one planter exceeded Townsend's crop. With 400 pounds of cotton to a bale, and because his premium Sea Island cotton was able to fetch $1 per pound, he grossed $60,000 minus the commission paid to the broker for the transaction. Such was the bounty reaped by his investment in the 272 slaves he owned, and it was more than enough to pay for the regular expenses of his operation—for cotton seeds; for plantation machinery and tools; for horses and mules; for peas, corn, and sweet potatoes; for beef cattle, pigs, sheep, and poultry; for Oqui's garden; and, of course, for the champagne and whiskey poured at the Oyster Roast.

Planters often sought political office, and Townsend was notably precocious in this regard. Before he reached the age of twenty-one, he won his first election to the South Carolina House, representing St. John's, Colleton, a Sea Island district that included Edisto. Because land ownership was required for holding office, Townsend's father arranged to put a parcel in the son's name. He served five terms in the House. He was neither part of any political machine nor an ambitious leader of any cause, but he was able to express himself sharply and lucidly and with rhythm and pace. In 1828, ten constituents sent Townsend a letter calling into question the young representative's opposition to the federal tariff. In dramatic response, Townsend reached for his purse and commissioned a Broad Street printing house to publish *A Reply* in pamphlet form. It was targeted not only to the constituents but also to all of the planters and businessmen with an interest in politics. Addressing "my intimate associates" and friends "both personal and political," he said he "had not supposed that there could have existed a doubt in this community" as to his stance. "My opinion" of the tariff is "that it is absolutely unconstitutional; that in its intentions, it is most iniquitous and unjust; that in its operations it is peculiarly oppressive to our interests" and "should be abandoned as speedily as possible."

As abstract as such matters seemed, politics was intensely personal for Townsend. At the end of 1845, he wrote to Calhoun in the Senate about his "painful anxiety" over what he saw as a possible British plot to destroy the cotton economy of the South. At the time, the US and British governments were involved in contentious negotiation over the boundary separating the so-called Oregon Territories, stretching from the Rocky Mountains to British-controlled Canada on the Pacific. Perhaps the mischief-making British, Townsend suggested to Calhoun, would see an opportunity to strike a blow against America with an attack on the Atlantic seacoast to "destroy our commerce, with all the exports of our agriculture" and "lay in ashes all our tidewater cities." Britain's objective also might be "to paralyze us in our slave labour institutions" and possibly even to seize Texas to gain a source of cotton for England's textile mills. "Pardon me, my dear Sir, for indulging in these speculations," Townsend wrote. "All of my family; almost all the friends I have in this world; and all the property I own, will be at the mercy of the enemy, in the event of war."

A war never came to pass, and the Sea Islands remained unmolested. Still, the "painful anxiety" Townsend confessed on this occasion never deserted him. He was at the pinnacle of a social order with everything to lose, and any threat from the British paled in relation to what the North, prodded by the abolitionists, might do to disturb his world. Yet Townsend's constituents were not wrong in seeing him as a moderate. He was willing to entertain Southern secession but only if the slave states went out as a bloc. In the 1850s, when he returned to Columbia as a state senator, no one was his equal at the pithy encapsulation of the Cooperationist perspective. Supporters of a freestanding South Carolina republic forget that "Venice is, at this very moment, under the iron heel of Austrian soldiery," he said. He regarded unilateral secession as "defunct." There was no need for such issues "to be dug up from their graves, and, like dead frogs, to be galvanized into a spasmodic life."

As a commentator, he placed himself in the tradition of his hero, the "profound" Edmund Burke, the eighteenth-century British philosopher and statesman who had published a memorable critique of the French Revolution in pamphlet form. He understood that the pamphleteer is not necessarily the propagandist. It is one thing to take a combative but well-reasoned stand on an issue, another to rally the public by appealing to raw emotion and especially to primal fears. The brute task is to destroy any middle ground, to present the common man with an unavoidable, "either or" choice. Townsend grasped that propaganda was not elevated work and denounced demagogues who "can hope for distinction only by keeping the people fretted." With his Princeton education and planter's refinement, the descent to propaganda was a last resort—a bow to the necessity of circumstance. It was a lowering of his standards of right conduct, and yet, six months into 1860, he stooped to it.

On the first Thursday of June, he addressed the citizens of St. John's, Colleton, at a public meeting called to consider matters in light of the fracturing of the Democratic Party in Charleston. The meeting was held in the village of Rockville on Wadmalaw Island. Mary Caroline was from the island, and the couple built a summer home in Rockville shortly after the marriage. Seaside Rockville was an idyll for planter families, a place to teach their children how to sail—the annual regatta was a highlight of the season—and a refuge from the malaria that plagued much of the Carolina coast. A steamer made a daily trip to Charleston and back, stopping at Edisto along the way.

A gathering like this one had the character of a family affair. Townsend would be speaking to men he had known for decades—men who had attended his Oyster Roast, men who in some cases had questioned his political fortitude. Whatever their quarrels, they were bonded by their joint interest in the Sea Island plantation economy. Or to put it another way, they were apt to share the same fate, for good or ill, depending on the political turbulence before them. At the same time, Townsend must have understood that he would be speaking to a much wider audience as well: his remarks were carefully crafted and had in them the makings of another pamphlet.

He began with a full-throated endorsement of the breaking up of the convention and of the Southern Democrats' unwillingness to accept anything less than explicit support of *Dred Scott*. "The causes which led to that rupture, so far from being temporary," Townsend told the gathering, "are permanent, and increasing, day by day, in number and strength. No union, then, on principles, may ever again be looked for in any Democratic Party." With the "Black Republicans" virtually certain to win the presidential election in November, the South, Townsend declared, must prepare to leave the Union as soon as the election results were known. "And here," Townsend cried, "I expect to be met with the babbling cry-out of the timorous—'Why this is disunion!' and with the stereotyped croakings of the old fogey 'Union-savers'—'Why this is revolution!' Even so, fellow citizens," he urged, "do not blink . . . look it full in the face. Become familiar with it; for the necessities of our condition require it. Let us hear no more of the sophomoric sentimentality about 'the Union'—'the glorious Union'—cemented with the blood of our father[s], and to be cherished for the memories of the past, etc., etc." It sounded like a battle cry. The plea could not have escaped Townsend's first son, who would be turning fifteen years old in 1860, nearly old enough to serve in the military.

Townsend was convinced cotton could be grown profitably only with the use of slave labor. For this reason alone, abolitionism, which he believed to be the work of religious fanatics, was an existential threat to the agrarian economy of the slave South and to the Sea Island cotton planters in particular. To purchase and maintain a slave was a proven financial investment. To pay a laborer to scrape out creek beds, cultivate the fields, pick the cotton, and pour the champagne for party guests was an unsustainable business method. An unsuccessful British experiment with hired black labor in the fields of the West Indies, launched after the abolition of slavery there in 1838, demonstrated "that these tropical productions cannot be obtained except by steady and continuous labor, which the freed negro will not give." The negro, of course, was naturally disposed to "sloth," Townsend reminded the assemblage at Rockville.

The breakup of the Union should start, he continued, with "the eight seceding States at Charleston"—the states whose delegations walked out of the convention. That meant South Carolina along with Alabama, Mississippi, Louisiana, Georgia, Arkansas, Texas, and Florida—but not Virginia

and the other slave states bordering the North. This bloc, he allowed, suf-
ficed to form a constitution, organize a government, and hold elections
for a Southern president and Congress. As for launching a "Southern
Confederacy" without Virginia and the others, "sooner or later, they must
make a choice," Townsend said, "and all the chances are in favor of their
uniting themselves with their brethren and natural allies of the South. The
Revolution will then be complete." With or without war, the Confederacy
would be set to take its place "among the foremost nations of the earth."

Townsend recognized that propaganda is not only about cultivating
fear but also about planting seeds of hope. "The consequences" of secession, Townsend declared, "will be those of a prosperity—financial,
commercial and manufacturing—which the South has never before
enjoyed." In support of this optimistic vision, he noted that "the eight
seceding States alone possess a territory more than three times as great
as France, more than six times as large as Prussia, and nearly six times
as large as England, Scotland and Ireland put together." The agricultural productions of this bloc were "the most valuable in the world" and
"objects of envy to every manufacturing and commercial people" on the
planet. Moreover, Southern independence, in this view, offered a permanent solution to the nagging problem of abolitionism. For "when the
South shall have taken our institution of African slavery under her entire
and sovereign control," he reasoned, "and no other people should consider that they are responsible for it, in any way, for its alleged sins, and
crimes, and disadvantages to them, as partners in this present Union, we
shall be rid of the impertinent intermeddling with it, with which we are
now annoyed."

He was optimistic, too, about how the world beyond America's shores
would treat a new Southern republic. "It is a mistake," Townsend said at
Rockville, "to suppose that England, France, Germany, Russia, and the
other commercial and manufacturing nations, are hostile to our African
slavery." Nations, he pronounced, "are not governed by sentiment, much
less by sentimentality, but by their interest; and these peoples . . . are too
deeply interested in procuring the raw materials, which the South, almost
alone, can supply them with . . . to embark in a silly quarrel with us about

the kind of labor by which these raw materials are acquired." Indeed, "no alliance would be more natural than one between these nations and our Southern Confederacy. There would be no cause of rivalry and jealousy." Here Townsend seemed to be on solid ground. Many political and business figures in the North shared the idea of cotton as a geopolitical trump card for the South. The South supplied nearly 80 percent of the raw cotton bales used in European textile factories—six times more than supplied by the East Indies. The British cotton industry, by far the largest importer, received more than 80 percent of its cotton from the South, consisted of more than 3,000 factories, and directly employed some 650,000 workers. Tens of millions of pounds sterling were invested in cotton.

Townsend insisted that the North was feeble and apt to crumble at the South's secession, to be "separated into two or more divisions" and no longer able to "plunder" the wealth of the South. He neglected to note that the North at this time accounted for more than 80 percent of the Union's manufacturing capacity and 65 percent of the nation's railroad mileage. Despite long-standing calls by Southern nationalists for the South to build textile mills to weave its raw cotton into finished, high-value products, the mills of the North accounted for 90 percent of the value of cotton textiles produced in the Union. New York was well established as the nation's financial hub, and many Southern planters were in debt to New York banks. Merchants in Southern towns typically went to New York—not to Charleston or any other Southern city—to purchase at wholesale the goods they sold to customers at retail. Northern shipping lines dominated trade with Europe. That included the South's cotton.

Townsend's speech evinced the worldview, the fears, and also the hopes of his class. His was a mind-set that had taken generations to develop and was as firmly rooted in the Lowcountry as the oaks and palmettos. His performance won over the assemblage at Rockville. Just two years after sixteen of his neighbors accused him of being soft on states' rights, one of these men moved that the speech, with its "subjects of deep interest to every Southern man," be widely published. The *Courier* ran an article on the persuasiveness of Townsend's vision of a "flourishing" South embraced by Europe and ascendant over a factious North. The *Mercury* printed the entirety of the speech in two installments, the first on June 13. Now his words would reach readers from New York to New Orleans. When the inevitable pamphlet was published under the title *The South Alone, Should Govern the South*, copies were devoured in cities and towns all over the South. Townsend gained renown for his Sea Island cotton but most of all, it proved, for his seductively spun words.

Chapter Fourteen

"TO SET US FREE"

O n July 4th, at three in the morning, Charleston awoke to the sound of cannon fire from the Citadel Green—the traditional Independence Day welcoming from the town. There were the usual parades of volunteer militia bands in colorful uniform—the German Artillery in its brass-mounted helmets sweltering in the 102-degree heat—and in the evening a banquet for town notables at Hibernian Hall. That might have been a time, amid the clanking of glasses, for fiery speeches denouncing the "cursed Union" to which Charleston was still bound. But as it turned out, the city was feeling unexpectedly nostalgic. The host of the banquet was the '76 Association, a group formed by elite Charlestonians in 1810 to pay homage to the Declaration of Independence. It was celebrating its fiftieth anniversary, and an ode composed for the occasion was read out loud:

> How uncertain our future, how cheerless the view:
> No beacon to light up, no bright beaming hue . . .
> The day, when dissevered from Union we be,
> In darkness will break, o'er the land and the sea;
> The Genius of Liberty, mantled with gloom,
> Will despairingly weep o'er America's doom . . .
> Once 'twas a Union, dearly cherished and loved—
> A Union, cemented by patriotic blood.

With its elegiac tone and weepy spirit, the poem was exactly what John Townsend had hoped to put a stop to in his "do not blink" speech to his Sea Island audience. Secessionists could only hope that this nostalgia was a last spasm of feeling for the Union and nothing more. Not every day is a good one for a revolution. Perhaps heads had been clouded by the wine. Perhaps the unremitting heat and the inescapable stench from dead fish and rats rotting on the mudflats had sapped resolve.

Five nights later, the radicals convened a political meeting at the theater. Wealthy planters and prominent merchants filed in along with others of lesser standing. Representative Miles, on hand to preside, looked out from the stage at scores of familiar faces. Some were close friends, men like merchant Henry Gourdin, brother of Robert and one of the original investors in the theater built twenty-five years before. The pugilistic ex-mayor, John Schnierle, was there, as was steamship baron M. C. Mordecai. And waiting to give the featured speech was Barnwell Rhett, who came with his son Edmund. Barny was not present. At the end of June, his wife Josephine had died suddenly of typhoid, and, just two years into his thirties, he was a widower. His health had suffered in his grief, and he had left Charleston to recuperate in the cooler climes of Saratoga.

The immediate purpose of the meeting was to endorse the presidential nomination of John Breckinridge of Kentucky at the Constitutional Democratic Convention of Southern delegates held in Richmond after the crackup of the Charleston convention. Breckinridge was serving in the White House as Buchanan's vice president and was the Southerners' counter to Stephen Douglas, successfully nominated by the Northern Democrats at the National Democratic Convention in Baltimore. The Democrats were now committed to a pair of rival sectional candidates. The radical secessionists' plan to concede the White House to the Republicans was on track—even with still another candidate in the race, John Bell of Tennessee, nominated by a group of former Whigs.

The Charleston men gave their unanimous approval to Breckinridge's nomination. The "Southern people," they resolved, "look for no power but their own to protect their rights," and "they require no other for their complete vindication and perpetuity to all time." Barnwell Rhett, a delegate to the Richmond convention, then addressed the hall. It was his first speech to a public gathering in Charleston in eight years—since his retreat from the spotlight after being defeated in his quest for South Carolina, on its own, to take leave of the Union. The *Mercury* reported that his "appearance on the stage was hailed with demonstrations of tumultuous applause" and printed his speech in its entirety. As was ever his wont, he took some time to clear his throat. He started with a review of constitutional history and the tyranny of measures like the tariff to remind his listeners of how the federal government, in the grip of the North, had become a monstrosity of unbounded appetite: "Everything that a man eats, drinks or wears, is taxed by its all-pervading pragmatical exactions." Washington had set its ravenous appetite on "the one internal object which it was supposed was beyond its influence or power—slavery in the Southern States," he declared. "Even that—belonging to us exclusively— the basis of our civilization and wealth . . . this Government embraces as an object of its control and legislation." Congress itself, for ten years running, had been spewing the "propaganda" of abolitionism.

Finally, he arrived at the election and the Republican ticket of Lincoln and Hamlin. "The last act, in the grand drama of consolidation, seems now about to take place in the next Presidential election. Sectional candidates, nominated by a sectional convention, upon sectional principles, are brought forward by the North, to rule the South. Hostility to Southern slavery, is the grand principle of their organization." It has come to this, he thundered: "A renegade Southerner, and a man with negro blood in his veins—as the papers state—are their candidates. . . . To reward a traitor to the South, and to insult the South, by placing over the Southern States . . . a man of negro origin, is the policy of this sectional party."

The "negro blood" swipe at Hamlin was a reference, apparently, to the senator's swarthy complexion. In stooping to this as a crude means of arousing the racial fears of white Charleston, Barnwell Rhett showed that his years away from the podium had not changed his familiar style of combining high-minded rhetoric about the Constitution with the jagged-edged politics of the personal. Yet the familiar doubts about his leadership abilities also persisted. "Mr. Rhett I hold to be the most un-trustworthy politician in the State," planter William Henry Ravenel wrote in his diary. "He is truly devoted to his State and to the South, but he wants judgement, and can never be relied on for statesmanship as a leader."

It was left to Miles to close out the meeting. He was not the featured speaker, but whatever he had to say was bound to matter more than the senior Rhett's diatribe. Miles had Charleston's affection and its respect. A cerebral man, once a professor of mathematics at the College of Charleston, he was not a natural politician. In fact, he almost surely would not have entered politics at all had Charleston not begged him to run for mayor—moved by reports of his heroic efforts as a volunteer nurse to combat an epidemic of yellow fever on the coast of Virginia. After he instituted municipal improvements like establishment of a sewage system, his grateful constituents sent him to Washington. His experience there amounted to nearly four years and convinced him the North would never leave the South alone. He was not a slave owner; his position on secession, which gradually hardened, was a matter of principle: the Constitution unambiguously permitted slavery, and if that principle was not to be enforced, then the South should leave the Union. Miles did not scoff, as many of his fellow radicals did, at the prospect of secession leading to a war. He thought an armed conflict with the North might well come and that a civil war was apt to be "so bloody, so terrible, that the parallel of it has never yet blotted the page of history." Still, his position was fixed.

Miles had celebrated his thirty-eighth birthday on July 4—and had been at the banquet at Hibernian Hall to listen, no doubt with clenched jaw, to the poem mourning the demise of the "cherished" Union. At the theater, his frustration poured forth. What if "Lincoln and his 'irrepressible conflict,' and 'higher law,' Constitution-ignoring party [were] elected to rule over us? What then?" he asked his constituents. It was a neat trick—inserting Seward's fighting phrase into Lincoln's mouth. "I am sick at heart of the endless talk and bluster of the South. If we are in earnest, let us act," he pleaded. "The question is with you. It is for you to decide—you, the descendants of the men of '76." Shortly after this "manly address," as the *Mercury* called it, Miles contracted typhoid fever and retreated to the Rhode Island seacoast to convalesce.

Lincoln's specter still remained the best means by which secessionist leaders could seek to rouse the people of Charleston, and the fears were indeed palpable. A conspiratorial haze seemed to envelop the city, from the tip of St. Michael's down to the alleyways along the waterfront, as if Lincoln's presence already could be felt. An editor for the *New York Times*, eager to follow up on "hints" of "secret" military preparations among peoples of the South, hit upon the idea of sending a young reporter to the region in disguise as a tourist from England. The correspondent made it through New Orleans and Memphis, Nashville and Atlanta, Mobile and Savannah without attracting suspicion. But not through Charleston: in a barroom, a local man, pumped up with whiskey, said the "tourist" looked to be not an Englishman but a "damned Lincoln spy." The reporter wisely fled town.

The suspicions were not groundless, for Lincoln did in fact have a secret set of eyes and ears in Charleston. He was stocky and broad-shouldered with an impressive mustache and a thatch of curly hair. He was a military man, acquainted with battle, and he was possessed of sensitive political antennae as well as strong political convictions, on behalf of which he was unafraid to take initiative. Such was Captain Abner Doubleday—a forty-one-year-old West Point graduate and veteran of the Mexican War assigned to the US Army garrison at Fort Moultrie, on Sullivan's Island. He was born in 1819 in Ballston Spa in New York, near Saratoga Springs, the same region, bursting with progressive fervor, that produced William Seward. The village of Auburn, in which the Doubleday family lived for a time, was a stop along the Underground Railroad. In 1848, women's rights activists met in Seneca Falls, some fifteen miles from Auburn, for their first-ever convention in the United States, organized by a pair of abolitionists. Although Abner was to become famous for the legend that he invented the game of baseball, his true passions ran to chess and map-making. He did not use alcohol or tobacco and cultivated his wide-ranging mind by reading the essays of Ralph Waldo Emerson and other moral and spiritual philosophers writing for the *Dial* magazine, to which he was a subscriber. He believed wholeheartedly in the Union and, like Emerson, found slavery abhorrent.

With his assignment as second in command to Fort Moultrie's garrison at the start of the summer of 1860, he became a regular visitor in Charleston. St. Michael's was easily visible on a clear day from the fort's harbor-side home on the western fingertip of sandy Sullivan's Island. He found Charleston, as he wrote years later, in a book of reminiscences, "far from being a pleasant place for a loyal man. Almost every public assemblage was tinctured with treasonable sentiments, and toasts against the flag were always warmly appreciated." As early as July, "there was much talk of secession," he noted, "and threats of taking the forts as soon as a separation should occur." Of Charleston's four federal forts, only ramshackle Moultrie—with its cracked, twelve-foot-high walls—was occupied, by a skeleton allotment of seven officers and sixty-one enlisted men plus a regimental band. The commanding officer was the aging Colonel John L. Gardner, a veteran of the War of 1812 sympathetic to the cause of the South who resided with his family outside of the fort.

Doubleday quickly judged Moultrie barely defensible. It shared the island with numerous summer residences and was abutted by sand dunes on which a sharpshooter might perch. "The contingency that the people of Charleston themselves might attack a fort intended for their own protection had never been anticipated," he noted. He was appalled by Barnwell Rhett's "violent speeches to the mob" as well as of "other Ultra men in Charleston" with their calls "to drive every United States official out of the State." He was likewise taken aback at the senior Rhett's attempt to stir the pot by calling Hannibal Hamlin a mulatto. And his apprehensions could not have been relieved by an island homeowner hoisting to the sky a custom-made flag with fifteen white stars, one for each slave state.

An opportunity to raise an alarm presented itself in his regular correspondence with his brother Ulysses, who worked at a New York City bank. Abner arranged to have his letters, which set forth his impressions of the situation in and around Charleston, forwarded by his brother to Lincoln in Springfield. Concerned that the letters might be opened by postal authorities in the South, Abner and Ulysses worked out a secret code that assigned numbers to words in a dictionary each of them owned. In one of the letters, Abner pledged his support for Lincoln—whom he assumed would be elected—and assured the candidate that "I shall never have any favor to ask of you as President." Another included a hand-drawn map of Charleston. He was worried not only about the security of the forts but also about the federal arsenal on the banks of the Ashley River in western Charleston, loaded with munitions and thinly guarded.

For all his anxiousness, Doubleday at first was not convinced the secession movement would triumph in Charleston. Even with the excitement raised by the talk of secession, sensible citizens, he figured, were bound to question the sales pitch—laid out by wealthy planters like John Townsend and amplified by the *Mercury*—that the South, with King Cotton on its side, would be more prosperous outside of the Union than inside of it. Even the secessionists might think twice, he drily noted, because many of them "were enjoying the sweets of Federal patronage" courtesy of Washington.

Much like an intelligence operative on a delicate mission in foreign territory, Doubleday made it his business to understand all parts of Charleston. He had to be careful because the secessionists viewed every Union officer in the city as possibly hostile to their cause. But Doubleday did his work artfully. He reached out to the temperate Memminger and the sympathetic Petigru, and he cultivated contacts among merchants, whom he saw as a potential source of pragmatic resistance to secession. He also burrowed into black Charleston. Free blacks were quite likely his best source of information. Some Northern journalists had lines into free blacks in Charleston, and Doubleday, as a Yankee and a stalwart Unionist, might have been seen as trustworthy. He probably conversed directly with slaves, as would have been possible in Charleston's many nooks, without drawing attention to such encounters. The assessment he developed certainly could not be found in the *Mercury*: Doubleday discovered that not only Charleston's secessionists harbored an outsized image of the man who might next be president. "The negroes overheard a great deal that was said by their masters," Doubleday learned, "and in consequence became excited and troublesome, for the news flew like wild-fire among them that 'Massa Linkum' was coming to set them all free."

Chapter Fifteen

"HUNTED DOWN"

A s summer passed, and with Lincoln's election approaching, white Charleston turned to increasingly violent domination of the black community. The knock on the door could come at any time, day or night. All of the free blacks of Charleston—over three thousand people— expected and feared it, including tailor James M. Johnson. He typically spent most of the year at his home in the dusty town of Stateburg, one hundred miles north of Charleston, but this summer he was living in the city, helping out his father, James D. Johnson, at the family's tailoring shop on King Street. His father was getting on in years and finding the work- load more than he could handle. The elder Johnson made room for his son at his home on 9 Coming Street. He also owned the larger house next door on 7 Coming, which he rented out.

Tree-shaded Coming, with its brick and wood-frame houses scrunched together and often turned sideways in the Charleston style, was the heart of Charleston's community of free blacks and, in particular, of the most successful among them—the so-called "brown elite" of mulattos to which the Johnsons belonged. The street ran from the edge of downtown, where James D. had his houses, into the upper reaches of the city. Here could be found many of the black Charlestonians' civic institutions, such as the Friendship Moralist Society, a group established to purchase burial plots for free mulattos and dispense financial aid to widows and orphans. Yet it was not quite an enclave for the brown elite because white families lived on Coming, too. A Jewish cemetery dating to colonial times occupied the northern stretch, and a German-owned grocery store was just three blocks up from the Johnson properties.

Johnson had grown up in Charleston, where his father had lived for some forty years. The King Street shop, a short stroll from Coming and Beaufain Streets, had been operating for about a quarter century. Clients included some of the most prominent figures in white Charleston, such as Judge Andrew Gordon Magrath, who had his measurements taken in his chambers in the courthouse. As was permitted by the law, the Johnsons owned their own slaves to assist in the shop and at home. Privileged families like the Johnsons also sent their children to special schools, three of which were on Coming and one of which was operated by a white man. Such schools were technically against the law, but they were an open secret. "Colored" children, some with golden hair and blue eyes, could often be seen walking along the street, books tucked under their arms. Men of consequence in the white community, such as Christopher Memminger, generally tolerated the schools. Although "the free colored man" may not vote, Memminger once told his fellow legislators in Columbia, "he has his rights just as well as any other citizen." And among the free blacks, he added, are "men of most estimable character." The Memminger and Johnson families worshipped at the same church, Grace Episcopal, a block and a half from the Johnsons' home. As members of the elite, the Johnsons were safe and secure compared with slaves at the bottom of the social order—or so they thought.

The knock would come, and at the door would be a policeman, in his blue cloak with brass buttons. His demand would be for documents, always the documents, to indisputably prove that the free black was just that— free. At a basic level, such a demand was absurd. Everything about a family like the Johnsons, from their ownership of real estate and slave property to their long-established trade as tailors, confirmed they were not slaves. But in the summer of 1860, none of that mattered. There were state and municipal laws and regulations on the books, pages and pages of them, as to the status and requirements of free blacks, and now the rules were to be enforced, to the letter. The free black had to show up-to-date payment to the city of Charleston of the annual capitation or "head tax"—and there had better be a receipt for every single past year as well. The free black also had to produce valid certification of an agreement with a white guardian who had stood up in court to attest to his or her "good character and correct habits." The state had enacted that particular rule in the wake of the Denmark Vesey insurrection plot of 1822.

If the free black could not fully satisfy these demands, all would be lost: property confiscated and sold off, freedom taken away. The free black would be reduced to a slave. For some, this would be a return to their earlier life; either their master, perhaps at death, had granted their freedom, or they had managed to purchase it. For those born free, slavery would be a new experience altogether. The Johnsons could easily be enslaved, as could barber F. H. Mark, whose prime location at the Charleston Hotel allowed him to pile up assets in excess of $20,000. He was deemed "a good credit risk" by a white credit agency in town. The Charleston police could also enslave the Holloway family, operators of a prosperous harness repair shop on Beaufain. The Holloway lineage in Charleston, meticulously recorded in the family bible, stretched back to the eighteenth century. Even Joseph Ellison Adger, owner of a hardware store on East Bay Street and the son of one of Charleston's richest white merchants, was at risk.

With their dreaded knock, the police were terrorizing Charleston's free black families one home at a time, as James M. Johnson well understood. "They have not visited Coming Street as yet," he wrote to his brother-in-law outside of Charleston on August 20, "but have declared their intention not to leave one family uncalled upon" in the neighborhood. "It is like the heat of this summer conceded to be the hottest and most deadly assault ever made upon this class," Johnson said in his letter, "and animal, like vegetable life, must wither and die from the shock."

On the surface, the enemy of the free blacks seemed to be the mayor of Charleston, Charles Macbeth. A wealthy attorney with a house on Legaré Street and ten slaves in his possession, Macbeth was from an old-line Charleston family with roots in the planter community. He had been elected to the office in 1857 to succeed William Porcher Miles. A free black whose papers were in doubt would appear before Macbeth in the

"Mayor's Court," over which he presided. It was part of a daily ritual: Charlestonians, black, brown, and white, were hauled in by the police for a variety of often petty charges—from selling "spirituous liquors" to stealing raw cotton off the wharf—and brought before Macbeth.

Although Macbeth had launched the crackdown on free blacks, he really was something of a tool, a front man. The true enemy of the brown elite, standing behind the mayor, was the white working class of Charleston. A blue-collar white man was apt to envy a family like the Johnsons, who could afford to own slaves as he could not, of whom the white gentry thought more highly than of him, and who married off their daughters in champagne-soaked festivities far beyond his meager means. It was hard, from the perspective of the white workingman, to see why any black person should be allowed to work at a trade—and, for that matter, to receive money for any type of work at all. All of those unskilled jobs on the waterfront long filled by free blacks—stevedore, porter, drayman—properly belong to whites. As the Southern politicians often emphasized, and as Yancey himself thundered in his celebrated speech at the Democratic Convention, was not the white man, even the poorest among them, part of a master race? Why should whites have to compete in a labor pool that included blacks?

These questions had a troublesome urgency the planter class would have preferred to ignore. Indeed, in Charleston's first century and a half, the question of labor competition between the races seldom came up in politics. Charleston had been a town with a very large number of black slaves, a small number of free blacks, and a white pleasure-seeking gentry. A free-black carpenter was no threat to a gentleman who would rather put a pistol to his head than hold a hammer in his hand. But in the nineteenth century, a wave of immigration from Europe upset the status quo. White laborers were pouring in, and they needed work for themselves and their families. Many lived in the Neck, the sprawling neighborhood situated above Calhoun Street and bordered on the east by the Cooper River. The Neck was not part of the original settlement of Charleston but was incorporated into the city in 1849. With its annexation came a growing number of votes, enough to sway the balance in municipal elections. By 1860, the planters were being forced to listen.

The white workingmen, feeling their collective muscle, banded together in the 1850s into a political movement to clear the field of black or
brown competition. The movement was led by mechanic Henry T. Peake,
a self-described "friend of the laboring man and the benefactor of the
poor" who managed a machine shop of the South Carolina Railroad, and
by James M. Eason, who owned a foundry near the railroad yards in the
Neck. Eason, at the age of forty, represented a new kind of wealth—and a
new kind of political kingpin—in Charleston. He was a slave owner, but
his status came not from what he could grow on a plantation but from
the steam engines, pumps, cotton presses, and other heavy machines his
foundry made with its eighty white, wage-earning employees.

Peake and Eason, each with their own political ambitions, were able
organizers, and their bloc of votes helped elect Macbeth to office. During
his first term as mayor, his city did little more than enact restrictions on
free blacks working as produce sellers. But upon Macbeth's reelection in
the fall of 1859, the white workingmen's patience was spent. They were
adamant in their calls for action. And by unleashing the police on the free
blacks in the summer of 1860, Macbeth, with a practical concern for his
own political survival, had acceded to these demands.

———

To his brother-in-law, the younger Johnson reported that the "higher
class"—the white gentry—was "quite incensed" by the attack on the
free blacks. Johnson related that ex-mayor John Schnierle, combative as
ever, came to the defense of a free black man "and defied" the police "to
touch him. . . . He would beat the one to death who did." But Schnierle,
in making his feelings known loudly around town, proved an exception
among his peers. The others seethed quietly. Even the *Mercury*, generally
reflective of the interests of the gentry and supportive of the rights of free
blacks, was uncharacteristically silent. There was not a word in the paper
about the crackdown on the brown elite.

The "higher class" had been outmaneuvered by the white workers'
movement. This was galling to the gentlemen of Charleston, for as a matter of sentiment or what might simply be called class prejudice, the gentry
had previously cared little for the white workingman, whose services had

no great value in a society with a surplus of skilled and unskilled black slaves and free persons. As immigration to America from places like Ireland surged in the 1840s, planter society was no more welcoming to the masses that clambered onto the Cooper River wharves than the Yankee aristocracy of Beacon Hill was to the multitudes that poured into lower Boston. In fact, old-line Charlestonians, largely from the Anglo and Huguenot communities, tried to stem this tide by joining with like-minded upper classes in the North in pushing for a federal law to make it harder for foreign-born immigrants to become US citizens. "In some parts of Europe," declared a group calling itself the American Republican Association of Charleston, "our country is regarded as a means of getting rid of the most vicious, disorderly, and burdensome population." Prominent merchants like Henry and Robert Gourdin were members of this group.

But the campaign had proved a futile effort, and now the wheel had turned: the gentry had need of the support of the white workingman to bring about the popular revolution that would liberate the South from the clutches of the North. For South Carolina to leave the Union in an orderly fashion, the Charleston secessionists required the cooperation and organization of the state legislature, in which the workingmen had influence. And for a Southern Republic to take its place among the mighty nations of the earth, as envisioned by the *Mercury* and planters like John Townsend, white laborers would be needed to stock the military and to manage and operate the factories, especially those that manufactured armaments. Even those once deemed "the most vicious, disorderly, and burdensome" rejects of Europe might be required for these vital purposes.

Eason and Peake, both of whom were running for seats in the South Carolina legislature, played their hand shrewdly. Preaching the gospel of Southern independence, Eason escorted a reporter from the *Courier* around his foundry. There was an urgent need, the reporter wrote in his article published in August, "to build up an entirely Southern manufacturing establishment" with the South "to raise their own workmen." The *Courier* pronounced hopefully that with the "determined spirit and enterprise of our mechanics," the citizens of Charleston in time would be able "to boast of having all their machinery manufactured on the spot." By late summer 1860, Old Charleston was willing to see its social mosaic shattered—and free blacks persecuted—for the sake of the revolution. Haircuts, custom tailoring, and harness repairs could be obtained elsewhere. White solidarity trumped all else.

James M. Johnson dolefully sized up this brute calculus. The freedom of the brown elite had always been provisional, a grant that could be revoked. Its members were the offspring, sometimes the acknowledged offspring, of the men who traditionally had run Charleston, but by mid-1860 the brown elite was politically expendable and on its own. "It is vain for us to hope that if it is not the will of God he will not permit it," the tailor glumly told his brother-in-law. "Hence it is that on earth wicked rule prevails." The free blacks must take charge of their affairs as best they could, he reasoned, "and not supinely wait for the working of a miracle by having a chariot let down to convey us away."

To save themselves, they had a few choices, none of them good. One was a kind of voluntary reenslavement. In Charleston, a slave owner could purchase a metal badge for his slaves from the city treasurer's office, enabling his property to work for hire at odd jobs around town. The males toiled at tasks like wagon puller, stevedore, and chimney sweep, the females at domestic positions like dressmaker, nursemaid, and washer woman. As police terror increased, free blacks rushed to purchase slave badges, each with its own identification number, to keep from being arrested and brought before Macbeth. In just a few days in early August, some four hundred badges were sold. "There are cases of persons who for 30 years have been paying capitation tax and one of 35 years that have to go back to bondage and take out their badges," the younger Johnson informed his brother-in-law.

Yet although the badge might stop the police from demanding a free black's papers, it did not mitigate the white workingman's bitterness. There was nothing in it for him to allow slave owners to earn "rental" income on hired-out slaves—much less to allow the slave, as was often the case, to pocket some portion of the "fee" for himself. Even as menial a task as ditch digger belonged exclusively to the white man, if the job was for pay. The black could be an unpaid slave and nothing else.

Another choice for the free black was to flee—to leave Charleston altogether. And many did so under the most frantic circumstances. The refugees hurriedly sold their homes—in some cases with no choice but to accept fire-sale prices—cleaned out their bank accounts, and packed the necessary belongings and treasured keepsakes that could fit into their trunks. "Those who are now hunted down have divined what is to be done with them and before their destiny is sealed . . . are wisely leaving by steamer and railroad too," Johnson told his brother-in-law. Some booked passage to Philadelphia aboard the *Keystone State*, which departed from the Cooper River dock every ten days. Five months earlier the steamer had arrived in Charleston piled with whiskey-soaked delegates from Pennsylvania in town for the Democratic Convention and a good time. Now, it was a means of tragic escape. A journalist in Philadelphia noted that some of the arrivals bore copper badges, one reading, "Charleston, 1860, Servant, 1,243."

In the "city of brotherly love," the arrivals from Charleston would find the largest urban population of blacks outside of the South—some 22,000. Yet although Philadelphia was a thriving center of abolitionism, it also had an immigrant, white working class determined to have all the best jobs, just as in Charleston. Hard, physical labor might be found for a paltry wage—but to work at a trade in keeping with one's experiences was apt to remain a dream. Riots, tension, and violence against blacks prevailed.

Another alternative was to leave America altogether. Canada beckoned, but what were the prospects for gainful work there? Johnson's brother Charley, also a tailor, already lived in Toronto, and he was barely eking out a living. "I have seen the most magnificent buildings," he wrote a friend back in South Carolina. "I have seen all colors and classes obtain admission to them and I have seen people apparently happy but I have not seen much money. It seems a scarce article."

If not Canada, how about tropical Haiti? Direct passage was available from Wilmington, North Carolina, some 170 miles from Charleston. The Haitian government had been formed by the largest slave rebellion in the Western Hemisphere, and the country was actively seeking the settlement of blacks from America, of all shades of color. The lure was a promise of food and shelter and tools for working the land—and more than that, according to the sales pitch, a life of dignity that could not be obtained in the United States. "Pride of race, self-respect, social ambition, parental love, the meanness of the North, the inhumanity of the Union, and the inclemency of Canada—all say to the black and the man of color, seek elsewhere a home and a nationality," an agent for the Haitian government said.

Haiti, though, was beset with practical problems. Its democratic ideals were compromised by violent infighting among those aspiring to lead the country. The land distribution program was rife with inequities. Emigrants from America were apt to encounter religious and linguistic barriers, and they stood a fair chance of contracting a debilitating and even fatal disease like yellow fever. Elite mulattos from Charleston would likely be resented by blacks of purely African descent in Haiti—and they were unlikely to be welcomed back to Charleston, ever. Nevertheless, Haiti was still the leading destination for Charleston's free-black emigrants.

The decision to leave Charleston altogether was hardest to make for the most well-established members of the brown elite, those with the most to lose. Even as they understood no miracle was apt to rescue them, Johnson and his father hunkered down in Charleston and said good-byes to friends of many years. The knock on the door would come—or not. That was the final choice for the free blacks: not to reenslave themselves, not to leave town, but to lay low and hope the pitiless assault would exhaust itself.

Chapter Sixteen

THE GENTLEMAN REVOLUTIONARY

" I am in despair," Robert Newman Gourdin wrote to his good friend William Porcher Miles on August 20. A bachelor with a white, Santa Claus–like fluffy beard, Gourdin lived with his older brother, Henry (also a bachelor), their widowed sister, Anna, and her three sons in a mansion tended by four slaves in an enviable spot by White Point Garden on the Battery. He was attached to his family, to his geraniums, to his collection of vintage wines, and to the wide circle of friends in Charleston and beyond he was fond of entertaining at the home on 2 Meeting Street. His social graces were unfailing—a glass of Madeira for a visitor, a bouquet of roses sent to a friend to welcome her return to town. And at the age of forty-eight, he had become, improbably, a revolutionary. Secession was the great passion of his life. It was not an impulse or a fashion as it was for some in Charleston nor a practical finance-driven decision as it was for Henry, the harder-headed of the two brothers in the merchant house they ran together. Rather, secession was the vessel into which he poured his emotional life, a determinant, even, of his daily mood.

His present anxiety, Robert told Miles, was this: with the presidential election just eleven weeks away, the ebbing of enthusiasm for the secessionist cause, as seen in the nostalgia that had surfaced at the Fourth of

106

July banquet, seemed to be ongoing. It had only been four months since
a packed gallery of Charlestonians had hissed and jeered at B. F. Perry of
South Carolina for calling himself "a Union man," committed to guarding
the South against "storms of secession." But now, as Robert mournfully
said to Miles, "you will find many here who endorse Major Perry's views."

Robert was prone to dramatic pronouncements. He had told Miles
on the eve of the convention that its result would "tell the future of the
South for weal or woe." Still, he was not wrong in his present assessment.
This was the dreaded torpor half expected by his radical friend US marshal Hamilton. Immersed as he was in the commercial life of Charleston,
Robert grasped that it was not only nostalgia that nourished a reluctance
to embrace secession with open arms. Secession, for many men of practical affairs, truly was an accounting exercise. When weighing the costs
against the benefits, some men still could see profitable opportunity in
amicable ties to the North. There was the promise, for example, of the
newly formed Boston and Southern Steamship Co. to establish a regular
line of transport between two cities that, in politics, seemed irrevocably
pitted against each other. Shoes might be sent down from Boston and
compressed cotton sent up on the return voyage from Charleston. At the
end of 1859, the substantial sum of $40,000 was raised in Charleston for
the purchase of shares in the venture. Additional funds had been raised
in Boston for the construction in a South Boston shipyard of a pair of
iron steamers of 1,150 tons each, outfitted for carrying passengers as well
as commercial goods.

Six months later, VIPs from politics and business, joined by the press,
gathered on the first of these vessels to be completed, the *South Carolina*,
for an inaugural voyage around Boston Harbor. A brass band supplied
the music while guests dined on chowder. "May the smoke of these chim-
neys," Boston mayor Frederick W. Lincoln, Jr., declared, "be a perpetual
calumet of peace between the two representative cities of the North and
the South." A few weeks later, the *South Carolina* puffed into Charleston
Harbor. Charleston repaid Boston's hospitality with an onboard repast lu-
bricated by "accessory liquids." At the end of July, the second vessel of the
line, the *Massachusetts,* reached the city.

Even if Lincoln is elected, "I don't think South Carolina will secede," Petigru wrote from his vacation spot in New York's White Sulphur Springs to his friend Alfred Huger, Charleston's longtime postmaster. As Petigru knew, Huger, from his perch on the federal payroll, harbored his own doubts about the wisdom of secession. "No possible issue could be more untenable than to make his bare election a *causus belli*, without any overt act against the Constitution or even, the *Dred Scott* decision," Petigru told the postmaster. "I don't believe they are going to set fire to the Union, although there are members, no doubt, that would like it." As far as Robert Gourdin was concerned, the bigger the conflagration the better, and even in his "despair" he held out hope that there were some in Charleston, and indeed all over the South, still convinced of the need for secession.

———

Robert did not fit the mold of a revolutionary as a hard-driven, lone wolf type. He was not particularly ambitious, and he had many close, personal attachments. Yet at his core he indeed nurtured a romantic, revolutionary spirit. He was given to misty-eyed thoughts of a future, better world after the South was rid of the North. Robert was the great-grandson of Louis Gourdin, a French Protestant, or Huguenot, emigrant to America. Like the Puritans who fled Europe in the early sixteenth century to settle in Massachusetts, the Huguenots who came to Charleston and the surrounding Lowcountry decades later were seeking refuge from religious persecution. In 1685, Louis XIV stripped the Huguenots of their rights of religious worship and ordered their churches to be razed, their schools to be abolished, and their children to be baptized and raised as Catholics. But despite his decree explicitly forbidding Huguenots to leave France, many in this population of nearly 200,000 defiantly did just that. The diaspora scattered into neighboring parts of Europe, and some number made their way for Britain's colony of South Carolina.

The Huguenots arrived at a fortunate time: the development of the lush soils and marshes of the Lowcountry into a cash-crop plantation economy was just getting under way. The members of this community had been known in France for their mercantile enterprise and acumen, and they established themselves as planters along with their fellow Protestant

settlers from England. They also became the backbone of Charleston's nascent merchant class, thriving in the business of placing the plantations'
harvests into the hands of customers in Europe. Slave trading, too, was in
their line. The English and Huguenots frequently intermarried, and many,
like the Gourdins, adopted the Episcopal Church as their own. Together,
they occupied the top rung of Charleston's social ladder.

Still, even with their rapid ascent in their adopted home, their heritage of oppression in France remained central to their identity. The stories
passed down from generation to generation tended to omit the material
splendors some of their ancestors had enjoyed in France—homes filled
with gold and silver wares and with exquisite furniture made by Huguenot artisans. And if the contradiction ever occurred to them between the
thirst for freedom that propelled their forefathers to the shores of America and the denial of liberty to the people who picked their cotton, served
their tea, and cleaned their privies, the thought was scarcely spoken. In
the mid-nineteenth century, one member of an old Huguenot family
wrote to a friend of how "all of us Huguenots felt great pride in our ancestry and descent, from such honest, poor, virtuous, and energetic people,
who abandoned homes, friends, and all they had to encounter such trials
and sufferings with fortitude and energy with a view of maintaining their
faith, and their liberty intact." Such was the story the Charleston Huguenots told themselves.

The son of a planter, Robert was born in 1812 at Buck Hall plantation
in St. John's Parish, Berkley, just to the north of Charleston. He was eight
years younger than Henry and seven years younger than Anna. With the
death of their mother in 1815 and father in 1821, Henry became head of the
family. He was of a pragmatic, energetic, resolute disposition with a head
for numbers, and in time he was able to establish his own successful trading firm with his chief clerk, Frederick Matthiessen. Located on Adger's
Wharf in Charleston, Gourdin, Matthiessen & Co. specialized in the sale
of raw cotton from the Sea Islands and the Upcountry to merchant customers in France and England.

Robert attended South Carolina College in Columbia and graduated in
1831 in a class that included future federal judge Andrew Gordon Magrath.
Robert was admitted to the bar three years later but shortly afterward

decided not to pursue the career of a lawyer. The reason was his chronically frail health. Thin and sallow, he consulted a doctor on a visit to Liverpool in the summer of 1835. "He advises me strenuously to abandon the law," Robert wrote Anna back in Charleston, and "is further of opinion that I will scarcely ever be enabled to endure our Summer climate. What I am to do under such perplexing circumstances I cannot say." The following day, Robert wrote Henry of the doctor's diagnosis. "My situation is a painful one but I must make the best of it," he told his brother.

Robert's heartfelt political convictions began to take shape in his time at college in Columbia in his late teenage years. The president of South Carolina College was the charismatic Thomas Cooper, who in a much-noted speech in the summer of 1827 sharply questioned whether the Union was worth keeping. In Cooper's opinion, the federal tariff demonstrated the government's intention "to sacrifice the South to the North by converting us into colonies and tributaries." Robert dated his political awakening to the crisis over nullification—in which the Convention of the People met in Columbia in the fall of 1832 to declare the tariff "null, void." Over the course of the year, President Andrew Jackson belligerently upped the ante by bolstering the US military presence in Charleston Harbor, the South Carolina legislature answered with a call to raise a 25,000-man army, and Calhoun dramatically resigned as vice president. All of this, which could have led to a violent confrontation and even secession without Henry Clay's compromise, must have thrilled him. There were many Unionists on Jackson's side in South Carolina at this time, but Robert seemed to have no doubts about where he stood. In 1832, at the age of twenty, "I was a nullifier," he said.

Even so, the young Robert agonized over what the unresolved tensions between the sections might mean for America's future. "Under what evil stars has our country been brought," Robert wrote Henry from Liverpool in September of 1835. "I find myself engaged in many unpleasant discussions on the subject of slavery." At this time, Robert still felt that the North, if only from "selfishness," would not demand that the South give up slavery. As he put it to his brother, he thought the Yankees would continue "to support us in our peculiar property." Still, the South could be torn by troubles within: "Yet I cannot but fear that the open and constant agitation of the question has brought it too distinctly before the mind of those who we should desire to hear it even alluded to." This thought, revealed to his brother in confidence, reflected a certain naiveté in his character. He seemed to believe that the blacks of Charleston, and throughout the South, were unaware that the whites of the North and South were in the midst of a quarrel over slavery.

In his wrestling over the matter, Robert developed into a committed secessionist—and there his grappling stopped. *"Il faut coupe"* (it must be cut), he told a friend in his fluent French of the tie binding the South to the North in the Union. It was a matter of honor. He could not see how the South could stay in a Union that refused to leave his native section unmolested in its chosen way of life. It wasn't obvious, though, what role he could play in advancing the cause. He was not a natural politician. In fact, Robert was so lacking in ambition and cunning that a friend once felt obliged to say, "You have always associated with honest gentlemen, your own nature is as open as the day, and it is just such men as you who are the victim of political tricksters."

Nor did he have a talent for the rousing speech making and pamphleteering for which the Rhetts and John Townsend had a knack—and indeed his genteel sensibility was uncomfortable with the occasional unruliness of the street. In August of 1835, on learning of the seizure of antislavery literature from the Charleston post office by a white mob and the incineration of the abolitionist leader William Lloyd Garrison at a boisterous public rally, he wrote Henry from Liverpool, "I am indeed sorry that they"—the mob—"treated this matter with so much passion. The slave question is of too high and grave an importance to be met thus. Decision and firmness which are alone the result of reason and calmness is the only mode by which to meet this subject."

As decades passed, and the secession movement continued in an endless cycle of rising and then ebbing, Robert must have felt some measure of frustration. He had a comfortable life as a partner in Gourdin, Matthiessen & Co. and spent parts of the year at the branch office in Savannah and on business in Europe. Robert had a specialty in the trade in Madeira—but the driving force at the firm was Henry. In fact, even though Henry had none of Robert's passion for politics, he managed to outstrip his young brother in this avenue, too. A founder of the Bank of Charleston, a leader of the chamber of commerce, and an executive director of the Jockey Club, the "old gentleman," as Anna's boys called him, had developed into a back-room political fixer. He threw his weight behind candidates for local, state, and federal office and coaxed subsidies from the legislature for his venture to build a railroad through the Blue Ridge Mountains. Whereas Henry had once been entreated to run for the US Congress, only to decline to the "regret of his friends," Robert's sole political accomplishment was election to the City Council in the mid-1850s. He reached that height only after the humiliation of running a dismal twenty-fourth in the elections held in 1853. (The top twenty vote getters in Charleston made the cut.) As a city councilor, Robert worked closely with Christopher Memminger and William Porcher Miles as mayor "to sweep away the remains of old fogeyism" in the civic life of Charleston.

Even within his household, Robert's fixation with secession seemed to be treated as something of a quirk by Henry and Anna. His sister was not among the Charleston ladies who heckled Perry and urged their men to seize the moment. She had qualms about the prospect of a violent disunion, of a battle that could engulf her own three sons. Her sympathies were with her native land, but still she bemoaned its apparent fate, "as though it were situated," she once told Robert, "at the base of some ever-threatening & never-to-be trusted volcano!" Her misgivings had no apparent effect on her younger brother.

Still, for all his shortcomings, Robert did in fact have something to give to the secessionist movement that a figure like Barnwell Rhett, so antagonistic and self-serving, did not: a far-flung network of powerful and wealthy friends who found him convivial company and had faith in his good intentions and discretion. Robert knew how to gather people for robust conversation and debate, even when the subject was politics. He was not a polarizing force; he argued that if secession could be accepted as the paramount goal, then all else was negotiable. He once told Miles there was no need to take up the controversial question of reopening the African slave trade, banned by the US Congress in 1807: "It will produce divisions in the South at a time when unity is absolutely necessary." And yet, even if it was not displayed in his gentile manners, the hardness in his character revealed itself in the determination he brought to his role as an organizer. For it was organization that the secession movement lacked with Lincoln's election approaching—and he had an idea for how to provide it.

Chapter Seventeen

SECESSION INC.

"The Society of Earnest Men will meet this day, at 12 o'clock, at the usual place." Consisting of this single sentence, the notice appeared near the top of page two of the Thursday, September 20, edition of the *Mercury*, directly below a posting for a meeting that evening of the Palmetto Loan and Building Association. As spare as the message was, several facts could be hazarded. First, whatever the society was, surely it was known at least to Rhett, Jr., the paper's micromanaging editor. Second, wherever the "usual place" was, it would be known to the group's members, who presumably were daily readers of the *Mercury*.

It all began, Robert later told a friend, with an "informal meeting" at his home in September of "several gentleman of Charleston." The idea was to discuss how to position the South "in the event of the accession of Mr. Lincoln and the Republican Party to power." Robert did not disclose who attended the first meeting and those that followed, but his brother Henry undoubtedly was involved from the start. Even though Henry had never shared his younger brother's ardor for secession, his practical sense of things suggested to him that, at this point, there was no better alternative.

Although it did not define itself as such, the Society of Earnest Men evolved into a kind of business venture—"Secession Inc.," in effect—with branches for marketing, promotion and publications, strategic direction, research and analysis, campaigns and elections, sponsorship and coordination of events, and last but not least fund-raising. The members would bring to the task of secession the same high level of discipline and attention to detail they had brought to the management of their profitable business enterprises—whether in brokering cotton sales to Europe, writing and peddling insurance policies, or overseeing slave plantations. It was an unusual enterprise in the sense that, if it successfully established a Southern Republic, it would automatically go out of business. The dividend for the investors would be the permanent protection of slave property and their way of life—for themselves, their families, Charleston, and the Lowcountry—which rested on the slave system.

Secession Inc. also had the flavor of a conspiracy. A group of men gathered for the purpose of plotting to take the South out of the Union—this was not the sort of thing, at least in the planning and development phase, to advertise, especially because some of the plotters might have been on the payroll of the federal government. An intelligence gatherer like Captain Doubleday at Fort Moultrie would be eager to report on such an enterprise to Lincoln in Springfield. Hence the discrete notice in the *Mercury*.

But Charleston was no good at keeping secrets. The appetite for gossip, and especially for any fresh tidbit that had to do with secession, was too large. Soon enough, a Charleston nephew of South Carolina senator James Henry Hammond wrote his uncle in Washington to tell him that "an association formed here. They are known as the Earnest men," and the group "comprises some of the wealthiest and most influential names amongst us, such as the Lowndes, Heywards, Middletons, and Aikens and a host of others. Their exact object I do not know." Those were indeed names redolent of social privilege, money, and power—the mix that makes for oligarchy. Robert had put together a spectacular collection of figures.

Charles Tidyman Lowndes, who had a home on East Bay Street, was president of the Jockey Club and the Bank of Charleston, founder of a Broad Street fire-insurance agency, and an investor with Henry in the Blue Ridge railroad project. The Lowndes clan, of Huguenot ancestry, had established itself in Charleston despite the impressive flameout of the founding patriarch, a spendthrift sugar planter from St. Kitts Island, in the Caribbean, who arrived in Charleston in 1730 with a plan to grow rice. Swamped by his debts and jailed for failing to support his family, he took his life with his own pistol. The Heywards, also Huguenots, had pioneered rice planting in the Carolina region in 1685 and later branched out into cotton. Charles Heyward was a friend of Robert with a home on East Bay, and he owned a rice plantation in the Colleton District with some 540 slaves. Williams Middleton, whose father had been a governor of South Carolina, had a rice plantation on the Ashley River and a Charleston home at 1 Meeting Street, next door to the Gourdins'.

As for the Aikens, William Aiken, Jr., might have been the single richest man in Charleston and indeed all of South Carolina, with property worth about $360,000, including his slaves. The Aiken family represented relatively new money: in the late eighteenth century, as a young boy, William's father had arrived in Charleston from his native home in Northern Ireland. He went on to found the South Carolina Railroad; ironically, he died at the age of fifty-two in a grisly carriage accident caused by his horse taking fright at the sound of a train. William, Jr., the only son, inherited a portion of his father's wealth and subsequently amassed his own fortune as a planter and an investor in railroads. He owned an island that produced vast quantities of rice and also served as governor, Congressman, and nearly Speaker of the House. He was married to a Lowndes, and the couple lived in a magnificent mustard-colored mansion with walled-in grounds lined with magnolia trees—a kind of urban plantation—on the corner of Judith and Elizabeth Streets. An art gallery on the second floor was equipped with a skylight and crammed with paintings and sculptures collected on their travels to Paris, Vienna, Florence, and Pompeii. French chandeliers lit drawing rooms in which guests gathered for sumptuous meals served on English porcelain in the Japanese Imari style. Hired-out slaves brought in income from carpentry jobs.

Nevertheless, Aiken was perhaps the most surprising of the names listed by Hammond's nephew, for William, Jr., was a moderate by temperament with a library graced by portraits of Calhoun, Webster, and Clay. He had long held an allegiance to the Union and to the Democratic Party as a national organization: one foot was planted in the free North, the other in the slave South. At the start of 1860 he had viewed Stephen Douglas as "the only man who could save the party." But like all the moderates in Charleston, he had underestimated the strength of the radicals. The party had not been saved, the Republicans were on the brink of power, and the middle ground was disappearing.

The total amount of wealth represented by the underwriters of Secession Inc. was staggering—a massive treasure chest that could be tabulated not only in stocks, bonds, and slave property but also in collections of jewels and antique furniture, closets of lace and silk garments, stables of thoroughbred horses, pleasure-boat rides on the crystalline lakes of the Swiss Alps. It could be thought of as the bottles of Madeira purchased from Robert Gourdin's lovingly assembled inventory; the banquets laid out for the guests at the Race Week celebrations in February; the bills for the French governess; the tuition paid to Mademoiselle Darry's finishing school for the daughters and to Harvard, Yale, and the College of New Jersey for the sons. It could be thought of, too, as the small comforts of this life of privilege—the slave boy always at hand to bring live hot coals to light the evening pipe, a fire blazing in the den. All of that was at risk—or so these men viscerally felt—if the Union remained.

For these Charleston barons, revolutionary activity was present in their bloodlines—as it was in the blood of Charleston itself. The family trees of the Heywards and Middletons each included a signer of the Declaration of Independence. To be both men of property and social rank as well as dedicated radicals, participants in a plot to overthrow an existing order, did not present a contradiction in terms. Was not Jefferson an icon of the type?

The Society of Earnest Men recognized that many of the materials for the aggressive and comprehensive promotion of secession already existed. They simply had not been given wide enough distribution. The Charleston oligarchs were enamored of John Townsend's speech at St. John's, Colleton, back in June. Townsend himself was one of this elite (and a future member of the society), and he was arranging to publish his galvanizing speech as a pamphlet, as was his usual practice. Why not paper the entire South with the pamphlet—circulate tens of thousands, or even hundreds of thousands, of copies in cities, towns, and villages from Richmond to New Orleans? To do so was a matter of checkbooks and an available printing press, neither of which was lacking. The publishing house of Evans & Cogswell, at the corner of Broad and East Bay Streets, could be enlisted to churn out the tracts. The proprietors were ardent secessionists with steam-powered presses able to run off tens of thousands of copies at a time. More challenging was distribution—but there the society could rely on the US postal system and on the organizers' numerous personal contacts all over the South, to whom bulk packages of pamphlets could be sent for circulation in churches, militia groups, universities, and other civic organizations. The abolitionists relied on the postal service and their friends to distribute their subversive tracts—why not the secessionists?

The society envisioned young men as the prime target group of the mailings—the men who might be called into battle and whose natural enthusiasm could help lift the more temperate spirits of their elders. Put "incendiary" pamphlets "in the hands of the youth and genius of the South," said the society's youngest member, twenty-two-year-old William Tennent, Jr., secretary and treasurer, and "stir the sleeping South out of the lethargy fostered by the poison called love of Union."

In order to continue selling the brand of secession, the society also needed boots on the streets—men parading, flags waving, and trumpets blaring on visible behalf of secession to excite the public and invigorate revolutionary consciousness. The South abounded in volunteer militias, but the groups did not have an explicitly political character, and not many had experience beyond rudimentary slave patrols and ceremonial musters for friends and family. The model in mind was the Minute Men of colonial Massachusetts, the bands that gathered renown for taking on the British redcoats at the outset of the Revolutionary War before becoming absorbed into a regular army. Minute Men bands had cropped up in South Carolina during the nullification crisis, and now, the feeling was, they needed to be revived with the explicit goal of rallying support for secession.

When considering their strategy, the Earnest Men easily agreed that there was no reason to pursue an orthodox Cooperationist tack. After all, the failed Memminger mission had already demonstrated that the

Southern states were incapable of coming together as a bloc to take up the question of secession. South Carolina needed to be ready to break away from the Union on its own. With elections for the state legislature on October 8 in sight, the society would help build support for the election of prosecession candidates—their own members among them. And as soon as the presidential election of Tuesday, November 6, was over, with Lincoln presumably the declared victor, they would aim to set the machinery of secession in motion. The legislature or some designated body of the legislature would establish an orderly process to bring the state out of the Union.

At the same time, the society resolved to conduct outreach among the "leading men" of the Southern states in order to gain an understanding of the public feeling for secession in each of these states, the level of military preparedness, and how the rest of the South was apt to respond to the unilateral secession of South Carolina. Identifying other states as sympathetic to South Carolina—Georgia, Alabama—could help persuade the state legislature in Columbia to move along the secession path.

With Robert Gourdin as the leader—chairman of the board—the society had a decidedly inclusive nature. Robert had no interest in relitigating the secession battles of the past. In this spirit, he welcomed the participation of Rhett, Jr., who began to write his contacts in the South, as did Robert, in the effort to gather and share intelligence on the mood and readiness for secession in the other slave states. The two men seemed to reach an accommodation, as Robert also took on the task of spearheading a fund-raising effort to help bolster the sagging *Mercury*. The senior Rhett, though, refused—or was not invited—to take part.

———

On September 20, Robert sent a note with a stack of Townsend's *The South Alone, Should Govern the South* pamphlets enclosed to Edward Clifford Anderson of Savannah, a prominent businessman, planter, and former mayor of that town. A sympathetic—but still skeptical—Anderson wrote back, "I question very much whether there is at the time enough gunpowder to fire a general salute" over the state of Georgia. "What then are we to do should the people decree secession," Anderson asked. "If we are to go into revolution on this basis or threaten resistance to be whipped into subjection with our arms folded, I am for letting things alone and trusting to Providence in the hope that better times may dawn upon us."

As ever, Charleston's leading role invited mockery from those who continued to believe agitation for secession among the town's unquenchable "firebrands" was little more than the usual table talk among idle dreamers with too little else to occupy their time. "In Charleston, S.C., there is an Association styled 'Earnest Men' who meet every Thursday at meridian," an item in the Atlanta *American* noted. "We have plenty of earnest men in this city who meet every day at that time to discuss fish, flesh and fowl." An unnamed "member" of the society responded, in a letter published on the front page of the *Mercury*: "Yes, there is an association of 'Earnest Men,' in Charleston, who meet on Thursdays at 12 o'clock, m., but they take ice-water only, and spot the traitors to the South, who may require some hemp ere long. I will inform the *American* that the said Association, by its constitution, is called the '1860 Association.'" Traitors and hemp—the aggressive phrasing was not of Robert Gourdin's cordial epistolary style. Townsend was capable of this sort of verbal pugilism, but the clipped voice and the suggestion of brute violence sounded more like the editor of the *Mercury*. Whoever the author was, the message of the Earnest Men of the 1860 Association was clear: this time would be different.

Chapter Eighteen

"A LARGE AND COARSE MAN"

With September, a menacing climate crept back into Charleston. It had been nearly a year since John Brown's raid on Harpers Ferry—and the threat of a broad-scale slave uprising, felt so palpably at the time, had not come to pass. Nothing in the crime blotters kept by the police suggested any serious troubles brewing. There were reports of a cattle thief ring led by a free black, a slave's theft of a canoe, and of several escaped slaves hiding out in town—"Anney . . . small, neat figure, full eyes, rather large teeth"—but that was nothing out of the ordinary. Nevertheless, it was as if the white community's free-floating suspicion had an irresistible need to latch onto something. In the heat of the summer, the target had been the free blacks. With cooler weather on its way, it became the Yankee in their midst.

On the seventh day of the month, US Army captain Samuel Wylie Crawford, an assistant surgeon, received orders to "proceed forthwith" from Rhode Island to Fort Moultrie on Sullivan's Island. He was to report to the garrison there as the new chief medical officer. Crawford, a Pennsylvania native, was thirty years old and slim of build with a thick mustache connecting to full sideburns. He arrived by train in Charleston in the dead of night, when the streets were deserted. Determined to have a night's rest in town before moving on to the island in the morning, he made his way to the Charleston Hotel, where a "rather dogmatic clerk" interrogated him as he registered his name. He recorded the event in his diary:

"You are an officer of the army to be stationed in this harbor—No?"
I replied in the affirmative.
"Where have you come from?"
"From Newport, R.I.," I replied.
"Don't you think you had better go down to-night?" he said to me, in rather a marked way.
"It is five miles or more; what means of conveyance is there?" I asked.
"I have never been here before in my life."
"None that I know of," he replied; "the steamers stop running after 3 o'clock, but you might get a negro to row you over in a skiff. It is dangerous to stay here."
"No," I replied, "that is out of the question. I shall remain overnight here."

Crawford got his room and proceeded without incident to Fort Moultrie at daylight, but the episode was evidence of a troubling—and threatening—disdain for Northerners in Charleston.

A few weeks later, Catherine Bottsford, a widow from New York living in Charleston and working as a seamstress, received a considerably more unpleasant dose of civic vigilance. "I was alone in my room, having hardly recovered from a severe illness," Bottsford recalled, when "a large and coarse man presented himself before me without permission or pronouncement. He demanded my name; I told him and asked what he wished. He stated that he was one of the Vigilant Police, and ordered me to go with him to the Mayor's Court, that officer having sent for me." When Bottsford asked why she had to go with him, the officer told her she was understood to be an abolitionist. This was an offense to the city of Charleston. "You must come with me or I will take you by force," he said.

Reluctantly, she went with the man to the Guard House at Broad and Meeting Streets and spent the night there, confined to a cell, "sick and faint from breathing the foul air," supplied a pail of water but no food. On the afternoon of the following day, she was taken to see Mayor Charles Macbeth for questioning:

"Mrs. Bottsford, you are accused of treason and sedition."
"I am not guilty of treason or sedition."
"I understand you have been tampering with slaves?"
"It is utterly false, Sir, I have had nothing to say to the slaves."
"You are an Abolitionist?"
"Yes."
"An admirer of John Brown?"
"Yes."
"You have expressed Abolition sentiments?"
"I have on a few occasions when asked; I can name all I ever conversed with, and what I said to them I will say here. I lived here nearly a year, attending closely to my business; I have not injured or offended any one, and have been well treated until now; I cannot see why I should be subjected to this outrage."
"You say you have been well treated?"
"Yes, until now."
"Then I think you have been very ungrateful; you have been well treated, been profitably employed, and have received our money while you hated us?"
"I have not hated the people; I am no friend to Slavery. . . . I have received what I have earned. I owe you no gratitude."
"I would advise you to go home."

Bottsford said she would be happy to return to New York. But she refused to pay, or attempt to raise, the $300 "bail" demanded by the mayor for her release because she did not consider herself guilty of anything. She was then taken to the courtroom of a city magistrate, who raised her bail to $2,000. If she defaulted, she would go to jail. "Why, if you had been a man you would have been hung up on one of the trees" on the Citadel Green, the judge told her.

As much, perhaps, for her honest defiance as for her actual offense, Bottsford was dispatched to the Charleston district jail, the dank four-story crenellated fortress on Magazine Street, built in 1802 and known not only for its rats and lice but also for its stench of stale sweat and human waste. The jail was a minute's walk from Reverend John Bachman's Lutheran Church, but it exuded misery. Twenty years before, the facility had held Denmark Vesey and his "conspirators" as they awaited their execution. Bottsford was lodged in the most grotesque section of the jail, an addition completed in 1855 known as the octagon, where she shared a cell with "two drunken, abandoned women" and had "nothing but a dirty blanket to sleep on." The "roar of the blood hounds" in the prison yard outside kept her nerves on edge.

With a report in the *Courier* of her detention, her case became the talk of Charleston. Doubleday felt "profound indignation" at her jailing "simply for stating that she did not believe in the institution of slavery," but he was helpless to intervene. Others felt disinclined to do so. Reverend William B. W. Howe, assistant minister of St. Philips' Episcopal, visited Bottsford in jail on hearing that she was a parishioner of the church. When she admitted to being an abolitionist, her minister replied, "That's treason." Bottsford pointed out that the Constitution still applied in Charleston—"you are not out of the Union yet"—and did not make abolitionism a crime. "Well, we have slaves, and we mean to keep them," Rev. Howe replied. "I own them myself." He advised the prisoner to petition the mayor and the state attorney general for release, but she refused: "I would not consent to be smuggled off in disgrace."

———

Until 1860, it was not usually in Charleston's heart to treat visitors from the North, and especially women, so ungallantly and unforgivingly. Meanness of spirit was a characteristic Charleston tended to assign to the Yankees. Even if the accusation of abolitionist activity could be proven, her detention, with an exorbitant demand for bail she could not possibly pay, was excessive punishment. She could easily have been put aboard a steamer headed for New York, and that would have been the end of the affair. That was how Charleston usually handled abolitionists—by chasing them out of town.

But Charleston was not in a generous mood. Perhaps the city's spitefulness on this occasion signified its spoiling for a fight, with Bottsford merely an available symbol of the larger conflict. She wrote a letter to the mayor of New York, Fernando Wood, in hopes he might use his influence to gain her release, but he would not do so. He quickly replied, "You have offended against the peace and good order of the community where you were sojourning." He advised the seamstress to go before Macbeth "in a spirit of contrition," for "no other power can aid you in the distress you have brought upon yourself, and you must rely solely on the mercy of those who administer the laws you have broken," he said.

Although Wood's refusal to intervene was in keeping with his view that the North, generally speaking, best let the South alone, Bottsford nevertheless was taken aback. "My astonishment only equaled my indignation on reading this absurd letter," she recalled. October arrived with the first frost, and she shivered in her jail cell. Justice, Charleston style, was on grisly view: "There was to be an execution in the jail yard, and the gallows was built and a negro hung just before my window." In her filthy cell she stayed.

Chapter Nineteen

"OUR LIVES, OUR FORTUNES ... "

The seamstress might have shuddered again had she been able to take in the newest sight on the streets of Charleston: the men of the blue cockade, also known as the Minute Men. She could probably hear from her window their brass bands and the martial anthems the men sang while they marched through the downtown area. Black Charleston no doubt trembled, too. But for the most part, white Charleston—with its craving for pomp and circumstance—was dazzled and thrilled.

The Minute Men bands embodied the vision of the rich men of the 1860 Association for a more galvanizing form of political action. The elders constituting Robert Gourdin's group understood secession could not be accomplished simply through speeches by professional politicians from the stage of the Charleston Theatre. The people of Charleston had been pelted with words for years. The ordinary man—the mechanic, the firefighter, the grocery store clerk—wanted his own stage, to feel like an actor in the drama, not merely a spectator. The daughters and wives, sisters and grandmothers of Charleston shared this desire for hands-on participation in the cause—the women composed "patriotic" odes and stitched the banners and bonnets that gave symbolic expression to their partisan Southern hearts.

Any white male with a gun was eligible to join a Minute Man chapter—as long as he took the oath adapted from the last line of Jefferson's Declaration of Independence, to "solemnly pledge, OUR LIVES, OUR FORTUNES, and our sacred HONOR, to sustain Southern Constitutional equality in the Union, or failing that, to establish our independence out of it." Leaving no doubt as to the combative secessionist spirit of the Minute Men, their constitution proclaimed that "submission" to the election of a "Black Republican" president "must end in the destruction of our property and the ruin of our land."

The emblem of the Minute Man was a knot of blue ribbons with a military button at the center, pinned to the left side of his hat. It was a public declaration that instantly became a fashion accessory, and Charleston ladies pinned the rosette to their own garments in solidarity. Improvised versions flourished, including one featuring a palmetto tree, a coiled rattlesnake, and a lone star. Young men wore blue cockades with plaited palmetto leaves in their lapels. "Let every son of Carolina prepare to mount the blue cockade," the *Mercury* instructed. Mary Walsingham Crean of Charleston composed a song:

> *There's many a gallant laddie who wears a blue cockade,*
> *Will show them what it is to dare the blood of Southern braves!*

Some in Charleston found the Minute Men difficult to take seriously. "A gentleman from the country, who had joined the Minute Men," Doubleday recounted, "came in one day to the Charleston Hotel, with a huge cockade on his hat, expecting to be received with great applause; but to his astonishment, he was greeted with laughter and ridicule." Horace Greeley's *New York Tribune* also took the opportunity to scoff in a comment titled "Cockades and Common Sense:" "The South knows perfectly well that nobody is going to attack her, and that she is going to attack nobody," it said. The *Tribune* did allow that "reckless politicians, whose trade is agitation, whose chief ability lies in brawling, who are without influence except in seasons of turbulence . . . will seize this occasion, as they have seized scores of others, to achieve notoriety, and to rise to a disgraceful eminence." But "their madness," the paper confidently predicted, would come to naught at the slightest flexing of federal muscle. In Charleston, "a revenue cutter off Charleston bar would be likely to make blue rosettes in South Carolina as scarce as blue roses."

Doubleday knew better. With his West Point training and experience in disciplined military units, he fully appreciated the risk posed by self-forming groups like the Minute Men. Such outfits, "from their very nature, were quite unmanageable," he believed, subject to manipulation for almost any end, apt to act on impulse sooner than reason. The Minute Men's own rhetoric confirmed his fears. South Carolina needed Minute Men, one recruit said, to ward off "mongrel tyrants" who aim "to reduce you and your wives and your daughters on a level with the very slaves you buy and sell." A rumor circulated that the true purpose of the men of the blue cockade was to prepare "to march at a minute's notice to Washington to prevent Lincoln's inauguration." The Rhetts themselves were said to be behind that plot.

The Minute Men could quickly become a "mob," Doubleday warned: "It was easy to raise the storm," but it could yet prove "difficult to govern it." At this point, though, the Minute Men were still only a militia. There were no unconstrained bands of political hooligans roaming the streets bent on anti-Unionist mischief and destruction. The mood in Charleston was both anxious and excited but not yet overwrought. Order—as much as the increasingly radical city could manage—prevailed.

On the 8th of October, voters went to the polls to choose representatives for the state legislature. After they were seated in Columbia, the new set of legislators could be expected to decide whether and how to speed South Carolina's exit from the Union. To make sure voters understood the stakes, secessionists touted their candidates by placing notices in the *Mercury.* "Strike the Blow, and Make the Iron Hot by Striking It!" declared "Many Planters." In a letter published by the paper, "Civis" of Charleston demanded that candidates pledge whether, in the event of Lincoln's election, they would "vote for an immediate call of a Convention of the State to secede from the Union" and, even without the support of the other

Slave States, "vote that South Carolina should alone assume the vindication of her rights and liberties, and secede from the Union."

In the Charleston district, thirty-six candidates were vying for twenty
assigned seats in the House of Representatives. Three days after the polls
closed, on Thursday, October 11, the results were printed in the newspapers. Secessionists rejoiced. At 9:00 in the evening, a large crowd accompanied by a brass band gathered in front of the *Mercury* offices on Broad
to call out Rhett, Jr., who finished a respectable eleventh place in the balloting. The outcome, he told the gathering after the music died down,
could be taken "as a good omen for the cause which is advocated in the
columns of the *Mercury*. I trust that cause is on the rise. It is the cause of
the South," Barny said. "Evade the crisis we cannot," he added, because "it
sweeps down upon us from the North." And, as if to answer criticism of
his paper and himself as intemperate and impetuous, he declared, "I am
no hot-headed revolutionist; I am a cold-blooded conservatist. My patriotism, like my charity, begins at home."

The election also demonstrated the power of the white-workingmen's
bloc: Eason placed third and Peake tenth, easily making the cut. Both
men campaigned as secessionists. Their triumph was a blow, if not a surprising one, to Charleston's free blacks, who could expect a fresh attack on
their rights from Columbia.

As the fourth-highest vote getter in Charleston, Charles Tidyman
Lowndes of the 1860 Association also won a musical visit to his home, on
East Bay Street. But no brass band showed up at the doorstep of 2 Meeting
Street. Robert Gourdin placed a dismal twenty-fourth despite warm support by the popular William Porcher Miles and enthusiastic backing by a
group that called itself Southern Rights at All Hazards. He conveyed the
bad news in a telegram to Anna, who was in New York. "My surprise was
inexpressibly great," she wrote back, "with sisterly love." She condemned
the Charlestonians who had rejected her brother in "their folly, their petty
feeling, their blunders and their lack of principle."

"I regret that you are not one of us in the legislature," Allan MacFarlan,
an Upcountry planter, railroad baron, and militia colonel, wrote Robert,
"My deliberate opinion is that virtually the Union is already dissolved,
and that we must form a new government." The public regard mattered to

Robert; he would not have put his name forward otherwise. Still, he had plenty of work on behalf of the 1860 Association to occupy his time. On top of these duties, he also was fulfilling a civic obligation as the chairman of the grand jury in the federal courthouse of his college classmate and friend Judge Magrath. With the state election over, the presidential election was less than one month away—twenty-nine days to the first Tuesday of November. Then the proof of all his labors would be known.

Chapter Twenty

"IS IT FOR MANLY RESISTANCE?"

"**M**EN OF THE SOUTH," began the first page of John Townsend's pamphlet, "The South Alone, Should Govern the South," which blanketed the entire region. With time rapidly "hurrying the question to your hearthstones . . . How then do you decide? Is it for manly RESISTANCE; to be followed, with security and a prosperous end? Or is it for SUBMISSION; and a short inglorious ease; to be followed with certain ruin? Say!"

The pamphlet was required reading in Charleston and beyond. In the run-up to the presidential election, with the steam presses at Evans & Cogswell at full employment, Robert Gourdin's 1860 Association managed to put some 200,000 copies of its pamphlets into the hands of Southerners. Baltimore and Richmond, Savannah and New Orleans, these cities, too, had industrial-scale printing presses. But none rivalled Charleston as a developer, producer, and distributor of secessionist literature. It was a classic propaganda campaign; nothing like it had been seen on American soil, for sheer volume and intensity, since the circulation in the winter of 1776 of Thomas Paine's call to revolt, *Common Sense*. That tract, too, was couched as a dare. "It is not in the power of Britain or of Europe to conquer America, if she does not conquer herself by delay and timidity," Paine wrote. "There is no punishment which that man will not deserve" be he "the means of sacrificing a season so precious and useful." So felt the Charleston secessionists.

Even with a run of 200,000 pamphlets, there appeared to be unmet demand. "'The South Alone'—Circulate the Documents!" cried the *Montgomery Mail* of Alabama. "The people take it and read it with avidity: We could distribute thousands of copies instead of hundreds. We call upon our State Rights friends, in every county of the State, to collect funds and forward them to the *Mercury* or *Courier* office, Charleston, for this and other pamphlets." The tracts had already helped "in promoting the sentiment of resistance to Lincoln," the *Mail* said, and could be even more effective if Alabama's own Minute Men groups amassed a supply: "They do far more good than stump speaking, for they are constantly speaking and never grow hoarse!"

An admirer wrote to the *Mercury* under the name of "Palmetto" to recommend John Townsend—with "his cultivated intellect, his high practical sense," and his "fixed and approved political opinions"—as an ideal choice for governor. A reader would never have guessed it from the pamphleteer's swaggering tone, but Townsend inwardly worried the secession movement might collapse. He confessed his anxieties in a confidential letter to Edisto Island's congressman in Washington. The "undefined dread of terrible consequences which must certainly follow any act of separate secession" by a single state, he wrote, "palsies" any one state "from taking the first step." Other ardent secessionists shared his concern, and there was talk in Charleston of South Carolina becoming "a French protectorate" should other slave states not leave the Union. Nevertheless, Townsend remained fully supportive of secession. Never again would the South possess "an opportunity so favorable for decisive action," the planter wrote.

In a speech to the Edisto Island Vigilant Association, he made his challenge to Southern manhood even more pointed. "Unmanly fears" must not keep the South from parting with the Union, he said. He worried that the South, like a "timid sheep," will "allow itself to be bound, whilst the butcher is preparing the knife for its destruction." The *Mercury* published an excerpt of the speech that became the basis of the 1860 Association's second pamphlet, *The Doom of Slavery in the Union: Its Safety Out of It.*

Captain Truman Seymour, from his station at Fort Moultrie, observed the propaganda campaign carefully. Seymour, the son of a Methodist minister, was a native of Burlington, Vermont, and a graduate of West Point who had served in the Mexican-American War. He must have known that at least some of the men in the garrison, born and raised in the South, harbored secessionist sympathies. But, like Doubleday, Seymour was a Union man, determined to thwart the secessionist message spreading through Charleston. All he could do was try to douse this fire with water in hopes of giving fresh life to reasoned doubts. His target was the practical minds of Charleston's merchants. He grasped, just as the leaders of the secession movement did, that the shopkeepers could not be considered altogether reliable, concerned as they were with the well-being of their hard-built enterprises, into which they had poured their sweat and ploughed their savings. A store owner might possess a few slaves and perhaps collect some rental income from hiring them out for odd jobs, but he was not dependent for his livelihood on the slave system. A man like George Walton Williams—a prosperous Haynes Street wholesale grocer and the number one vote getter in the 1857 City Council elections—was well known to be skeptical about secession. There was a market for his Cuban molasses and Baltimore hams, his Rio coffee and Tennessee lard, whether Charleston was in the Union or out. Seymour met personally with men like Williams to remind them that if South Carolina managed to secede on its own, it would have to equip and maintain a professional defense force. There could be no avoiding "the enormous expenses involved in keeping up a standing army," and the taxpayers would be responsible for them.

Then there was the risk to the banking system, for America in 1860 had no central bank. The economy was afloat with dollar-denominated notes printed by individual banks, convertible to coined money—specie, typically gold—on presentation to the issuing bank. There was an active market in such notes involving banks as well as speculators, so that a speculator, say, might buy notes at less than face value in hopes of reselling them at a profit or with the plan of obtaining their full value in gold. What if anxious Northern capitalists holding notes issued by Charleston banks lined up to redeem the bills in gold? What if Northern banks cut off dealings with customers in Charleston? What if a Southern bank decided not to accept as payment a note issued by a New York bank? These were not idle questions: in mid-October, Henry Gourdin heard of an instance of a bank in Savannah refusing to accept any New York bank notes, pending the presidential election. "The enthusiasm of the moneyed men in Charleston began to cool" when they reflected upon such unwelcome but undeniable facts, Doubleday observed.

Yet secession's propagandists were meticulous guardians of their argument and, like all effective political operatives, left no counterclaim undisputed. On the question of the economics of secession, they advanced a brief of their own contrivance. The *Mercury* pointed out that Charleston's shopkeepers, like many in the South, typically purchased their inventories of goods on credit from suppliers in the North. Those debts would be suspended in the event of secession and "obliterated forever" in the event of war. The constitutional compact that required account settlement between US citizens would no longer be in force, Barny's paper explained. "It is they, the Northern people—the Northern creditors—who have driven us out of a union with them. Let them bear the consequences of their oppressions and persecutions."

This was an argument even a planter without a zeal for secession might find enticing. "Why do you wish to go out?" a *Tribune* reporter asked a planter, the owner of some two thousand slaves, in a conversation one evening at the Pavilion Hotel on Meeting Street. The reporter then suggested Lincoln might make a good president. "That is not the thing," the planter replied. "Most of us planters are deeply in debt; we should not be if out of the Union."

As for any threat to the banking system, here, too, secessionists had soothing answers. Whatever immediate financial difficulties they might experience as a result of the rupture with the Union—or of its anticipation—these would soon pass. Charleston's own banks were known for their prudent lending practices and would be able to keep the economy prospering. In fact, "our banks, disconnected with the North, would no longer be embarrassed by its crazy speculations, or more crazy panics," the *Mercury* said. There would be no shortage of specie because South

Carolina still could obtain gold for its raw cotton from Europe and, if need be, insist on payment in gold from buyers in the North as well. If gold reserves somehow, against all expectation, became depleted, even that would not be cause for worry: "Cotton is specie. It comes from the earth like gold, and is convertible into gold wholly independent of the North," the paper told readers.

Capital would flow to Charleston's banks, the *Mercury's* argument went, with monies available for productive economic investments like the expansion of the South's network of railroad tracks. Carpenters, brick-layers, shipwrights, blacksmiths, machinists—all would have gainful employment. And they would be able to buy their own slaves, should they so desire. When a Southern Republic reopened the African slave trade, there would be a glut in the supply of slaves and a resulting plummet in price. What is more, in the free-trading, tariff-free Southern nation of the future, Charleston would be the prime port of entry for European manufacturers bringing their goods to the South. "Great jobbing houses"— wholesalers, dealing in imported goods—"would accumulate"; the city's warehouses would be filled to capacity; real estate values would rise; and the Rothschilds, no less, would have agents based in Charleston, the *Mercury* assured. "Those that have ears to hear, let them hear what a calculation of dollars and cents teaches."

This vision of the future was in some ways nostalgic of a lost past—of the bygone days at the close of the eighteenth century and start of the nineteenth, when Charleston was a prime storage center for European traders in West Indies coffee and sugar, and when, on a given day, the harbor might contain more than one hundred ships involved in foreign trade. Charleston had since been eclipsed by growth in rival ports like New York and New Orleans, but still the memories tugged.

As for the idea of South Carolina growing its own money, that spoke to the overworked imaginations of Barny's *Mercury* readers. What would happen to the supply of money in a drought or when the soil was exhausted? But to those already disposed to believe in such fanciful notions, such questions were unwelcome. There was an insistence on optimism.

Chapter Twenty-One

"GOD HAVE MERCY ON MY COUNTRY"

I t was one thing to laugh at a country bumpkin strutting down Meeting Street with a blue cockade pinned to his wide-brimmed hat and a worn rifle in his sweaty grip. In contrast, a man of the Washington Light Infantry commanded respect in his expensively tailored, dark-blue frock with black-silk trim and brass-ball buttons and his red-striped trousers. The militia took its name from George Washington, whose birthday the men heartily celebrated on February 22 with a banquet attended by the city's notables. Founded in 1807, the rolls featured eminent Charleston names like Lowndes, Ravenel, and Gilchrist. An honor guard of the infantry greeted Lafayette, in French, on his visit to the town in 1825. Infantrymen fought the Seminole Indians in Florida in the 1830s and marched into Mexico City as part of the Palmetto Regiment in the 1840s. Their motto was "Virtue and Valor" and their crest a winged angel with horn in mouth, triumphantly soaring through the clouds.

From the start of 1860, the Washington Light Infantry had been a visible presence drilling and parading on the streets of Charleston. In May, its members had marched off to the train station for a visit to their rural campsite and were later welcomed home with banners suspended across Meeting at Hibernian Hall. Two companies of 144 men in all had turned out for a Fourth of July procession through downtown Charleston.

On the evening of Saturday, October 20, with the election nearly two weeks away, the men assembled to consider "the threatening aspect of affairs and the necessity of preparing to meet the emergency." The commanding officer, Captain Charles Henry Simonton—a thirty-one-year-old native of Charleston, a practicing lawyer in town, and an elected member of the state House of Representatives—proposed that the unit undertake preparations "to take the field at a moment's warning" and even to go into battle, if need be, against Union forces. The men agreed and unanimously adopted a resolution offered by Sergeant William Ashmead Courtenay—a twenty-nine-year-old Charleston businessman and future mayor—to make one hundred men of the Washington Light Infantry immediately available to the governor of South Carolina as Minute Men, with a pledge to raise the number to two hundred, if desired, to form a battalion of light infantry. In Columbia, Governor William Henry Gist accepted the offer.

The Charleston Light Dragoons, a mounted regiment, was equal in prestige and costume to the Washington Light Infantry. Its men wore helmets of brass-trimmed, black patent leather with a large plume of white horse hair and bottle-green jackets trimmed with red cashmere. With origins predating the Revolution, this militia also drew from old, upper-class Anglo and Huguenot families—names like Manigault, Heyward, Middleton, and Huger. Its members tended to be known as much for their capacities for quaffing champagne as for their battlefield exploits, but by October their blood was up with an impatient desire to confront the North. One member of the "Drags," as the Light Dragoons were called, William Lee Trenholm, wrote to a friend of the "improving" election prospects of the Breckinridge ticket. That, of course, was the ticket upon which Southern nationalists had decided in June after breaking with Douglas and the Northern Democrats. Back in August, Trenholm had dreaded thought of Breckinridge's defeat by Lincoln. But his emotional calculus had shifted. "If he is elected," Trenholm said of Breckinridge, "we will have four more years of agitation, of Federal corruption, of Southern spoliation and of Northern aggrandizement. If he is defeated the struggle will be sharp and soon over, and the South will either enter upon a career of prosperity and security, or sink into degradation and ruin. God have mercy on my country."

"Do not blink," John Townsend had instructed, and young Trenholm embodied this imperative. No one, it seemed, was more eager to put their lives on the line for secession than the youth of Charleston.

———

Eight days to the election and the circus came to town—Nixon's Royal Circus of London. Thousands of spectators streamed into an enormous tent on the Citadel Green to laugh at the clowns, gape at the contortion-ist, and marvel at the daredevil acrobatics of the Hanlon Brothers and the dashing equestrian exploits of the "renowned" Ella Zoyara. Still, the sight of the Hanlons suspended from ladders and of Mr. Charlton on stilts failed to divert Charleston from its political fixation. The *Courier,* for so long a tribune of moderation compared with the *Mercury*, was becoming nearly indistinguishable from the latter. "It is well known that our city is at the present time overrun with Abolition emissaries disseminating in-cendiary principles among our negroes, deluding these credulous people with the belief that the election of Lincoln will be their millennium," a writer called "Caution" declared on the first day of the circus. Perhaps the author had in mind the seamstress Bottsford—although from her jail cell she was hardly in a position to spread the abolitionist gospel. "Our safety lies in extreme measures," Caution urged.

On the last day of October, the Drags were on the streets for their first parade of the fall. The German Fusiliers drilled at Military Hall in the evening, joined by the Washington Artillery, the Palmetto Guards, the Meagher Guards, and the Charleston Riflemen. The Charleston Zou-ave Cadets, a newly organized militia made up mostly of young men and outfitted in natty uniforms of white cross-belts and red-trim pants, drilled on the Battery before a large throng of admiring spectators. "We are rejoiced to find the men of Charleston—young and old—up and do-ing, in the cause of State defence," the *Mercury* said. "The military spirit of our people is thoroughly aroused, and not a night passes that the mea-sured tramp of disciplined platoons is not heard echoing through our otherwise quiet streets."

The assault on Lincoln's image intensified, with the *Mercury* describing him as "the *beau ideal* of a relentless, dogged, freesoil border-ruffian—a

Southerner by birth, and a Northerner in feeling and association—a fanatic in philanthropy and a vulgar mobocrat and a Southern hater in political opinions." As ever, the *Mercury* and its home city had surpassed all others in the South: a more memorable diatribe against Lincoln was not composed during the presidential campaign.

Barny and his father must have felt some satisfaction that Charleston was finally arriving at consensus in favor of secession. They had always believed public opinion was a product to be manufactured, and they had proven master assemblers. "The issue before the country is the extinction of slavery," the front page of the *Mercury* declared on Saturday, November 3, the final weekend before the vote. "The Southern States are now in the crisis of their fate; and, if we read aright the signs of the times, nothing is needed for our deliverance, but that the ball of revolution be set in motion." To back up that claim, the paper wrote, "We have innumerable assurances that the men of action in each and all of the Southern States, earnestly desire South Carolina to exhibit promptitude and decision in this conjuncture."

This was misleading. Barny knew that the "men of action" in fellow slave states were by no means sure their states were ready to follow South Carolina out of the Union. In fact, if *Mercury* readers had been paying careful attention, they knew this, too. The paper had printed a letter back in October from a "Distinguished Georgian" on this very matter. In "candor," the author said, "there will be a large party in the State who will oppose any action" in favor of secession if Lincoln is elected, and whatever South Carolina does on her own "will not influence" the people of Georgia, one way or another.

Such "candor" seldom crept into the *Mercury*. Yet on the last weekend before the election, another exception appeared. In its back pages, the paper published a bracing letter accusing the secession movement and its leaders, although not by name, of an almost criminal recklessness. The author was identified as "Festina Lente," the slogan of Roman emperors meaning "make haste slowly." As an instructive example for the would-be revolutionaries of 1860, the writer invoked the prudent conduct of the leaders of the American Revolution nearly a century earlier. Even after the Battle of Bunker Hill, "the resolute, moderate, patriots of Congress kept open the door of conciliation," Festina Lente pointed out. "From September, 1774, to July, 1776, they made every effort that was honorable to preserve the Union. They still hesitated to abolish it, even in the midst of battles, sieges, and frequent bloodshed," and what is more, "there was no boyish petulance, no indecent haste, no blind rushing into the mire of revolution, with a vague dependence on some contingent Jupiter to assist them in getting out of it."

The letter was published at the request of an "old subscriber," the *Mercury* cryptically said. The author must have been someone of stature with a taste for classical allusions and in the good graces of the Rhett family. Petigru would have qualified on all counts.

Perhaps Barny published the letter because he was confident nobody who mattered would agree with it. There was good cheer at the *Mercury's* offices. With "the crisis" approaching—always the crisis—agitators prowled the streets, and on this Saturday they staged a public rally in Charleston. There they raised the alarm that the Fort Moultrie garrison was busily strengthening its defenses and prompted a large group of Minute Men at the gathering to make off for Sullivan's Island. They clambered aboard the harbor ferry, and on landing streamed into the fort for a detailed inspection of the works. There was, in fact, repair work in progress. The Union men stonily endured the impromptu "visit," with Doubleday inwardly fuming. "November had arrived," his pen recorded. "The muttering of the storm was heard all around us."

The *Mercury* closed the campaign season with an exhortation from "a young Carolinian" cadet at West Point. "I would like to hear something positive about what our State is going to do in the event of Lincoln's election," he said. "I think that she should leave the Union at all hazards, let come what may, and if she does, I am coming home instanter." He presumably would have company from a Charlestonian residing in Texas, who sent in a letter also published in the *Mercury,* saying, "I hope Lincoln will be elected and that we will get face to face with those d----d Yankees. If he is elected, and my native State faces the music, I will be home by the first train." As for the *Courier,* its headline of Monday, November 5, was as enthusiastic as it was unequivocal: "If Lincoln Is Elected, South Carolina Will Lead Boldly for a Southern Confederacy!"

"My own countrymen here in South Carolina are distempered to a degree that makes them to a calm and impartial observer real objects of pity," Petigru wrote despairingly to his old friend Edward Everett of Massachusetts. "They believe anything that flatters their delusion or their vanity; and at the same time they are credulous to every whisper of suspicion about insurgents or incendiaries." Yet even with the election imminent, Petigru believed a calm consideration of self-interest would prevail over a revolutionary fervor. "If Lincoln is elected it will give the Union a great strain; yet still I don't think that this State will secede alone; because the country is too prosperous for a revolution," he told Everett. He wrote likewise to his sister Jane, "I don't think the hazard so great as many do, for it is not easy to undo the complicated machinery of that great engine of government." Not for the first time during this year and not for the last, his habit of applying a prism of reason to the events unfolding before his eyes was to prove unreliable.

Chapter Twenty-Two

"HURRA FOR LINCOLN"

J ust about anyone, it seemed, could jostle his or her way into the offices of the *Mercury*. Early in the evening of Tuesday, November 6, Election Day, the *Mercury*'s newsroom at 4 Broad Street began to fill with "anxious expectants" of the tidings from New York. Everything depended on the telegraph and the Associated Press (AP)—on dispatches of the results, state by state, confirmed by the AP and wired from New York to the American Telegraph Office at 49 Broad. There, chief operator O'Bryan, who lived around the corner on Church Street , was stationed with a three-man crew of assistants. As the wires came in they would be decoded and run over to the paper, which had set up a bulletin board on the sidewalk in front of its building.

By midnight, the crowd of men numbered in the thousands, some attired in fine suits and black stovetop hats, standing shoulder to shoulder on Broad from the telegraph office to the *Mercury* office, spilling over to the plaza by City Hall. In the light of the gas lamps their shadows flickered on the office buildings and storefronts lining the sidewalks. They were spared any rain, but the thermometer was headed toward the forties. Police patrolled the area to keep prostitutes and black people—it was after curfew—off the streets. Reporters from out-of-town newspapers were dispersed throughout the crowd. Charleston at this moment was the most important dateline in America. From nowhere else in the nation was the immediate reaction to the election results more eagerly anticipated. Because of the hazards of operating in the city for Northern papers, especially for those like the *Tribune* identified with abolitionism, their correspondents planned to file their stories in code at O'Bryan's office.

In this throng could be found James Dunwoody Brownson De Bow of New Orleans. J. D. B. De Bow was a forty-year-old native of Charleston, born and raised in the city, whose father had been a grocer with a shop on East Bay Street. The younger was an acclaimed expert in economics and statistics and had been appointed by President Franklin Pierce to serve as superintendent of the US Census in the early 1850s. He was also the editor of *De Bow's Review*—a magazine he founded in New Orleans in 1846— and was one of America's most ardent and sophisticated advocates for the cause of Southern nationalism and independence. If only the South could mill its own raw cotton, he once said, the region could "hush the sound of every spindle in New England." At the request of Robert Gourdin, he was writing a pamphlet for the 1860 Association on how even nonslaveholders in the South had a core interest in the institution of slavery. There was plenty of secessionist enthusiasm in New Orleans, but it was no rival for the fervor of Charleston. De Bow had come home to Charleston to stand among his brethren and help give history a shove.

The first dispatch flashed the results from Connecticut—to Lincoln by several thousand votes. The second was no surprise: North Carolina to Breckinridge. At 2:00 a.m. the third dispatch carried the crucial news that Lincoln had beaten Douglas in battleground New York. It was over, the AP declared. A man from O'Bryan's crew posted the notice on the *Mercury*'s board: Lincoln's election was certain.

———

"Hurra for Lincoln!" men shouted as they ran through the streets, alerting the entire city to the remarkable tidings for the benefit of those who had gone to bed. By dawn scarcely a person in town could have been unaware of the news, including Catherine Bottsford in the jail that had been her home for more than a month. In the strangeness of the moment—in the incongruous harmony of feelings between those on opposite sides of the question of slavery—she must have felt elated on behalf of Lincoln's triumph, too.

Across the harbor at Fort Moultrie, Doubleday could also take satisfaction in the election outcome. The recipient of his secret dispatches soon would be in power. Still, in finding, as he put it, "the Disunionists were wild with delight," the officers of the garrison were mindful this was a dangerous kind of joy. At 9:00 in the morning, Captain Seymour and a small detachment of his men, clad in civilian clothes, noiselessly departed from Sullivan's Island aboard a small schooner. Their destination, an expected six hours away around the Battery and up the Ashley River, was the federal arsenal, a four-acre site on Bee Street in Charleston just off the wharf. They planned to make off with the facility's thirty thousand rounds of musket ammunition and cartridges—before secessionists in Charleston got it in their mind to take the ammo for themselves. But unbeknownst to the crew, they had already been spotted leaving the island. Charleston may have been "wild with delight," but it remained watchful. Joy and suspicion managed to mingle together, strange bedfellows.

Shortly after Seymour and his men set off on their stealth voyage, the US District Courthouse at 23 Chalmers Street opened for business. Lincoln's election offered no interruption to the peddling of human flesh at establishments like Ryan's Mart, located a block and a half down the street from the courthouse, and it may have seemed business as usual at 23 Chalmers as well. In the courtroom on the second floor sat the members of a grand jury, gathered for the last day of their term.

Before turning to his jury, Judge Magrath, presiding, read from the bench his decree awarding compensation to the owner and crew of the steamship *Nina* and the Eagle Fire Company for the help they gave the *Huntsville*, a steamer that had caught on fire on a voyage north from Savannah and had to be towed to the Charleston docks. With that item taken care of, he asked the grand jurors if, as was the custom on the completion of a term, they wished to offer what was known as a presentment, a general commentary on dealing with crime in the community and any particular recommendations for improvements.

Answering on behalf of the grand jury was its foreman, Robert Newman Gourdin. He told the judge—his old college classmate and, possibly, a covert advisor to his 1860 Association—that it had been the intention of the grand jury to offer such remarks, "but the events of yesterday seem to render this unnecessary now" because "the verdict of the Northern section" of the nation "has swept away the last hope for the permanence—for the stability of the federal government of these sovereign States." And so, Gourdin said, "in these extraordinary circumstances, the Grand Jury respectfully decline to proceed with their presentments."

The courtroom fell silent. All eyes turned to the bench. Reporters from the *Mercury* and the *Courier* were poised with pen and notebook in hand. "The business of the term has been disposed of," Magrath began, his gaze fixed on Gourdin. "And, under ordinary circumstances, it would be my duty to dismiss you to your several avocations, with my thanks for your presence and aid. But now I have something more to do."

Chapter Twenty-Three

THE JUDGE

How does a revolution choose its heroes? Some eagerly bid for consideration, chin thrust forward, like Barnwell Rhett. But this self-aggrandizing tactic is seldom successful. It is more often simply a matter of the ripe moment arriving for the candidate—who, presented with the invitation, grabs it. Andrew Gordon Magrath did not seem made of heroic fiber. With his close-cropped, carefully combed hair and his square jaw and custom-made suits, he could have passed for a staid banker. He was a loyal creature of the South Carolina political machine constructed by James Orr. Machine politics in Charleston emitted a stench, and Magrath's character was not above reproach. Robert Gourdin's nephew told his uncle that only by holding his nose could he vote for Magrath during the judge's ill-fated bid for Congress in 1856. "The elevation of such men as he, so well-known to the community as no great stickler for either morality, honesty or political fidelity, must, it seems to me, tend to lower the community's morality," the nephew said, "There are too many rumors about Magrath's having defrauded others and used too much money for elections, etc., for them not be entirely without foundation."

As for his political views, they gave no sign of being radical. This, of course, was why he was regarded with such distaste by the Rhetts. The Orr men were national Democrats, bent on keeping the party together. Unless he remained moderate, Magrath never would have been nominated for a seat on the federal bench by President Franklin Pierce, a Pennsylvania Democrat. On secession, Magrath had well-established credentials as a Cooperationist. When Barnwell Rhett's first wife, Elizabeth, railed against this "cowardly, stupid State" for siding with the Cooperationists in 1851, she had men like Magrath in mind.

A closer look at the man, though, revealed traits of a more subversive and less pliable character. Perhaps these attributes were an inheritance. Back in eighteenth-century Ireland, his father, John Magrath, was a soldier in the Society of United Irishmen. With chapters in Belfast and Dublin, the society aimed to unite Protestants and Catholics from the middle and the working classes in the fight for independence from the British, by force of arms if necessary. But in the society's 1798 uprising, the revolt was quashed and the elder Magrath captured and jailed. He managed to escape on a boat bound for America and arrived in Charleston as a fugitive from the law and an exile from his homeland.

Andrew, the oldest son, was born in Charleston in 1813. His mother was Scottish, and the Magrath family worshipped at the First (Scots) Presbyterian Church on Meeting Street. While making a living as a small-time merchant, John Magrath devoted his abundant energies to the Irish independence movement, which had a vibrant following in the city's Irish community. As one of the "men of '98" and as an absconder from the British, his credentials were impeccable. He served as president of the St. Patrick Benevolent Society for thirty-two years from its founding in 1817 and was elected captain of the Irish Volunteers militia by the mostly working-class members. That was how he liked to be known around town.

The father's creed became the son's. Andrew was a standout student, mastering his Latin at the Bishop School in Charleston, run by an Irish Catholic prelate. He graduated from South Carolina College in Columbia, along with Robert Gourdin, in 1831 at the age of eighteen. He read law under Petigru in Charleston, attended Harvard Law School, then returned to Charleston and gained admission to the bar. Two years later, at the age of twenty-four, he delivered a speech in the Cathedral of St. Finbar—before a joint audience of the Hibernian Society, the St. Patrick Benevolent Society, and the Irish Volunteers—and revealed where his youthful political passion lay. His theme was "justice" for long-suffering Ireland. Nothing, he said, could be left unremembered from the uprising of 1798, crushed by the heartless British nearly forty years ago. "Those wounds have no cure. That rebellion will never be forgotten. Might trampled over right. The battle was to the strong."

"Might trampled over right"—Andrew, like his father and also his younger brother Edward, felt an affinity between his childhood-imbibed Irish nationalism and the cause of Southern nationalism. Both movements, after all, were animated by a sense of a distant and arrogant power, whether in London or in Washington. The young attorney also held a nearly religious belief in the "right of property" as the basis of civilization—the only true barrier to outright chaos. Perhaps this conviction came from his legal training. Or perhaps, as for many educated Southerners, the sacred right of property was merely sophisticated legal cover for the unstinting defense of slavery. At Harvard, he encountered implacable opponents of the very idea of "human property." His instructors included Joseph Story, an antislavery man who at that time also served as a US Supreme Court justice. But for Magrath, each and every practice of the slave system was sacrosanct, from the auctions at Ryan's Mart to the insurance policies taken out on the field hands. The slave might have been a plot of land or a mule; the law of property applied to all. And no threat to the law could be brooked.

He was, however, sensible to the possibility that the slave, unlike the mule, might arrive at his or her own opinion on the majesty of the law and act accordingly. Andrew was nine years old when the "conspirators" in Denmark Vesey's slave-uprising plot were strung up by the noose in Charleston and the free blacks' African Church burned to the ground. A quarter-century later, in 1847, John Adger, a white Charlestonian, revived the idea of a black church whose parishioners, free blacks and slaves alike, could worship together apart from whites. This would be a long overdue act of spiritual empathy, he told his fellow congregants at the Second Presbyterian Church of Charleston. In response, Magrath took the scheme as

R. B. Rhett, Jr., editor of *The Mercury*, a "gigantic Ogre, whose supreme delight consists in treason, stratagem and spoils," an admirer wrote teasingly.
Courtesy of the Library of Congress.

ert Barnwell Rhett, Sr., a forerunner of the
ssion cause with "a vast quantity of cranks
a small proportion of common sense."
tesy of the Library of Congress.

Charleston slave mart. "Negroes are to this country what raw materials are to another," a Charleston planter said.
Courtesy of the Library of Congress.

(Clockwise, from upper left)

John C. Calhoun. His gospel of states' rights was holy writ in Charleston.
Courtesy of Wikimedia Commons.

Christopher G. Memminger, reluctant convert to secession. "It was a whirlwind, and all we could do was to try to guide it."
Courtesy of the Archives and Special Collections, Dickinson College.

Rev. John Bachman, dean of Charleston's clergy, he blessed secession.
Courtesy of Wikimedia Commons.

Mary Amarinthia Yates Snowden led the project to build a monument to Calhoun.
Courtesy of Internet Archive.

Institute Hall, renamed Secession Hall. South Carolina's Ordinance of Secession was signed here. Photograph.

Courtesy of the Library of Congress.

THE NATIONAL DEMOCRATIC NOMINATING CONVENTION IN SESSION AT CHARLESTON, SOUTH CAROLINA, ON APRIL 23, 1860.—[FROM A SKETCH BY OUR ARTIST CORRESPONDENT.]

Democratic National Convention, Spring 1860, Institute Hall. Southern delegates bolted the convention, fracturing the party. *Harper's Weekly* illustration.

Courtesy of Internet Archive.

John Ferrars Townsend. The planter as propagandist, declaring that "unmanly fears" must not stop the South from leaving the Union.

Courtesy of the South Caroliniana Library, University of South Carolina.

James Louis Petigru. "My own countrymen are distempered to a degree that makes them real objects of pity," declared Charleston's last Unionist.

Courtesy of the South Caroliniana Library, University of South Carolina.

Andrew Gordon Magrath. On resigning as a federal judge, he became the Charleston uprising's folk hero.

Courtesy of the South Caroliniana Library, University of South Carolina.

Robert Newman Gourdin. Gentleman revolutionary of Huguenot descent. *Il faut coupe* (it must be cut), he told a friend of the bond between North and South.

Courtesy of Henry Gourdin Young, Jr.

Henry Gourdin. Robert's older brother, the leader of their merchant firm, had practical concerns about secession.

Courtesy of Henry Gourdin Young, Jr.

(left) Abraham Lincoln. As presidential candidate, 1860.

Courtesy of Wikimedia Commons.

(below, left) Captain Abner Doubleday, front row, furthest left, with fellow Uni officers stationed at Charleston harbor. staunch antislavery man, he secretly fe dispatches to Lincoln.

Courtesy of the South Caroliniana Library, Unive of South Carolina.

(below, right) Charleston Mercury. "The Union is Dissolved!" Published minutes after passage of Ordinance of Secession.

Courtesy of Wikimedia Commons.

Fort Moultrie. The Union garrison stationed at Fort Moultrie feared
an attack from a Charleston mob. Illustration by Frank Leslie.

Courtesy of Archives and Special Collections, Dickinson College.

THE GOVERNMENT ARSENAL IN CHARLESTON, S. C., GUARDED BY DETACHMENTS OF THE WASHINGTON LIGHT INFANTRY.—From a Sketch by our Special Artist.

Federal Arsenal. Guarded by Washington Light Infantry
who kept munitions out of Union hands.

Courtesy of the Library of Congress.

Ruins in Charleston. Charleston, 1865, after the war.

Courtesy of Mathew Brady image, National Archives.

an invitation for an insurrection that could soak Meeting Street in blood. He waged his assault in an anonymous letter published in the *Mercury* in the name of "Many Citizens." "They will owe a spiritual allegiance to their Church," he wrote of black congregants of a newly organized church, "and will learn the lessons of zeal." After their minds were imbued with zeal, "what shall be the language of the master or owner? To spirits thus excited, what will be the interference of the master or owner?" Thus emboldened, the congregants, Magrath predicted, would undoubtedly pursue an alliance with the church-based abolitionist movement of the North: "Are they not at liberty to adopt the creed of the Church of the North, instead of that of the Church of the South? And if you have gone with them so far, who will dare question their right to go further?"

On top of his Irishman's readiness to embrace a need for rebellion and his evident alarm at even the most remote threat to the legal right to human chattel, there was a third quality in Magrath that suggested the possible making of a hero: his subtle ambition for public acclaim. Like his father before him, Magrath became a president of the St. Patrick Benevolent Society and captain of the Irish Volunteers, and he won election to the state House of Representatives in Columbia in 1842. He was sent back two years later for another term.

Of course, this was a modest accomplishment. He lost his bid for a seat in the US Congress after his brother's duel with the former *Mercury* editor, and his career in electoral politics ended abruptly. Still, as a judge he was determined to use his platform at 23 Chalmers Street to have his say on the more politically charged matters in his courtroom. And so it was, with his politician's sense of timing, that he issued a controversial ruling opening the door for a resumption of the African slave trade just as delegates were arriving in Charleston for the Democratic Convention in April. Copies of the decision were made available for sale as 15-cent pamphlets in hotels and bookstores around town. His ruling rankled federal prosecutors but won applause from the *Mercury*. Southern rights was an urgent enough cause, it seemed, to transcend the ill will between the Rhetts and Magraths.

After Lincoln's election, with Robert Gourdin and the other members of the grand jury declining to proceed with their duties, and with US District Attorney James Conner standing wordlessly by, Magrath had the rapt attention of his courtroom. "In the political history of the United States, an event has happened of ominous import to fifteen slaveholding States," he began. With Lincoln's victory, there could be no doubt of South Carolina's imminent departure from the Union. His responsibility, then, was clear: "Feeling an assurance of what will be the action of the State, I consider it my duty, without delay, to prepare to obey its wishes. That preparation is made by the resignation of the office I have held. For the last time I have, as a Judge of the United States, administered the laws of the United States, within the limits of the State of South Carolina." And "so far as I am concerned," Magrath added, "the Temple of Justice, raised under the Constitution of the United States, is now closed." The judge had caught the contagion. Transformed from Cooperationist to a full-blown secessionist, he would become a hero of the revolution in the making.

Magrath ended his speech with a warning for any citizen who might have it in mind to challenge a newly independent South Carolina, soon to be the master of its own domain. "Let us not forget that what the laws of our State require, become our duties," he said. "And that he who acts against the wish, or without the command of his State, usurps that sovereign authority which we must maintain inviolate." Then he removed his gown and laid it aside. And with "few dry eyes" in the courtroom, the *Courier* reported, he departed from it.

Magrath, of course, could have closed the "Temple of Justice" before delivering his decree on the *Nina* steamship matter, but instead he waited for a cue from his friend Robert Gourdin. And he could have stopped short of an outright resignation and instead simply suspended the work of his court, but that would have lacked dramatic punch. The duo's performance suggested a staged, set piece of political theater for which they had carefully prepared. South Carolina's secession was not, as Magrath told his courtroom, at that point imminent. After all, the legislature had yet to set a timetable or even a procedure for the state to vote on its departure from the Union, and it was nearly four months before the president-elect would assume power on the 4th of March, Inauguration Day. The immediate effect of Magrath's resignation, thanks to Gourdin's handy prompt, was to dramatically boost chances for secession and so help make South Carolina's exit a done deal. Perhaps personal considerations entered into his calculation as well. In selecting the most drastic path available to him, Magrath also was adopting the course most likely to advance his prospects in a transformed political landscape. Moderate ground was fast becoming dangerous terrain in Charleston.

District Attorney Conner, startled or not by Magrath's resignation, immediately followed by announcing his own. The chain of resignation continued outside the courtroom with William Ferguson Colcock relinquishing his post as director of the federal customs house at the port of Charleston, along with an underling named Meyer Jacobs. US Marshal Hamilton also stepped down from his post and might well have known what Gourdin and Magrath planned for this day. As Gourdin's friend, he sometimes supplied him confidential advice on how to advance the secession cause. The only prominent federal officeholder in Charleston to remain on the job was the longtime postmaster, Alfred Huger. Accused of being a traitor, he prayed to God for "protection" in "this emergency." The *Mercury* defended Huger, saying "the interests of our State and community would be jeopardized" by his leaving office. The paper asked him to remain "until the State assumes, in her sovereign capacity, the management of her postal arrangements."

All through the morning of November 7, a crowd kept vigil in front of the *Mercury*'s building as the paper kept posting the latest news on its sidewalk bulletin board. Upon notice of the resignations of the judge and the other federal officials, men, total strangers, embraced each other in the street. At noon, an enormous South Carolina flag—the palmetto tree and a lone star on a red background—was unfurled from an upper window of the *Mercury*'s offices and stretched across the street. "Tremendous cheers" greeted the sight. A merchant brought a suggested design to the *Mercury* for a new flag for the Southern Republic, a blue banner with a golden rattlesnake wrapped around the trunk of a palmetto, "its rattle sprung, head erect, and tongue protruded." A single golden star graced the flag, accompanied by the hopeful words "Room for More."

America's telegraph wires buzzed with the riveting news from Charleston, and offices in cities across the country received one bell-ringing alert after another. In Washington, news of the resignations, and Magrath's courtroom performance in particular, brought a profound shock to James Buchanan in the White House and his attorney general, Jeremiah S. Black. Neither man could have been surprised, of course, at the popular reception in Charleston to the news of Lincoln's election. Everyone in Washington understood the city to be the leading center of rebellion in the South. Nevertheless, Buchanan and his team had not anticipated this immediate and brazen act of defiance by a sitting federal judge. Magrath's deed could be an example for the rest of the South. Few men could be found brave enough to replace these defected officials, to stand up for the rule of US law in an aroused and threatening Charleston.

At 3:00 in the afternoon, in sync with the timetable, Capt. Seymour's schooner reached the dock by Bee Street, and the men made their way to the federal arsenal. There they found the keeper of the ordnance, A. A. Humphreys, agreeable to the plan of removing the munitions for safe hauling back to Fort Moultrie. But as Seymour's team started lugging the boxes of musket rounds and cartridges out of the facility, they were beset by an excited mob demanding a halt to the operation on the pain of force. The mission had been compromised from its start. Seymour considered reaching out for help to Mayor Macbeth, with whom he had amiable relations, but decided against it, given the need to get back to Fort Moultrie against the falling tide. Reluctantly he told his men to return the ammo to the arsenal, and the party retreated to the schooner empty-handed for an unhappy return voyage. The mayor later apologized for the unauthorized action of the "committee," but Seymour never attempted a return to the arsenal for fear "the mob might be beyond the control of the mayor."

———

That very day, Robert Gourdin called a meeting of the 1860 Association to plot next moves. Needed to keep the momentum going, the men decided, was a public rally to pressure the legislature in Columbia to take up the question of secession without delay. The association determined to rent

Institute Hall for the event on the evening of November 9 and issued in-
vitations for Magrath, Conner, Colcock, and Hamilton to speak. Several
hours later, Townsend gave notice for the rally at the regularly scheduled
monthly gathering of the Charleston Quadrille Association, of which he
was the chair.

Charleston, though, did not want to wait two days to hear from its
heroes. At nightfall, a crowd of about five thousand gathered on Meeting
Street in front of the Charleston Hotel. Among them was J. D. B. De Bow,
still on his feet, unable to extract himself from the fraternal grip of his
compatriots. There was a brass band and, for an escort, the Washington
Light Artillery, a militia organized in 1844 that had resolved, as of this day,
"All the stars, save one, should be erased from the flag of the company—
the single star to represent South Carolina, and other stars to be added as
the other Southern States fell into line."

The revelers called on Colcock and Conner at their homes, paying
them the honor of a serenade and receiving the reward of a few remarks
in return. On stopping by the *Mercury*'s offices, where the Lone Star flag
was still suspended over Broad Street, the crowd found not Rhett, Jr., who
was with his fellow legislators in Columbia, but his brother Edmund. The
younger Rhett obliged with a speech, and his theme amounted to "trust
in the *Mercury*.' "Gentleman," Edmund said, the "*Mercury* stands vindicated this day from all vain and foolish aspersions that hate, and malice,
and fear, have attempted to put upon it. . . . You all stand up on the policy
and platform of the *Mercury*" and "soon will dawn upon you the great
Southern Confederacy!"

The star of this nocturnal procession across moonlit Charleston, the
man whose words were craved above all others in the city, was Magrath.
The judge lived on Bee Street, near Bennett's Pond, half a block from the
federal arsenal, with his wife, Emma, a Charleston lady with whom he had
raised five children. When the crowd reached Magrath's home, De Bow
announced he was there to congratulate "their late ex-Judge." Magrath
spoke to the assemblage for ten minutes in plain, blunt, unscripted language. He stood before the gathering as "a citizen of South Carolina,
ready to defend her rights at any and all hazards." This day, he said, represented "the first gun of the revolution, the sound of which will be vibrated

back from the fifteen Southern States." And "if the action of the Southern States, forced upon them by the North, should bring ruin and desolation to the country, it could not be charged upon the South."

The captain's son had made good. He was truly a rebel, forever to be despised as a traitor by the Unionists in the North. Across the Atlantic, Ireland still suffered under the boot heel of the British. But a Magrath in Charleston was blazing a trail to the liberation of the South.

Chapter Twenty-Four

"WILL NOT DELAY COOL THE ARDOR?"

The tea has been thrown overboard—the revolution of 1860 has been initiated," the *Mercury* declared on its front page of Thursday, November 8. And so Charleston sped along on its voyage of excitement with a collective understanding that there could be no turning back. To hold a one-way ticket, purchased seemingly without cost, to a dream destination—what could possibly be more exhilarating?

But the revolution was only initiated—for much work remained to be accomplished. On this morning in the port of Charleston lay, as usual, dozens of vessels—schooners and steamships, brigs and barks—many of them flying the Stars and Stripes. A throng descended on the docks and made it a task to replace the banners to cleanse the waterfront of the intolerable sight of soiled Unionism. The first to comply was the *James Gray*, a brig owned by the Cushing brothers of Newburyport, Massachusetts. The Palmetto flag was raised to the masthead, and an iron gun fired off a salute for each of the fifteen slave states, three cheers from the crowd for each blast. Afterward, the captain and guests celebrated in his cabin with champagne toasts.

There was no rulebook for the mob to follow on how to impose its will. Yet before long a rough set of stipulations emerged, including that no ship enter the harbor flying a US flag. The *Keystone State*, sailing out of Philadelphia, was kept from docking by a greeting party comprising "boys of the city" until the captain complied. Had he refused—well, he did not. For the compliant there were rewards: a gold-topped cane was presented to Captain Michael Berry of the steamer *Columbia,* who sailed into Charleston from New York displaying a South Carolina flag. Most people did not need to be told how to conduct themselves. Downtown merchants raised the Palmetto on their own. The owner of the carriage depot on Meeting Street flew a white flag with a single star and pledged "to add a star for each State as they fall into line." The Zouaves Militia marched to the offices of the *Mercury* to present the delighted staff with a new "States Rights Resistance" banner. The flag depicted a crouching tiger—the emblem of the militia—with a serpent representing the abolitionist dangling from the predator's jaws. Charleston, it seemed, was seceding in advance of the state.

———

To be sure, the city's giddiness was not universally shared, even by those sympathetic to secession. Mary Boykin Chesnut, the wife of US Senator James Chesnut of South Carolina and the daughter of a former governor of the state, considered herself "a rebel born" but nonetheless felt a "nervous dread" at the prospect of a break "with so great a power as [the] U.S.A." She was on a train bound for Charleston when she received word of Lincoln's election. "Now that the black radical Republicans have the power I suppose they will 'Brown' us all," one passenger exclaimed, in grim shorthand for John Brown's raid on Harpers Ferry. "No doubt of it," Chesnut tersely wrote in her diary on the following day from Charleston.

With the abrupt collapse of federal authority in Charleston the possibility of mob rule had to be taken seriously. That prospect troubled Edmund Ruffin. After Lincoln's election, he had made his way from his home in Virginia to Charleston to add his voice to those calling for South Carolina to leave the Union on its own. On learning of the orders put to the captain of the *Keystone State* by "the boys" at the docks, he recorded in his diary his "fear that the people will run ahead of the government" and "make a disruption of the Union by revolutionary and illegal action, instead of by deliberate and legal secession." Ruffin was also distressed by the report of citizen-volunteers taking it upon themselves to stop Capt. Seymour from carting off the munitions at the federal arsenal. The Virginian was relieved Seymour's effort was thwarted but alarmed by the unsanctioned action of the roving band of irregulars. Governor Gist tasked the Washington Light Infantry, now adorned with the blue cockade, to stand guard over the arsenal—to keep Union forces at bay should they return and also to keep any ragtag crew from helping itself to the munitions.

Memminger, too, was appalled at the prospect of civic chaos. His mission to Virginia at the start of the year in search of a cooperative solution for the South's political dilemmas had failed, and Charleston was descending into mayhem. Even in the midst of a revolution, which he had come to accept as preferable to the status quo, his cherished goal was regular order. He seemed to take personally the menace in the air—to take the hooliganism as a threat to private and public property and as a direct affront to the city that had nurtured him as a ward of its orphanage, given him a profession in the law, elected him to office, and claimed his heart. Always the diplomat, he kept open a channel of communication with the Union officers in charge of the garrison at Fort Moultrie, and they in turn felt gratified by his efforts "to prevent any irregular and unauthorized violence."

It was too easy, though, for men like Ruffin to blame "the people" for civic unrest. The leaders of the Charleston uprising were responsible for inciting the crowd because they too seemed to lose themselves in the excitement of the moment. Free from his judicial robes, Magrath seemed to find a new calling in provocative and theatrical oration. It was as if he had been bottled up for years and the cork at last released. He was the main attraction at the rally sponsored by the 1860 Association held at Institute Hall on the evening of Friday, November 9. The building was packed, and the throng spilled out the door onto Meeting. Here assembled were the most devoted of the devoted of white Charleston—three thousand or so souls, men and women, who left their homes on a cold, rainy night to join the assembly. Among those present was a young Charleston minister, A. Toomer Porter, chaplain of the Washington Light Infantry. At thirty-two years old, Porter was a former rice planter who had grown "very tired of the plantation life" and found a new calling in the clergy. He had no history of involvement in political affairs. In fact, only the month before, he had frowned on talk of secession as "a second nullification madness." And yet, he confessed, "day by day the excitement increased" in Charleston, and "we had all become crazed."

Porter fixed his eye on "The Judge," as Magrath was still called, standing on the left side of the stage facing the audience. "The time for deliberation has passed," Magrath began. He paused and then began slowly walking across the stage. As he did so, he passed a handkerchief through his hands. "He said not a word more," Porter noted, "and the audience waited until, in an impassioned voice and gesture, he added, 'The time for action has come.'" Up went "a universal yell," Toomer recalled, a deafening, spine-tingling holler that sounded like a battle cry. The chaplain "yelled with the rest of them, and threw up my hat, and no doubt thought we could whip creation."

The Judge's enraptured audience understood him to be calling for a direct rising up of the people against all forms of federal authority, following his own example. A day later, with his voice still hoarse from his performance, he recast his words. He claimed that his real message to the people of Charleston was not to act now but to "await the action of the State—She will tell us the hour of deliverance and liberty." Yet this episode was not the first of his dramatics—given his earlier evocation to the crowd outside his Bee Street home of the "first gun of the revolution"— and it was not to be his last.

"The Grand Secession Rally," as the *Mercury* called it, certainly fulfilled its purpose of impressing the intense public desire for secession upon legislators in Columbia. "The city which is most exposed and must bear the brunt in great part, is clamorous for secession," William D. Porter, the president of the South Carolina Senate and a Charleston man himself, observed. Still, Columbia was also seeking assurances that South Carolina, if it acted first, would not be abandoned by other Southern states. Those assurances were not easy to come by, even in the uproar created by Lincoln's election. In response to a letter sent by Barny before the election on the likelihood of Mississippi's secession, US senator Jefferson Davis, writing from his plantation home just a few days after Lincoln's victory, offered a deflating reply. If Mississippi were to call a convention, "the proposition to secede from the Union, independently of support from neighboring States, would probably fail," Davis began. "If South Carolina should first secede, and she alone should take such action, the position of Mississippi would not probably be changed by that fact," he continued. A "powerful obstacle," he explained, was his state's continued need to conduct its trade through ports controlled by the Union. And pouring even colder water on the matter, Davis advised South Carolina to wait on secession, at least until it secured Georgia's commitment to join.

The Charleston secessionists rejected that advice as unsound: a revolution, any revolution, could be advanced only by continuous action, to keep the public "clamorous" and give the citizenry as little time as possible to reflect on the possible consequences of their deeds. So far as the radicals were concerned, a state convention was best held immediately, if not tomorrow, then the day after tomorrow. In order to make a revolution, the leaders must leave no "time for re-action on the part of the people," Barnwell Rhett wrote in a letter drafted for the *Mercury*. "Will not delay cool the ardor of our people, who incensed now would resist promptly?"

Luck intervened at a previously scheduled banquet to commemorate the reopening of a direct railroad line between Charleston and Savannah. At 5:30 p.m. on Thursday, November 9, the same day as the rally planned for Institute Hall, some two hundred dignitaries from the political and business elites of the sister cities gathered at Mills House for a feast arranged by Robert Gourdin, the master of just about every ceremony in Charleston. The guests started with turtle soup and progressed through a staggering array of dishes including lobster salad, French game pie, broiled lamb chops, wild turkey, saddle of venison, and omelet soufflé, all washed down with champagne, Madeira, claret, port, brandy, Scotch, and bourbon. By the meal's end, and the beginning of the rounds of toasts, the talk was not of railroads and commerce but of the immutable bonds of Southern civilization uniting Charleston and Savannah—and of the ripe future of a Southern Confederacy, "the consummation of Southern welfare." The men stood in silence to honor the memory of Calhoun, and Savannah mayor Charles Colcock Jones, Jr., promised the Charlestonians that, in taking the lead in secession and exposing themselves to the wrath of the North, they would not be left alone in their struggle. "The first rude blast that rustles your Palmetto, will vibrate among the sturdy oaks on our shore, and I tell you now that your Palmetto has been rustled and that our oak is sending out its arms in a brawny defense," Jones proclaimed to loud cheers all around.

Savannah's message, it was decided, needed to be heard directly by the assemblage just up the street at Institute Hall. The banqueters staggered out of Mills House and made their way to the rally, which was by this time well under way. Magrath had already stirred the flock with his plea for action. They were ready to be stirred more. Savannah's Francis Stebbins Bartow—planter, Yale Law alumnus, and militia captain—spoke: "I am tired of this endless controversy between the sections of our country," he declared from the stage. "If the storm is to come—and it seems to me as though it must, be its fury every so great and its havoc ever so dire—I court it now in the day of my vigor and strength," Bartow said on behalf of his forty-four years of age. "And let it come now," he repeated. "Put it not off until tomorrow or next day."

Others from Savannah joined in these effusions of support. The question might have been asked wherein lay the greater source of inebriation: the wines and liquors consumed at Mills House or the high spirits of the audience at the hall. It did not matter. The Charleston secessionists finally had in their possession a gift with which to impress legislators in Columbia—a fraternal call for "secession today" from weighty voices of a leading city of Georgia. At 10:30 in the evening, Magrath, Colcock, and Conner jointly sent a telegram to the members of the Charleston delegation in the capital: "The greatest meeting ever held in this city is now assembled in Institute Hall. . . . They [the Savannah guests] have pledged their State, and our people cannot be restrained. . . . The feeling is alike unprecedented and indescribable. . . . We expect to be with you by train tomorrow."

Of course, the pleas from the Savannah group did not in fact constitute a pledge of Georgia's support for South Carolina's secession bid. Robert Gourdin later received a letter from a minister and farmer in Kingston, Georgia, advising him, "The gentlemen from Savannah who made speeches in Charleston had no right to speak for the State. . . . I fear they have greatly misled our friends in Carolina." Unilateral secession by South Carolina "may provoke civil war" in Georgia, the farmer warned: "If it be not too late I would beg, I would implore Carolina not to secede alone." But this note was written more than three weeks after the rally on November 9—three weeks too late. The morning just after the rally, Magrath, Colcock, and Conner had boarded their specially arranged train to Columbia to press the initiative. It was a Saturday, but the legislature was at work preparing to pass a bill to schedule the Secession Convention for January 15, 1861. But under pressure from the Charlestonians, the members agreed to shorten the timetable considerably. They voted to begin the convention in Columbia on December 17. An election for delegates to the convention would be held in less than a month, on December 6. The revised bill made clear that although Columbia may have been the formal seat of power in the state of South Carolina, Charleston held the whip setting the pace for the revolution. The city had seized the initiative, and it would not be relinquished.

Chapter Twenty-Five

"TO ARMS, CITIZENS!"

C harleston rose on Saturday, November 10 to a patriotic poem by one of its ladies, published in the *Mercury*:

> *Up, up! Ye Southern freemen,*
> *Rouse yet at the trumpet's call;*
> *Past is the hour of dreaming,*
> *Break ye the oppressor's thrall.*
> *No longer idly daily,*
> *No more your duty fly;*
> *Under the Lone Star rally,*
> *Ready to "do or die."*

In the evening, the townspeople, thrilled by the legislature's call for the Secession Convention to start five weeks hence, staged a spontaneous celebration outdoors. An effigy of Lincoln, adorned by a placard labelling him "First President, Northern Confederacy," was carried through the streets, raised by a pair of slaves onto a scaffold, and torched.

The city's slaves watched as their putative hero, Lincoln, went up in flames. Although there were many literate slaves in Charleston, none, it seemed, dared put their feelings to paper. The oldest among them undoubtedly had personal memory of mob violence in Charleston—of the Vesey plot of 1822, when the black congregants' African Church was burned down; of the summer of 1835, when a mob torched William Lloyd Garrison in effigy; of that incident in 1849 when a rabble, frightened by the escape of black inmates from the Charleston workhouse, threatened to set fire to another "nigger church." But as alarming as these episodes were, they were intermittent. In 1860, the aggression of white Charleston was continuous, and there was no reason to think the level of violence had peaked. So Charleston's slaves retaliated with their traditional weapon: arson. It was a deed almost impossible to trace, and in October and November there was a rash of suspicious fires by likely arsonists, according to the fire commissioner. It was impossible to officially blame the slaves, but white Charleston had its assumptions.

Even in its mood of triumph, the white community continued to justify itself. "For distribution amongst their friends," the owners of Evans & Cogswell printed a ghoulish broadsheet titled "Epitaph on the United States of America" that proclaimed in the upper-left column, "Here lie the mutilated and disjointed remains of the noblest form of government ever contrived." It was not the South that killed the Union, according to the broadsheet. This was the deed of "ambitious and unprincipled leaders" of the North who would "elevate the negro race to an equality" and make America a "government of black men." Street bands played Verdi's requiem "Miserere," from the opera *Il Trovatore,* to mock the Union's death.

At services at Saint Michael's on the following Sunday, the pastor omitted his usual prayer for the health of the president—an office still held by James Buchanan and not yet by Lincoln. An indignant Petigru rose from his pew and stalked out of the church. The startled eyes of his fellow congregants followed him. The tentative optimism he had shown before the election in evincing his doubts that South Carolina would secede on Lincoln's triumph was evaporating. "We have fallen on evil days," he wrote his sister Jane. "It is sorrowful to see things that impair our respect for our countrymen, and nothing can be more efficient to produce that feeling than the scenes that are passing." Petigru well understood that the leaders of the secession movement, in their demand for a hurried timetable, betrayed their own anxieties. "The South Carolina men," he told Jane, "show by their precipitancy that they are afraid to trust the second thought of even their own people."

In Springfield, Lincoln had much the same thought. "Disunionists, per se, are now in hot haste to get out of the Union," he said shortly after South Carolina called for its convention, "precisely because they perceive they cannot, much longer, maintain apprehension among the Southern people that their homes, and firesides, and lives, are to be endangered by the action of the Federal Government. With such, 'Now, or never,' is the maxim."

Petigru feared that the "now" was imminent. "We shall be envied by posterity for the privilege that we have enjoyed of living under the benign rule of the United States," he mused to his daughter Susan. "The Constitution is only two months older than I. My life will probably be prolonged till I am older than it is."

Petigru's behavior at St. Michael's outraged and embarrassed his wife. In frail health, Jane Amelia seldom attended church, but she made a point of doing so on the Sunday following her husband's much-noted performance. She went alone, and the church's congregants could only wonder about the state of affairs in the Petigru household as she stood by herself in the family pew and made a conspicuous show of joining in the hymns.

Petigru's isolation contributed to his despondency. Longtime Charleston friends who never before had shown enthusiasm for secession now surfaced as eager converts to the cause. "My old friend, Dr. Porcher, has not escaped the contagion," he reported to Jane, using the same word B. F. Perry invoked to describe the popular excitement at the Democratic Convention in the spring. Petigru was referring to Francis Porcher, of Huguenot descent, who was in the habit of dropping in on him Sunday at breakfast time. In the case of another friend, also stricken, Petigru simply could not fathom how a "sober man" could avow "his readiness to sink the welfare of his country forever . . . rather than submit to the rule of Abraham Lincoln, even if he were assured that Lincoln would prove a constitutional and conservative ruler!"

Petigru could see that the "contagion" extended beyond his gentry friends to all segments of white Charleston. Spokesmen for the German community publicly declared their support for immediate secession in a statement published in the *Courier;* the commander of the German Fusiliers showed where he stood by planting a palmetto in front of his house. The Jewish community also was onboard—how could it not be? The Jews had roots in Charleston dating to the end of the seventeenth century. The British crown encouraged them to settle there "in this land of milk of honey," as one Jewish migrant called his new home. Jews, many of them merchants, owned slaves and served in elite militia alongside Christians. Their hearts beat together for secession.

Charleston's workingmen shared the buoyant mood. When freshman legislator Henry Peake returned to his job as head of the South Carolina railroad's machine shop after voting in Columbia to speed up the secession timetable, the men halted their work and gathered in a circle around him. "Well done," they cried, with no fewer than "nine vociferous cheers." Overcome with emotion, Peake could not find the words to respond and retreated to his office to compose a letter to his men. "When I see those with whom I have been intimately acquainted and working side by side for the past twenty-five years, approve my course, I feel perfectly satisfied," he said. He admitted to having once been a "cooperationist." But no longer, he assured them, because "the only thing left for the South is secession or submission. For my part I am ready to see South Carolina out of this cursed Union, and hope the people in convention will take her out by the first of January, 1861."

For the 1860 Association, the *Mercury,* and their allies, the next objective was to organize support for an approved slate of committed "secession now" candidates in the election to be held on December 6 for delegates to the convention. Voters needed to be motivated to get to the polls and to vote as urged. If the wrong men were sent to Columbia, the sort of men apt to hesitate at the last moment, then the entire effort could collapse. On the evening of Monday, November 12, the dedicated again filled Institute Hall for a secession rally. Magrath thrilled them with the announcement that James Henry Hammond had resigned from the US Senate. Hammond was an Upcountry planter, fifty-three years old, who had served as governor of South Carolina in the 1840s. Senator James Chesnut had given up his office two days earlier, and South Carolina no longer had representation in the Senate.

The crowd would not have been delighted, and Magrath would have been less than pleased, to hear Hammond's true thinking on the events playing out in Charleston. "I thought Magrath and all those fellows were great asses for resigning and have done it myself," he told his brother Marcus in a letter written that day. "It is an epidemic and very foolish. It reminds me of the Japanese who, when insulted, rip open their own bowels." Another bloody parallel that came to Hammond's mind was the French Revolution and its mob-pleasing demagogues: "We shall soon have the guillotine at work upon good men," he worried. Tales of the terror were well known to many Americans through popular works like Charles Dickens' *Tale of Two Cities*, which had been published in 1859. (Hammond had once called Rhett, Sr., a Robespierre.) Yet even though he did not regard the "affront" of Lincoln's election alone a good reason for secession, Hammond nonetheless gave the crowd what it wanted in renouncing his federal office. Perhaps the menacing climate and the seeming inevitability of secession had weakened his resolve. The guillotine had not made an appearance on the streets of Charleston, but the H. F. Strohecker gun shop on Meeting Street was advertising Smith & Wesson Seven Shooters in the *Courier* under the slogan "Southern Rights at All Hazards. Fire Arms!"

Had Hammond attended the rally on November 12, the night of his resignation, his fears would have been further confirmed in the frenzied keynote speech delivered by his nemesis. "The long weary night of our humiliation, oppression, and danger is passing away," Rhett, Sr., told his listeners, "and the glorious dawn of a Southern Confederacy breaks on our view." With the coming breakup of the Union, the North would suffer, and suffer grievously, as "their whole system of commerce and manufactures will be paralyzed or overthrown," causing stocks and real estate to plunge in price. Amid this "confusion and distress," he said, "mobs will break into their palaces, and society there will be resolved into its original chaos." Desperate for relief, "many of the free States," he predicted, "will desire to join us," and they would be welcome so long as they accepted the institution of slavery in the Confederacy and agreed that "taxation should be light."

The rally goers got what they came for, but as they trudged home, and with a moment to reflect, they might have asked how long it would take for Barnwell Rhett's remarkable prophecy to be fulfilled. Their Charleston, at this very time, was in the grip of an unhappy set of economic circumstances, seemingly beyond the city's power to correct. Lincoln's election, in making the South's secession a more plausible prospect, had unsettled financial markets all over the country. Charleston's frightened banks refused to trade in notes brought to them by merchants. And as the banks tightened, some merchants in town suspended their usual practice of extending credit to customers. They demanded "cash only" for the purchase of goods. No one could say when this downward spiral would end. "They painted the future in glowing colors," Doubleday observed with disgust of the leaders of secession, "but the present looked dreary enough." In his assessment, "financial ruin was rapidly approaching" in Charleston. Wealthy property owners were fearful that the state would resort to "forced loans" to pay for military preparations. Doubleday felt that "intimidation and threats prevented any open retrograde movement" against the "Rhett faction" to block the drive for secession.

It was true, Mrs. Charles L. Pettigrew, a Charleston lady, told her husband, that "numbers of men" skeptical of the "secession now" position "did not like to speak openly, so violent is the opposite feeling." At a dinner in town, she was "astonished" to even hear a son "reprove his mother for her expressions"—less than wholehearted on secession—"really sharply. He is a rabid secessionist!" Still, the passions vented at Institute Hall and on the streets and at the dinner tables also could be found in private correspondence, in letters written from friend to friend, not out of calculated desire to manipulate the public mood but simply to share feelings. Before the election, young William Lee Trenholm of the Charleston Light Dragoons had written to his friend in Russia of his worry that Lincoln might not win. On November 15, he again picked up his pen, this time to report that his "political despondency" of that earlier letter "I am happy to say is now dispelled." In the new circumstances, "we of the disunion sentiment are of course elated at the arrival of the crisis for which all have waited so long and so restlessly. South Carolina will secede from the Union as surely as that night succeeds the day." Trenholm saved his greatest praise for Charleston, piling the superlatives on top of each other. "Never before in the history of any people was there such unanimity as that which now prevails in our community," he wrote. "Never before has the shadow of an approaching revolution cast less gloom upon those whose fate is bound up in its issues," so much so that "there is no complaint in any quarter, no impatience on the terrible monetary stringency, no popular violence" on the streets. "You will no doubt see the sneers and taunts of the Northern papers—do not be disturbed by them," he told his friend. "Banners are waving in every street, the very boys and women are wild with enthusiasm, and every man, indeed every youth, has gone thoroughly into military organization." And in his euphoria, Trenholm persuaded himself that there could be found "no servile disaffection" in Charleston, although he was hardly in a position to know what was on the lips of the city's slaves in the privacy of their backyard cabins and cellar grog shops.

The militia rolls were indeed swelling. And woe, it seemed, to the boy who hesitated to sign up. "I am myself a widowed mother, but I have said to my three sons, that if any one of them should be craven enough to desert their State now," a "Carolina Mother" declared in a letter to the *Mercury*, "let him never look upon my face again."

The secession throngs were sipping from the most intoxicating cup of all: they were feeling imbued with a sense of historical destiny. If Charleston was demonstrably more ardent in its passion for secession than any other Southern city, then so be it. To be in the vanguard and to be, perhaps, the most exposed to danger was to occupy a place of honor. Their Charleston was blazing the path of righteous rebellion, like Boston and Paris in the century before. On November 16, the day after Trenholm wrote to his friend about "the approaching revolution," a ninety-foot-high "Liberty Pole" made of pine was planted on Meeting Street outside the Charleston Hotel. For the dedication ceremony at 11:00 a.m. on November 17, thousands cheered the raising of a white palmetto flag to the top of the pole. One chronicler put the size of the gathering at twenty thousand. Surely that was too high, even allowing for those attending from out of town, but it was the largest show of public support for secession since the election—and proof that the movement still was growing. As the crowd vowed for the Stars and Stripes never again to fly in Charleston, the Lafayette Artillery fired a fifteen-gun salute and a military band played *La Marseillaise*:

> *To arms, citizens!*
> *Form up your battalions*
> *Let us march, Let us march!*

Chapter Twenty-Six

THE GOSPEL OF SECESSION

N ow God was invited to offer his thoughts. On Wednesday, November 21, Charlestonians assembled at their respective houses of worship. They had been asked to do so by a resolution of the legislature, endorsed by the governor, for clergy and people of all denominations to come together "to implore the direction and blessing of Almighty God in this our hour of difficulty, and to give us one heart and one mind to oppose, by all just and proper means, every encroachment upon our rights." It was to be a day not of marches and martial jingles but of fasting and prayer.

The Almighty, it turned out, had nothing but encouragement for the people of Charleston in their quest—at least as his will was understood by the pastors of the city. At St. Peter's Episcopal, on Logan Street, Rector William Otis Prentiss supplied a rationale for secession drawn from his interpretation of Paul's first epistle to Timothy. The "farseeing" Paul, Prentiss said, "has warned us to withdraw ourselves from men who disturbed the relations existing between masters and servants, because they are unholy persons, men of corrupt minds, destitute of the truth, identifying gain with godliness." Should the South remain in the Union, Prentiss warned, the section would invite the "awful doom" that awaited the North. A native of the Lowcountry, forty-five years old, the rector had a considerable investment in his message because he was also a planter with some 170 slaves to his name. Congregants liked his address so much that they asked him to repeat it for his Sunday sermon on November 25—and such was the renown of the sermon that he was requested to deliver it yet again, this time to the legislature in Columbia.

Prentiss was sure to include, as a digression, observations on the "African race." "History assures us," he said, "that this race has been, from its earliest records, a nation of slaves, and that the African has joyfully acquiesced in slavery as his normal condition. Physiology proves that he is utterly ungovernable by men of his own race" and is suited best to be "a reliable cultivator of tropical products." The sermon was not lost on the black people of Charleston. The tailor James M. Johnson mentioned it in a letter to a friend, tersely noting, "One of its distinguishing features is the inferiority of the Race."

At the Second Presbyterian Church, Reverend Thomas Smyth took sharp aim at "the infidel, atheistic French Revolution," identified as "the evil and bitter root of all our evils." Parishioners present at the playing of *La Marseillaise* four days before at the Liberty Pole's unveiling might have felt puzzled at this assault. But Smyth made his point plain enough: to believe in God was necessary to accept slavery as a divinely ordained institution. In this vein, he took a swipe at the Declaration of Independence as another testament of a fallen, secular spirit. "All men are not born equal," he said, apropos of the truth that Jefferson, in 1776, described as "self-evident." His tone was somber, and he described the Union as being at a "dreadful eclipse," at "the consummation of a tragedy which has been long progressing to its last act."

Unlike St. Peter's Prentiss, Smyth was not of the Lowcountry and had no direct tie to planter society. Born in Belfast in 1808, he immigrated to America and graduated from the Princeton Theological Seminary in 1831. He moved to Charleston as a "perfect stranger" and was crowned the Second Presbyterian Church's pastor by 1834. Smyth was a stranger to slavery as well, but his acquaintance with the practice did not seem to trouble his spirit—much to the dismay of a Belfast friend who wrote, "I find that a few years' connection with a slaveholding Church" had so "blighted your sensibility of conscience" as to countenance "the blackest opinions that ever disgraced not only a professing Christian Church but humanity it-self." As he aged in the pulpit, stricken by a paralysis that forced him to deliver his sermons from a custom-made, saddle-like seat, Smyth yielded not an inch. He considered himself an eloquent representative of the Southern Christian perspective—and was sufficiently proud of his "fast day" peroration to send copies to pastor friends in the North. He could hardly have expected a favorable reception, and he was not met with one. "Is it a fact that you feel authorized to put the whole Republican Party into a conglomeration of atheism, infidelity, communism, bible-hating anti-Christian men! This—or even the remote implication of this—I must say, astounds me," the pastor of a church in New Jersey told Smyth. "No, my beloved brother, this is not the way for us to speak of each other."

A few blocks down Meeting from Smyth's Second Presbyterian, Rev-erend William C. Dana of the Central Presbyterian Church took as his theme the title of Townsend's pamphlet *The South Alone, Should Govern the South.* "It is permitted us, then, my brethren," he said, "to feel that it is a righteous cause on which we invoke blessings." Dana was a native of Newburyport, Massachusetts, a graduate of Dartmouth in New Hamp-shire's snowy White Mountains, and, by 1860, a secessionist.

Rev. Bachman was a familiar sight at secession rallies, and he had attended the Liberty Pole ceremony with Ruffin. However, at St. John's Lutheran on Archdale, Bachman had resisted preaching on secession, in keeping with his long-standing reluctance to direct his flock on politi-cal matters. Back in the 1830s, during the crisis over Nullification, South Carolina's governor also had called for a day of fasting and prayer, but Bachman, unlike some of his colleagues, had steered clear of the subject. "I will not disgrace my pulpit by preaching a political sermon," he had told a student. But now, with an even greater crisis facing his state, and before a gathering that included visiting cadets from the Citadel seated in the gallery, Bachman declared that secession was appropriate—valid even. Because the rights of the South were no longer protected in the Union, "our cause is just and righteous," he said.

Afterward, in his office, Bachman seemed spent. With a friend he rem-inisced about his life in science—his meeting of thirty years before with the young Charles Darwin, who was by this time famous for *The Origin of Species*. Then he broke off: "My mind is not on these things." He spoke of his father, a soldier in the Revolutionary War. "I was taught from my earliest childhood to venerate my country's flag," he told his friend, who spotted tears in the reverend's eyes. "I have this day done the saddest act of my life. . . . I love the Union but I must go with my people."

Charlestonians emerged from their churches empty of belly but fortified with spiritual morsels for their political march forward. November 21 might have been a day for sober reflection, but on November 22 the streets were rowdier than ever with a throng of people filling them for a torchlight parade and firing off colorful rockets into the sky. An alarmed German merchant described the mob "as a great turnout of urchins and ragamuffins, quite a motley crew." Petigru wrote to Jane of his "awful foreboding of what is to come when the passions of the mob are let loose, and the truth is our gentlemen are little distinguished in a mob from the rabble."

In Charleston Harbor, a Union flag still hung at Fort Moultrie, but only there, and for how much longer? As the uprising searched for a point of fixation, Fort Moultrie—with its garrison, guns, and federal power— became the natural target. The fort, after all, rested on sacred ground— the turf on which the original American revolutionaries had defended themselves against the mighty British in the battle of Sullivan's Island. The Minute Men began visiting the fort on the eve of the presidential election, and they continued to hold "noisy demonstrations" just outside the walls in the weeks following. Officers were told point-blank by "prominent citizens of Charleston" that as "the people were greatly excited," no reinforcement of the garrison would be allowed. With his own ear, Chief Medical Officer Crawford heard calls for an attack on Fort Moultrie "loudly proclaimed" in nighttime marches of armed militia through the streets of Charleston.

"The approaching battle of Fort Moultrie was talked of everywhere," Doubleday noted, "and the mob in Charleston could hardly be restrained from making an immediate assault." The men of the garrison were exhausted by their need for constant vigilance to the point that the wives of Captains Doubleday and Seymour, who had joined their husbands at the fort, "took turns in walking the parapet, two hours at a time, in readiness to notify the guard in case the Minute Men became more than usually demonstrative." Except during the night hours, not a move could be made inside the fort that could not be seen from the top-floor windows or roofs of the nearby homes in the village of Moultrieville. Unoccupied Fort Sumter, on its uninhabited granite island—one mile away but close enough to look almost swimmable from the Sullivan Island shoreline— must have appeared a tempting sight to the federal soldiers. Bricklayers brought in from Baltimore were laboring to strengthen Sumter's walls.

As a warning to anyone in Charleston who might have seriously considered attempting the seizure of Fort Moultrie, Doubleday began a habit of loading an eight-inch howitzer with a double round of cannonballs and firing in the direction of the sea. "The spattering of so many balls in the water looked very destructive and startled and amazed the gaping crowds around," he observed with satisfaction. He also concealed small mines under planks around the outskirts of the fort. The mines did not pack any explosive charge and were harmless, but they did make a loud noise if stepped on. "These experiments," Doubleday felt, "had a cooling effect upon the ardor of the militia, who did not fancy storming the fort over a line of torpedoes."

The garrison had a new commander, Major Robert Anderson, who had arrived on November 21. A native of Kentucky and married to a Georgian, Anderson was a supporter of slavery. He was personally acquainted with Robert Gourdin, who amiably welcomed him to town with an invitation for a get-together at 2 Meeting Street. Although the major and Robert might find much to agree with, Anderson, a West Point graduate who had fought for his country and been badly wounded in the Mexican American War, was implacably opposed to secession and determined to take every step to protect his men. It was becoming a hazardous chore to visit Charleston to obtain fresh provisions for the garrison. The federal soldiers found the streets decorated with banners bearing insulting slogans like "Good-bye, Yankee Doodle" and "Let Us Bury the Union's Dead Carcass." Charleston's largest maker of bread and biscuits, the South Carolina Steam Bakery, run by German immigrant J. C. H. Claussen, was also unfriendly ground—the establishment promoted its goods to "all who are true to SOUTHERN RIGHTS and SOUTHERN INTERESTS."

For their own reasons, the leaders of the Charleston uprising also worried about the possibility of a mob assault on the Fort Moultrie garrison. In a letter written by D. H. Hamilton to Robert Gourdin on November 26 marked "private and confidential," the former marshal said an "overt attack" on the fort would "destroy the moral effect of South Carolina upon the other Southern States, and leave her but with little sympathy from her sisters of the South, in what will be termed a mere popular outbreak." All the more reason, he said, for South Carolina to act on secession as rapidly as possible to divert the attention of the masses away from the garrison and toward an orderly political process the rest of the South would accept as legitimate. He was now far from doubting the willingness of the common people to act on secession, as he once did. "The people are ahead of their leaders," he told Gourdin, and as soon as the Secession Convention began, "the people will force the Delegation to instantaneous action."

Hamilton did, however, doubt the will of the radicals' leaders. He expressed concern that Gourdin might falter at this critical juncture by joining with moderates on a "temporizing ticket" of candidates in the December 6 election for the convention delegation. "Should you appear on a ticket" with the likes of Memminger, "you will find that you will exclude yourself from the ranks of your old friends and allies," he warned the merchant. Even with the work Gourdin had done in organizing the "Earnest Men" of the 1860 Association as the South's leading secessionists, still, somehow, Hamilton was suspicious. Gourdin was certainly committed to disunion, and Hamilton was obviously on edge. The spiritual assurances their pastors had supplied them as they sat earnestly in their pews, listening to pledges of God's blessing for their cause—had they not been enough to calm the rebels' nerves?

Chapter Twenty-Seven

CATCH ME IF YOU CAN

A s November neared its end, Mayor Macbeth, whether because of belated mercy or admitted defeat, finally let seamstress Bottsford out of jail. She had resided there in miserable conditions for nearly two months but had not admitted to any crime or begged for her release despite pressure to do so. "Others," she later recounted, had been "tarred and feathered, whipped, and hung, while they asserted their entire innocence of Abolitionism; yet I was released." The only condition was for her to depart the city permanently, which she always had agreed to do. "Of course I was not sorry to leave Charleston," she recalled. Her final memory was of bands of Minute Men with their "terrible oaths" lurking on the wharves. Her passage was paid for in a cabin of the steamer *Columbia,* and she was back in New York on the last day of the month. There, on safe ground, she spilled her story to the *Tribune.*

The North was ravenous for news of the Charleston uprising. It was America's single biggest story apart from news concerning Lincoln, and the *Tribune,* proud of its role as the country's largest and most influential paper, was determined to get it firsthand. The subtext, and often enough the overt text, of the paper's coverage long had been that Charleston, as ground zero for secessionist fervor in the South, tilted toward the unhinged—but in a benign sort of way. Like many others, the *Tribune* failed to see the infectious enthusiasm that seized the town at the "secession" of the Southern Democratic delegates in the spring for what it was: a harbinger of a popular insurrection—a revolt that would stop at nothing short of tearing the bonds of the nation.

The *Tribune's* managing editor, Charles Anderson Dana, commanded the effort to organize coverage of the events in Charleston. Although not as well known to the public as publisher-editor Greeley, Dana was a weighty presence in his own right. He was forty-one years old, a New Hampshire native, a Harvard dropout, and a charter member of the utopian Brook Farm community, a commune established in 1841 outside of Boston "to ensure a more natural union between intellectual and manual labor than now exists." Nathaniel Hawthorne also signed up for the experiment, supported by the likes of Ralph Waldo Emerson, but it did not last. Dana, described by Walt Whitman as "a man of rough, strong intellect," decamped for the harder-boiled world of newspaper journalism. At the *Tribune's* grimy offices at Nassau and Spruce by City Hall Park, he reigned over a cadre of correspondents all committed, as he was, to antislavery principles. He believed that a managing editor was "a being to whom the sentiment of remorse is unknown." To a man asked to go to New Orleans, Dana noted that it was "precarious business" and that with six *Tribune* reporters already in the region, "it wouldn't surprise me, this very hour, to receive a telegram announcing the imprisonment or death of any one of them." The man went anyway.

For the Charleston job, Dana selected a trusted, veteran hand, Charles D. Brigham—"a subtle and utterly unprincipled rascal," as an admiring colleague at the paper described him. A native of upstate New York, Brigham was forty-two years old and a former editor and proprietor of the *Troy Whig.* He was familiar with Charleston from his coverage of the aborted Democratic Convention and made his way there just after Lincoln's election.

From Brigham's eyes, and through Dana's filter, the *Tribune's* readers—and many other Americans, for the paper's dispatches were reprinted by many other newspapers—received the best information available on Charleston, superior to the glossy dispatches of the *Mercury* and the

Courier. The *Tribune* informed the nation of Charleston's gathering economic woes. In "A Letter from Charleston" dated November 26, Brigham
reported, "There is much financial distress among the mass of the people
here, especially with a large number, amounting to several hundreds, of
mechanics and laboring people, who have been thrown out of employment, for whom, it is said, provision will have to be made, through some
plan of concerted action." In a follow-up, he noted, "All kinds of property,
save cotton, have gone down fifty percent" and that "Charleston, which at
this season of the year is usually very much the resort of strangers from
the North, is now literally deserted. The arrivals at the hotels are next
to nothing, and the proprietors groan audibly. There is a corresponding
falling off in every other branch of business. The railways especially suffer
from the absence of Northern travelers."

Yet the correspondent and his paper did not play down the support
for secession in Charleston. Brigham described it as "universal," with
"flags and banners that everywhere greet the eye" bearing slogans like
"Immediate Separation" and "Free Trade and Southern Rights." He noted,
"The mighty parades of the Minute Men and other military organizations and the universal substitution of the Palmetto Flag for the Stars
and Stripes have a meaning which cannot be disguised and which cannot well be overestimated, as indicating that already, in their hearts, the
people of South Carolina are out of the Union." Only back in October
the *Tribune* had ridiculed the Minute Men as feckless, strutting cowards,
but by November Brigham attested to the climate of "vigilance" in and
around Charleston, with suspicion of any literature circulating short of
the bible "or indeed almost any publication other than 1860 Association
documents." He also perceived that the goal of the secession movement in
Charleston was to "bring on"—or if not to bring on, then to keep minds
focused on the possibility of—"a collision" between "citizen-soldiers" and
the federal garrison at Fort Moultrie. "The supposed or real prospect of
collision has kept up the excitement, prevented deliberation, forestalled
everything like reflection, and raised a swell by which the whole community has been carried right onward," he wrote.

This was shrewd and accurate reporting—and it infuriated Charleston, especially City Hall and the *Mercury.* The mysterious *Tribune* corre-

spondent in the city's midst was understood to be a threat of a different order than a widowed seamstress from the North seeking, maybe, to spread her abolitionist views around town. He was delving into matters of strategy and tactics secession leaders aimed to keep confidential, and his reports made it harder for the story of the uprising to be told as the rebellion's champions wanted it. In the *Mercury* staff's mind, there was to be no counternarrative of the rebellion. There was to be a single narrative, a heroic and pure one—of a determined, unified resistance by the people of Charleston, to be followed by a bloodless withdrawal from the Union, with an independent Southern Republic thereafter living peacefully and prosperously alongside the great nations of the world. This narrative belonged exclusively to the makers of the revolution. It was their property.

Like any professional reporter, Brigham took good care to protect his sources. By making use of disguise, he could have picked up scraps from any number of unsuspecting people in Charleston, from merchants to Minute Men. And it seems likely that he had help from sources who knew his true identity as well in places like the French and British consulates in Charleston, which were as interested in tracking developments in the city as he was. He probably knew Robert Bunch, the longtime British consul and a treasure chest of information on the city's leading political figures and their plots. Bunch, who despised slavery and was vehemently opposed to the reopening of the African slave trade, cultivated contacts with journalists through whose dispatches he sought to spread his perspectives unsourced.

It is also conceivable Brigham had help from a second *Tribune* man— one secretly embedded at the *Mercury*. Years later, Doubleday made just such an astounding claim—that "an abolition correspondent" of the *Tribune* had managed to get himself employed in the *Mercury* newsroom, professing "to be the most loud-mouthed secessionist of them all." Doubleday said he had personally spoken with the man. But he never named him, and it is difficult to believe that the sharp-eyed Rhett, Jr., alive to the point of paranoia to the presence of the "enemy within" Charleston, would not have spotted such a traitor to the cause in his own office. But then again, Doubleday, a judicious recorder of events, was not in the habit of making up things. In fact, it would have been in the character of the crafty Charles Dana, "to whom remorse was unknown," to attempt such a daring gambit. He approached newspapering in the hostile South, after all, as a kind of intelligence operation conducted behind enemy lines. As a node, a central point of connection for so many involved in the secession uprising, the office of the *Mercury* would have presented a tantalizing target. Surely Dana would have taken immense delight in embedding a reporter and pulling off such a feat against an archrival. The possibility of a *Tribune* mole planted inside Barny's paper in the tumult of 1860, then, cannot be dismissed.

———

Dana's crew, in any case, was far ahead of its competitors in coverage of the Charleston uprising. Eventually, other correspondents arrived in the city, including a man from the New York *Evening Post*. The paper's editor had chosen to ignore Rhett, Jr's, warning that "he would come with his life in his hands and would probably be hung." The *New York World* sent a reporter, fortified by a letter sent to the *Courier* stating that the paper was not a "Lincoln sheet." No one in the newsroom had voted for him, and the paper's owner was personally not opposed to slaveholding. The *World*'s editor later disavowed the letter, and the reporter, on arriving in Charleston, spoke daily to his comrades in the press of his desire to return to the safety of his hometown.

From across the Atlantic, noted illustrator Thomas Butler Gunn of the staff of the London *Illustrated News* arrived. "Mr. Gunn brings credentials and references of the best import, and is himself a gentleman who would need no reference beyond a good acquaintance," the *Courier* informed its readers. Gentleman or not, Gunn, who also secretly filed dispatches for the New York *Evening Post,* instantly attracted the suspicion of authorities, as he wryly noted in his journal. The president of Charleston's Vigilance Committee, "a square-set man with an unpleasant face, rather Irish in character," he wrote, "jocularly took me by the beard and told me that he knew all about me and what I had come to Charleston for—that he had been informed as to these particulars within two hours of my arrival!"

True enough, Gunn detested slavery and approved of abolitionists. He felt himself surrounded by trigger-happy zealots not apt to take kindly to his opinions and did not leave his room at the Charleston Hotel without his pistol. On the same corridor of the hotel was a young man of twenty recently arrived from Alabama "to offer his services to South Carolina in the holy cause of secession." The fellow spoke happily of lynching abolitionists distributing literature "among our niggers," and his countenance profoundly spooked the journalist. "There was a look of latent, dangerous fanaticism in it which fascinated and repelled you," Gunn observed. "Whenever I met him, I always had a curious consciousness of the loaded revolver in my pocket and a strong conviction that if I were at any time discovered, and he of the discoverers, I would assuredly put a bullet into his skull, taking especial care of my aim in so doing."

<hr />

It was one thing to keep Alfred Huger's post office from distributing copies of the *Tribune* and another to control the flow of information to the outside world. It could not be done. Brigham likely slipped his stories out of Charleston not by telegraph—even a coded dispatch would draw suspicion from the wire-service operator—but by express mail addressed to a "blind drop" in New York. With Brigham's granular portraits of the streets of Charleston, Doubleday's coded messages, and Bunch's incisive reports (also in code) to his superiors in the British Foreign Office—the word seeped out. The elites of business and politics in places like New York, Washington, and London and the president-elect in Springfield, Illinois, knew the contagion for secession was spreading in Charleston.

Charleston made strenuous efforts to find the *Tribune*'s hidden correspondent. A notice placed on the door of a Broad Street bank even urged the populace to root out the fellow and "administer tar and feathers." Brigham took relish in this game of cat and mouse. "If the *Mercury* is still in doubt as to my identity and whereabouts," he taunted in one of his pieces, "let him look into one of the big guns in Fort Sumter. He may find me there." He remained on the loose.

Chapter Twenty-Eight

"I HAVE, DOUBTLESS, MANY FAULTS"

The December 6 election to choose Charleston's twenty-two delegates for the Secession Convention was fast approaching, and the run-up to the vote largely consisted of the candidates jockeying among themselves to prove their singular eagerness to take South Carolina out of the Union. "All are galloping down the same road and every one striving to be ahead," Petigru told Jane in an election-day letter.

The contest drew a high and vigorous turnout. "I saw a melee at one of the polls between a customer of ours and others," Coming Street's tailor, James M. Johnson, said to a friend. If anyone had entertained hopes of a "silent majority" in white Charleston, patiently waiting to use the ballot to express a collective wish to slow the pace of the rebellion, those hopes were dashed. The result was a total victory for the "secession now" slate, a boost for the radicals and a thrashing of moderates like M. C. Mordecai, the prominent Jewish merchant and civic baron who, to the fury of the Rhetts, had helped mobilize public opinion against unilateral secession in 1851. In past elections, Charlestonians were pleased to send him to the state Senate, but on December 6 he finished thirty-third place despite his pledge for disunion. Another moderate, the merchant and alderman George Walton Williams, scrubbed his name from a ticket. Despite his proven ability to win votes in City Council elections, he did not feel favored by the public mood.

The top vote getter was Judge Magrath. His owed his triumph in part to his devoted Irish base but even more to his new role as a folk hero of the uprising. In vividly colored, larger-than-life banners stretched across the streets of Charleston, he was depicted in that eventful scene in his courtroom as defiantly tearing off his judicial robes, a mythical heightening of his actual, considerably more restrained performance. In the weeks since his resignation, he had taken his "secession now" stump speech from Institute Hall to a gathering outside the Congaree Hotel in Columbia to meetings of citizens in the Upcountry. To a group assembled in a courthouse in Greenville, the home turf of Unionist B. F. Perry, he asked, "Shall we kneel down to Mr. Lincoln, and plead for an assurance of his favor? Perish the thought! Shall we petition Congress? Kiss the hem of Mr. Seward's garment?" The sole remaining "hope," he said, "is in ourselves. How? By coming out of the Union—by immediate secession!" In Abbeville, a crowd of thousands, with palmetto cockades pinned to their garments, heard his signature call—"the time for action has arrived"—at an outdoor rally site known thereafter as Secession Hill. A cannon fired a salute.

Surely "The Judge" could find satisfaction in outpolling William Porcher Miles, occupant of the congressional seat he had aspired to fill, who finished in second place. Third went to John Townsend, placed on the Charleston ballot in honor of his smashing success as a pamphleteer even though his home was Bleak Hall and he had always run from the Sea Islands in his career as a legislator. Six months before, he had declared in favor of South Carolina's secession with a core of eight deep-South states. By December, his stance had shifted, and he pledged in a statement published in the *Mercury*, "I am unalterably opposed to South Carolina being re-united, after secession, with any non-slaveholding state, under any form of government whatsoever." The season of excitement, it seemed, had concentrated his conversion to radicalism to a more distilled essence.

Robert Gourdin finished fourth and at last was acknowledged as a leader of the rebellion. His part in the Magrath courtroom theatric had won the hearts of voters, and he had left no doubt about his position:

South Carolina "should leave this Union as soon as practicable, even unsupported by a single Southern State. Such will be my vote, if I am honored with a seat in the convention," he informed the *Mercury*. Miles congratulated him on his "high position on the ticket. It is a fit and just tribute on the part of old Charleston," his friend wrote. "I would not delay the secession of South Carolina a day . . . all our best friends in the entire South urge it upon us as the step best calculated to advance the great cause of the South in all their States." Congratulations to Gourdin also came from an old friend in Savannah: "Upon your election to the most important Congress convened since '76"—that is, since the Second Continental Congress, which met in Philadelphia in July of 1776 and voted for independence from Great Britain.

Robert had followed D. H. Hamilton's advice not to join a ticket with moderates like Memminger, and that seemed like sound counsel because Memminger finished in eighth place. But that was good enough for Memminger to win a seat at the convention—and a respectable result considering the radicals' chronic suspicion of him. Unlike Gourdin, he had refused to sign the pledge demanded by the *Mercury* of all candidates, to commit to "immediate and permanent dissolution of the Union." There was still no fire in his belly for secession, and there never would be.

Yet he also felt it important to close ranks, for Charleston to present a united front to the South and the North. He saw the uprising in the city as akin to a hurricane—a sudden, powerful, and unstoppable force of nature. As an elder, the best he could do was to try to contain the damage. And so he stepped forward and spoke on behalf of secession to the people of Charleston, not in heated emotional terms, not as a way to take revenge on the North and the viperous abolitionists, but in crisp, lawyerly language. His were soothing words, intended to give comfort to anyone worried the state was behaving illegitimately. For South Carolina to secede, he told an assemblage at Institute Hall on the Friday before the election, "nothing more" was required "than the repeal of the enactment by which she became a member of the Federal Union." The work done on that day seventy-two years earlier in 1788—the ratification of the Constitution by a conclave of delegates—could be undone in like manner. It was a beguilingly simple description of the matter: secession, so momentous sounding a word, could be accomplished by a mere few sentences not even filling a single sheet of parchment. In his statesmanlike guise, unflappable as ever and projecting unshakable resolve, Memminger said at Institute Hall, "We are advancing on a track on which there must be no step backward." Memminger presented himself as one who could be of immense service to a Southern Republic that, once established, was apt to have a greater need of proficient technocrats than of fiery speechmakers.

The most conspicuous embarrassment in this competition for Charleston's acclaim was reserved for Barnwell Rhett, who came in seventh, just ninety-one votes ahead of Memminger, an especially dismal performance considering the *Mercury's* tireless promotion of his every utterance. He had been eclipsed: the great cause of his life was no longer dividing his community, but he still was. The wound went deep, and he could not mask it. "I have, doubtless, had many faults—many errors to answer for, both in opinion and conduct, in my political course," he told a crowd that stopped at his house as part of its rounds, accompanied by the Palmetto Brass Band, to hear from the delegates bound for the convention. It had taken him some time to emerge from his quarters. He had gone to bed early, suffering from "indisposition," as he told the assemblage. He roused himself enough to proclaim, "The bugle blast of our victory and redemption is on the wind."

Soon Barnwell Rhett was to suffer another blow, in his hopes to succeed William Henry Gist as the governor of South Carolina. Gist's term would expire shortly, and his replacement would be in a pivotal position to manage South Carolina's exit from the Union. It was the job of the legislature in Columbia to pick the governor. "Elect Robert Barnwell Rhett, if you would have the other Southern States believe you to be in earnest," a letter writer to the *Mercury* urged legislators. "Elect him, and you throw out, at the same time, the flag of defiance to the North." But that was a distinctly minority opinion. One lawmaker, Samuel McGowan, from Abbeville, got an earful from a constituent concerned that the choice of the senior Rhett would actually undermine the secession cause. "For God's sake and the sake of our beloved State don't let Rhett be elected Governor," the critic told McGowan, disapproving of his "rashness, impracticability, arrogance, selfishness." It was even possible that Georgia might quail at secession should Barnwell Rhett fill the governor's seat in Columbia, McGowan was warned. On the first ballot, Rhett, Sr., finished a distant third. By the fifth ballot he was out of the race altogether. To add to Rhett, Sr.'s, embarrassment, the eventual victor was Francis W. Pickens, a man with a reputation as a national Democrat just returned from a posting as the US ambassador to Russia. Pickens was tolerable to the Charleston radicals because, as a condition of his candidacy, he committed himself to a "secession now" posture.

The balloting painfully exposed Barnwell Rhett's diminished political standing. A friend of his old rival Hammond called the senior Rhett a "spavined old horse." Miles confided to Hammond, "It is undoubtedly the fact that nothing coming from him carried any weight or accomplished any good." The *Tribune* could not resist the opportunity to mock him. The paper sarcastically registered its "regret" at "the gross injustice that is done to the Hon. R. Barnwell Rhett, the real leader and soul of the whole secession movement. . . . There is certainly a danger that this devoted patriot may be made to feel the sting of his country's ingratitude." Although neither Charleston nor Columbia crowned him as a leader of the secession rebellion, there still remained a reservoir of affection for the senior Rhett. He was popular as a symbol, if not so much in the flesh and blood. The Charleston Restaurant commissioned a full-length portrait of him, a transparency that glowed at night when illuminated from behind by a lamp. A quotation from one of his speeches, "The Union is dissolved; henceforth there is deliverance, peace and liberty for the South," completed the work.

Rhett, Sr., well understood the brutal realities of politics, truly a blood sport. He must have realized that his ultimate ambition to lead a Southern Confederacy was fast receding from his reach, even as his dream of an independent republic was on the brink of fulfillment. If his peers would not elect him governor of his state, he surely would not be made president of a Republic of South Carolina or of any larger Southern entity yet to be formed. But then again, he was an incorrigible optimist when it came to his destiny. His fortune had waxed and waned for decades; perhaps time would permit one last ascendency, one last, glorious act.

Chapter Twenty-Nine

THE FLIGHT OF REASON

66 **T**he air smells strongly of gunpowder," Charleston attorney Edward Laight Wells wrote to his brother, John, on return to the city in the first week of December after a long absence in Europe. "The excitement here is intense." To his father, he reported, "The all-absorbing question at present is secession. Men, women and children talk of nothing else." So they did. With business activity at ebb, weekday blended into weekend, sleep was suspended, and social gatherings began and ended with ceremonial oaths of loyalty to the cause. A group of young ladies assembled for tea "became warmly imbued with the spirit of the times" and dashed off a set of resolutions placed at the disposal of the *Mercury* and duly published:

> *Resolved,* That we, though by Divine authority termed the "weaker vessels," are nevertheless endowed with resolute wills. . . .
>
> *Resolved,* That [with] the election of Lincoln to the Presidency, we consider our allegiance to the North as ended, and will therefore use our influence in favor of an immediate secession.
>
> *Resolved,* That we honor all men who are for this movement, but are determined to secede ourselves from all who are opposed to it.

Resolved, That at present the best "feather in the cap" of any young man, is the "Palmetto Cockade," and it makes our hearts flutter to see one mounted above a manly brow.

Resolved, That "gunpowder tea" shall be our favorite beverage, and "percussion caps" the only ones that we shall set.

Resolved, That "Yankee Doodle" is now defunct.

Young men, whose Southern "patriotism" the ladies had no reason to doubt, carried Charleston's secession spirit to the countryside. At 7:00 a.m. on Tuesday, December 11, a contingent of the Charleston Light Dragoons and the German Hussars boarded a train of the Charleston and Savannah Railroad to the sound of "three rousing cheers for Charleston and secession" followed by the band playing Dixie. The train chugged thirty-three miles west to Jacksonboro, and upon disembarking the regiments marched eighteen miles northwest to Walterboro with "the men indulging themselves in songs, races [and] secession speeches" along the way, recounted one of their number. They reached Walterboro at 3:30 p.m., quaffed "refreshments," then attended the raising of a secession flag as their band struck up *La Marseillaise* ("the most appropriate air upon patriotic occasions"). The evening's program featured a stag ball and more secession speeches, including one by a local delegate bound for Columbia who pledged, to cheers "lustily given," to vote South Carolina out of the Union and keep her out "forever." Upon return to their hotel, it was time for "fun, noise, mischief," the object of which turned out to be knocking down the walls of their lodging. (The rooms were deemed too narrow for comfort.) The hijinks came to a conclusion at 4:00 a.m., and at daylight, upon the blast of a bugle, the men "bade adieu to Walterboro" and "the numerous ladies who graced the occasion with their smiles." They arrived back in Charleston hours later "without anything occurring to mar the pleasure of one of the most delightful trips which was ever participated in."

"Secession now" meant the state could end up standing alone for some length of time, conceivably for all time, as a sovereign entity. "South Carolina," a despairing Petigru wrote to B. F. Perry in Greenville, "is too small for a Republic, but too large for an insane asylum." It was a quip, of course, the kind of clever and biting comment of which he had a seemingly inexhaustible supply, and yet there was something deeply serious behind it. In truly considering his compatriots in some way deranged, Petigru meant not simply that he adamantly disagreed with their course of action but that reason, the value he prized above all others, had left them. He was thinking along the lines of a much talked about book of the era, *Extraordinary Popular Delusions and the Madness of Crowds*, by London journalist and songwriter Charles Mackay, a friend of Charles Dickens. "Men, it has been well said, think in herds," Mackay said in the preface to the 1852 edition. "It will be seen that they go mad in herds, while they only recover their senses slowly, and one by one." Drawing on examples like the medieval Crusades, he wrote of "seasons of excitement and recklessness" for "whole communities," when "they care not what they do." Had Petigru been acquainted with the idea of a death wish, perhaps he would have applied the notion to his Charleston—but such psychological thinking, advanced decades later by the likes of Sigmund Freud, was not part of the vocabulary of his times. Humankind was commonly understood as possessed of its faculties, or not.

Charleston had started to "go mad," as was apparent in its imperviousness to certain emerging realities. The insurrectionists persisted in the belief that a Southern Republic, built on a slave economy, would win the favor of the world—even as evidence mounted that this would not prove to be the case. "I dare say you are well aware that English sympathies are not much with you in the South," a Manchester acquaintance politely wrote to Henry Gourdin in mid-December. "Public opinion here," he added, "think[s] you South Carolinians are unreasonable in not giving Lincoln a trial, that you are prejudging the question, and that you are altogether wrong in not waiting to see what the new government will propose." The letter writer asked Henry to "briefly as you can point out a few of the leading difficulties which you think will make it absolutely necessary to leave the Union."

Charleston, though, was well past believing it had "prejudged" anything. Indeed, the city saw itself as the soul of patience for sticking with the Union for as long as it had. There was little interest in hearing even from familiar voices in the North—men like Richard Lathers, a native of the Lowcountry who had moved to New York and amassed a fortune in cotton brokerage, banking, and insurance. In a letter addressed to Henry Gourdin, Memminger, and Magrath, "my old fellow-citizens," he wrote, "the grave aspect of the secession movement in your State alarms a large class of your friends in this State, and induces the fear that the usual influence of conservative men, like yourselves, has not been exercised to check undue excitement." A delegation of "leading men" from New York, "in the capacity of consulting and sympathizing friends," might prove helpful, he suggested.

With Memminger's approval, Henry Gourdin and Magrath responded to Lathers in a letter written on December 8. "There is no 'undue excitement'" in South Carolina, they insisted. The "conservative men" all believed in the state's secession "as the necessary and only mode of 'Southern resistance'" to the situation. "Our purpose is fixed; our course is certain"—and for this reason, a visit even from the sympathetic men of New York "would be unprofitable and unpleasant." In a follow-up letter to Lathers four days later, Henry wrote, "If war is to be forced upon the South, to compel her submission, her condition will be no worse than that which will be ultimately forced upon her by Republican rule." Always the more hesitant of the two brothers on secession, Henry had at last been swept up by the cause.

———

For every well-meaning Englishman and Yankee pleading patience, a larger number of fellow Southerners urged haste. Robert Gourdin's mailbox filled with desperate entreaties. From Macon, Georgia, James Mercer Green, a Philadelphia-trained physician distributing 1860 Association pamphlets, wrote to Robert of "fears expressed" in Georgia that the Columbia convention might get put off until January. "For God's sake do not allow this. You will in all probability be demoralized, and we certainly shall," Green said. "South Carolina from her unanimity and from the superior patriotism of her leaders (as a mass) must force the issue." He offered, unsolicited, to send along $40 for the pamphlets—not a small sum for a man of his profession. "Pray heaven that you don't listen to the wheedlings of Virginia and Kentucky," John M. Richardson of Perry,

Georgia, a professor of higher mathematics, begged Robert. "It is absurd to suppose that either they or Georgia will lead in this matter. May God give us speedy deliverance from this accursed Union!" And from Tuscaloosa, Alabama, John W. Pratt, a clergyman at the University of Alabama, wrote, "Sir, if Alabama refuses to stand by South Carolina, I shall renounce my citizenship here and seek a home in Carolina, and share her glory and her fate," even if allotted nothing more than "soil enough to stand on and wave my hat over the head of a free man. . . . My wife and I have talked the matter over and she agrees with me that poverty and hardship are to be preferred to the certain vassalage that awaits our posterity if Alabama refuses to strike one manly blow for freedom."

Green's fears of a delayed convention were unwarranted, but a debate did arise as to the setting. Concerns were raised by what appeared to be several cases of smallpox, liable to spread, in Columbia. The backup plan was to stage the proceedings in Charleston—a possibility that, as the *Tribune* observed in a sardonic aside to a December 13 dispatch, would be welcome to leaders of the secessionist movement in the city because, "as you must understand, Charleston has for some time been running the State on her own account." The *Tribune* correspondent assured his readers (and informed "the *Mercury* . . . the Vigilance Committee and the police") that he would be on the heels of the delegates wherever they might be found: "I will state farther that I wear a dashing cockade, eat fire like sweetmeats, and am always around whenever there is anything going on."

The question arose too, the *Tribune* noted, of whether the citizenry would have any say over decisions taken by the delegates. "Thus there exists a wish to have the Ordinance of Secession submitted to the people—a wish that will probably be crushed out," the paper asserted. The language was pungent as ever, but truly enough the delegates believed they possessed the legitimacy to act on their own. The people, after all, had elected them.

On Friday evening, December 14, with the convention three days away, the Moultrie Guards paraded through Charleston's streets in fatigue dress offering salutes to the *Mercury* and the 1860 Association. A rally was held at Institute Hall, where the stage was decked out with a colorful banner: "South Carolina May Well Be Proud of Her Delegates." The Charleston representatives, all twenty-two of them arrayed like belles at a beauty ball, were given their instructions: "Go to the Convention, gentlemen, and do your duty." Each tendered a few remarks, interrupted by thunderous cheers at any mention of South Carolina's impending secession.

On a frigid Saturday, Rhett, Sr., called at the home of British consul Robert Bunch for a private conversation on how England might treat a Southern Confederacy eager for good relations with Europe. It was a mission of diplomacy on the part of the senior Rhett, and yet, as ever, diplomacy was beyond his reach. When Bunch pointedly asked whether a confederacy would pledge not to reopen the African slave trade, "which Great Britain views with horror," Rhett, Sr., replied to the consul as if addressing a doltish student from the rostrum of a lecture hall. "No Southern State or Confederacy will ever be brought to negotiate upon such a subject," he said. "To prohibit the Slave Trade would be virtually to admit the institution of slavery is an evil and a wrong, instead of, as the South believes, a blessing to the African Race and a system of labor appointed by God." Bunch accepted the lesson dutifully and saved his opinion of Rhett, Sr., for a letter to the British Foreign Office: He "indulges in an abundance of utterly absurd invective against all who differ from him."

Sunday found Robert Gourdin at home with time to write a "few lines" to Major Robert Anderson at Fort Moultrie. The two had struck up a correspondence since Anderson's arrival in Charleston nearly a month earlier. The notes were respectful but frank. Each man stood his ground. On December 11, Anderson had told Gourdin, "You need no assurance from me that, although I am exerting myself to make this little work"— Moultrie—"as strong as possible and to put my handful of men in the highest state of discipline, no one will do more than I am willing to do to keep the South in the right and to avoid the shedding of blood. . . . Would to God that the time had come when there should be no war, and that religion and peace should reign throughout the world." To this letter, Robert replied, "Your sentiments in reference to war and bloodshed are such as I know you to hold." Nevertheless, the South would not and could not, at this point, stand down: "The secession movement cannot be suppressed; it pervades the South. I trust in God that we will be allowed to seek our peace and happiness as a people according to our own convictions of right and duty, unmolested by the government at Washington and by the peoples of the North."

At Bleak Hall, miles of seacoast away from the brass bands and fireworks of Charleston, a deep silence pervaded the weekend before the convention. The cotton-picking season that had started in August was approaching its end. The heavy work of dragging the pluff from the salt marsh to the fields to prepare for another year would not start for another two months. "It seems strange that we should be, in the midst of a revolution, so quiet, and plentiful, and corn for table up here," Meta Morris Grimball, a Sea Islands neighbor of Townsend, wrote in her journal. Grimball was the wife of a rice planter and a descendent of Lewis Morris, a signer of the Declaration of Independence. "Everything goes on as usual," she wrote; "the planting, the negroes, all just the same, and a great Empire tumbling to pieces about us."

Chapter Thirty

"TO DARE"

olumbia was selected as South Carolina's capital at the end of the eighteenth century because of its central, inland location. There was not much to the town apart from the statehouse, the railroad junction, and South Carolina College. At noon on Monday, December 17, the 169 delegates to the Secession Convention assembled at the First Baptist Church. Their ranks included five former governors and four former US senators, numerous former judges, more than one hundred planters, a handful of railroad barons and a dozen clerics. Nearly all of the men were slaveholders. Most had once identified as Cooperationists. They were "the gravest, ablest, and most dignified body of men I ever saw brought together," pronounced Joseph LeConte, a professor of chemistry and geology at the college and among those in the floor seats and galleries set aside for spectators. The flue had burst, and the red brick building was cold. A banner hung over the pulpit: "The Lord of Hosts is with us, the God of Jacob is our refuge."

Barnwell Rhett yearned to chair the convention, but there was practically no support for that. Instead the delegates elected as their president David F. Jamison, a planter from a rural district with two thousand acres and seventy slaves to his name. In his opening remarks he encouraged the men, in the motto of Georges-Jacques Danton, a leader of the French

Revolution, "To dare! And again to dare! And without end to dare!" If anyone felt puzzled by this declaration, considering that Danton had his head lopped off by the guillotine in the revolution he helped launch, the sentiment was unexpressed. Members next agreed to a resolution stating their "opinion" that South Carolina "should forthwith secede" from the Union—and calling for the drafting of an ordinance to accomplish this purpose. The vote, a kind of test poll, was nonbinding, not representing an actual decision to secede, and left the work of the delegates ahead of them.

And then they fled to Charleston.

Ostensibly, the reason to abandon Columbia was the worry over smallpox. Some people in town did have the disease. A notice affixed to the door of the statehouse, where the legislature was in session, asked "all persons visiting the sick with smallpox" to stay away. Still, the smallpox threat in Columbia had been addressed at least five days earlier—and the delegates had gathered there anyway. "To a New Yorker who at home is accustomed to blandly read in the weekly summary of deaths of ten or a dozen cases of [smallpox]," the correspondent for the *New York World* wrote, "the panic which has beset the good people of Columbia on that head, seems altogether unaccountable." Besides, if the smallpox was in Columbia, then it stood to reason, as some pointed out, that it could be in Charleston, too.

The bolt to Charleston was not just about fear of a sickness. Delegates, more than half of whom were over the age of fifty, were also griping about the meager accommodations in Columbia. Charleston, unrivalled in the splendors of its hospitality, offered more comfort for aging bones. Political calculations were at work as well. Columbia was not, like Charleston, single-mindedly fixated on secession. The town's most influential figure, Wade Hampton III, a planter with vast holdings extending to Mississippi, was thought to still be "a Union man," unconvinced that the moment for secession had arrived. In submitting to the convention his proposal to reassemble in Charleston, John A. Inglis of Upcountry Chesterfield County asked, "Is there any spot in South Carolina more fit for political agitation? Is there any spot more sacred to patriotism?" His resounding answer to his own question: "No!"

Even as Inglis thundered forth, Charleston delegates were wiring their contacts in the city to secure Institute Hall for a meeting place and Mills House, with its proven ability to put turtle soup and lamb chops on the table for hundreds at a time, for lodgings. Yet there was at least one member of the Charleston contingent emphatically opposed to the move. William Porcher Miles told his peers that decamping Columbia would make all of them look weak and timid. "We would be sneered at," he said. "It would be asked, from all sides, is this the chivalry of South Carolina? They are prepared to face the world, but they run away from the smallpox." His remarks met with laughter and applause, but when it came to a vote, delegates backed the move to Charleston.

Miles was exactly right. As soon as Jamison gaveled the convention to adjournment at 10:00 p.m. and delegates sprinted to the depot to secure tickets on the 4:00 a.m. train to Charleston, the mockery commenced. A friend dashed off a ditty to B. F. Perry:

> *Our brave secessionists have met, and*
> *Tarried but a day . . .*
> *Like children scared and terrified . . .*
> *They broke and ran away.*

A Columbia paper joined in the scorn. "Charleston Police Look Out!," the headline blared. "By a letter from New York, there is reason to apprehend that the Lincoln men have been gathering up all the rags they can find from the small-pox hospital, and intend an incursion in the South, to chase the secession conventions and legislatures from place to place until they are made powerless."

———

It was a seven-and-one-half hour journey by rail from Columbia to Charleston through pine forest, plantations, and small towns. Late on the morning of Tuesday, the 18th, bleary-eyed delegates stumbled onto the platform at the Charleston rail depot to the sounds of drum taps and a fifteen-gun salute courtesy of the Washington Artillery. A military escort stood ready to take them to their lodgings. Charleston was rapturous at the prospect of hosting the last act of the secession drama—and the delegates might have been excused of thinking they had wandered onto the set of a stage for an especially colorful and lively, perhaps somewhat fantastical, play. Downtown was a dense splotch of blue for all the cockades adorning the hats and cloaks of the men and women assembled in the streets. Some ladies also wore white cotton "secession bonnets" with streamers decorated by emblems of palmetto trees and a lone gold star. Institute Hall was now known as Secession Hall, and inside, awaiting the call to bring the convention to order, was a polished ivory gavel. In black letters carved deeply into the ivory, the head bore the word "Secession." Just up the street, a wrought-iron railing set in stone had just been constructed at the base of the Secession Pole to make it a "permanent institution," the *Mercury* said, as well as "the most handsome and complete flagstaff in the country." Over on East Bay Street was the Secession Gun, an artillery piece to be fired on ratification of the ordinance. (The gunpowder had been stored by a Charleston lady since the nullification crisis three decades before.) Henry Seigling's music store at King and Beaufain Streets was selling the five-page score for "The Grand Secession March," Opus 17 in the key of C major by Thomas J. Caulfield, "composed for and dedicated to the Charleston Delegation." On Meeting Street, Salcedo & Bierck, importers of Havana cigars, were hawking their latest brand, "Southern Confederacy."

The outdoor street art featured a coarsely painted canvas of Judge Magrath in his library, firing off a gun. Another depicted Lincoln, axe in hand, laboring without success to split a palmetto log. Amateur artists also painted romanticized images of postsecession Charleston—the wharves piled high with cotton tended by slaves, the harbor crowded with ships. A thirty-by-twenty-foot painting of a liberated Charleston graced the façade of the theater. At the Pavilion Hotel, a rendering of Hiram Power's statue of Calhoun could be found with one important modification—the tablet grasped by Calhoun, with the words "Truth, Justice and the Constitution," was shattered.

It was white Charleston's pageant, of course. Over at Coming Street, where the welcoming gun salute no doubt could be heard, the elder Johnson, James D., had his mind set on fixing up his houses, now on the selling block. "I only want to beautify the exterior so as to attract Capitalists," he wrote to a friend. The exodus of free blacks from Charleston that had started in the summer was continuing, and the "whole of our people," Johnson said, are "debating where to." Haiti was still the top choice. "Don't suppose I will be the last because I have replaced a missing tree," he said in his letter.

His son shared his woe. "It is now a fixed fact that we must go," James M. Johnson told a friend, of Charleston's free black families. "I hope it will meet with the sanction and support of us all. Our situation is not only unfortunate but deplorable, and it is better to make a sacrifice now than wait to be sacrificed ourselves."

Still, many of the free blacks could not tear themselves away from Charleston. "We are by birth citizens of South Carolina," thirty-seven of the men, paragons of the brown elite including the senior Johnson, declared in a desperate petition to authorities. "In our veins flows the blood of the white race—in some, half, in others much more than half, white blood," they said. "Our attachments are with you; our hopes of safety and protection from you; our allegiance is due to South-Carolina, and in her defence, we are willing to offer up our lives, and all that is dear to us."

The petition was in earnest in the sense that the men truly were willing to serve in the military on behalf of the Southern cause of independence. Of course, they must have realized that white authorities were not likely to accept this offer. The petition also represented a frank effort by the brown elite to separate itself from the slave population—to allay anxieties that white authorities might have about the loyalty of Charleston's mulatto community as South Carolina bolted from the Union.

———

At 4:00 p.m. on Tuesday, December 18, Jamison hushed the delegates and spectators packed into Institute Hall—Secession Hall—with a bang of his gavel. The Reverend J. C. Furman offered a prayer: "We ask to be heard in Christ our Redeemer. Amen." The senior Rhett moved that a committee be formed "to prepare an address to the people of the Southern States," and so it was agreed. Rhett, Sr., was appointed to head the panel. The delegates, though, quickly determined that the hall was too "commodious," as one put it, "to debate intelligently" the matters at hand, and they resolved to find a smaller place to meet. After just an hour, the delegates adjourned for the day. But they committed to staying in Charleston, despite continuing rumors of smallpox. City Hall's Committee on Health and Quarantine flatly denied the presence of the disease, insisting that there had not been a single case of smallpox for a year.

Passersby of the Charleston Hotel might have been startled by the sound of gunfire. Captain A. H. Colt, an agent of the Colt Company of Hartford, Connecticut, had commandeered a room on the top floor of the hotel to use for pistol practice. Colt, a New Yorker, was in town to sell his wares. This was his stock in trade. He had previously sailed to Italy to sell guns to the insurrectionists organized under Garibaldi. In Charleston he frequented the company of visiting journalists, including Thomas Gunn of London, and he had little sympathy for the South or for secession, notwithstanding his willingness to sell the rebels his revolvers.

Colt barely made it out of Charleston alive. He was accosted as a "Yankee" while making his way through the lobby of the Charleston Hotel. His assailant had slapped his face with a glove hard enough to draw blood. It was a case, it seemed, of mistaken identity: his attacker had taken him for Charles Brigham, the *Tribune's* wily correspondent. The combatants brawled with their fists in full view of dozens of spectators crowded in front of the hotel bar, and Colt decided to keep in check the Sicilian knife he always had on him. He retreated to Gunn's room, aided by a one-eyed Georgian who had taken pity on him. Colt felt sure that his attacker would issue a challenge to a duel with pistols that he had no desire to fight. Gunn soothed him by reading out loud from Dickens's *Great Expectations*, and Colt soon stole away on a steamer to New York.

Chapter Thirty-One

"WINE AND REJOICING"

or those with a belief in secession as just and pure, a holy cause, the idea that it might contain a base element was impossible to accept. The Rhetts and their friend William Porcher Miles could not acknowledge that something deeply primitive and seemingly irresistible had taken rude, unshakable grip on Charleston. The prevailing fiction was that Charleston desired only to defend itself against attack, not to strike the first blow. The fact that the outnumbered men of the Fort Moultrie garrison were still alive—when "some crowd on any night . . . could have massacred them"—was proof of Charleston's peaceful nature, Miles maintained. "The excitement here is a deep, calm feeling," the *Mercury* insisted on its front page on Wednesday, December 19, as the "secession now" delegates, permitting themselves a leisurely morning, prepared to reassemble. Although it admitted that the city "may be said to swarm with armed men," the *Mercury* assured readers in Charleston and beyond, "we are not a mobocracy here, and believe in law, order, and obedience to authority, civil and military."

At 11:00 a.m., delegates elbowed their way past the crowd into St. Andrew's Hall, on Broad Street. Eight months before, the renegade Southern Democrats had assembled in the main room under the watchful gaze of Thomas Scully's Queen Victoria for what the *Mercury* dubbed the "Seceding Convention." At that time, the spectators squeezed among them were asked to leave the hall to permit quiet deliberations. Now, when a Charleston delegate suggested the convention "sit with closed doors," James Chesnut objected: "It seems that a popular body should sit with the eyes of the people upon them." But when Chesnut proposed a change to a larger venue like the theater, he was met with cries of dissent from his cohorts. They were tired of moving about. The carpeted floors and velvet-cushioned chairs of their quarters at St. Andrew's suited them fine. "I protest," John Richardson said to Chesnut. "If there is one sentiment predominant over all others, and truly the mind of the people of Charleston, it is that this Convention should proceed." The doors were shut and a police guard stationed at the entrance to keep it clear.

———•———

Locked out! There scarcely could be a reason at this point to doubt the imminent delivery of an Ordinance of Secession, and yet somehow the crowd did doubt it. Charleston was like an expectant father, pacing and waiting for the child to be born. On this occasion, the waiting was done in a downpour that muddied the city. "The Union is being dissolved in tears," a Charleston lady told her daughter. "The feeling exhibited was intense; each man, through the day, as he met his neighbor, anxiously asked if the Ordinance had yet passed," Capt. Crawford of the Moultrie garrison recorded in his diary. "The public offices were all thronged by earnest men awaiting the final action of their State. Deep-settled purpose was apparent upon the countenances of all."

The people continued to express their enthusiasm with an afternoon parade by the Vigilant Rifles, escorted by the Washington Light Infantry, that stopped at Society Hall. The two-story brick building, with a ballroom and a musician's gallery, served as the headquarters for a benevolent association founded by French Huguenot businessmen and artisans. Inside, Mayor Charles Macbeth awaited to present Captain S. Y. Tupper of the Vigilant Rifles a flag sewn for the militia "by a number of the fair daughters of Carolina." The mayor read aloud a letter from one of the daughters: "Take this flag. If it be the will of Heaven that you never carry it amid clashing swords and rending balls, our hearts will rejoice. But if the call to arms should come, as come we fear it must, then we solemnly charge you to unfurl these colors . . . dare to do, and, if need be, dare to die for the sacred cause you have espoused."

With the flag in hand, Capt. Tupper responded, "Soldiers! Behold your standard. It comes from the hands of those whom we love, and whose earnest supplications will ascend to Heaven for your honor and safety in the hour of peril."

At the reception following the parade, Capt. Tupper raised his glass to Fort Moultrie. "It is ours by inheritance," he declared. "It stands upon the sacred soil of Carolina, and the spirit of our patriotic fathers hover about it. Infamy to the mercenaries that fire the first gun against the children of its revolutionary defenders." The "mercenaries" would presumably be the federal soldiers standing watch over the fort, accompanied by the wives of Captains Doubleday and Seymour and others, several dozen children of these families, plus Mrs. Rippitt, the housekeeper attending to the un-married men. Society Hall resounded with cheers. But where was the or-dinance? Wednesday went by and passed with still no action.

On Thursday morning, Robert Gourdin wrote to North Carolina gov-ernor John W. Ellis, "Before the sun sets this day, South Carolina will have assumed the powers delegated to the federal government and taken her place among the nations as an independent power. God save the State." The delegates planned to assemble at noon, and as the hour approached, crowds streamed toward St. Andrew's and set up watch in front of the hall.

The ordinance was a short, legalistic statement, just as Memminger had promised Charleston. Inside St. Andrew's, John Inglis, the lawyer who three days before had called for the convention to move from Columbia to "sacred" Charleston, reported to the delegates that the spare text would offer "in the fewest and simplest words possible to be used . . . all that is necessary to effect the end proposed and no more." It said: "We, the peo-ple of the State of South Carolina, in convention assembled, do declare and ordain . . . that the union now subsisting between South Carolina and other States, under the name of 'United States of America,' is hereby dissolved." There was no further debate; the call of the roll started at 1:07 p.m. and ended at 1:15 p.m., every delegate a 'yea.'"

From a window at St Andrew's the signal was given to the throng that the measure had passed. "And then a mighty shout arose," Reverend A. Toomer Porter recorded. "It rose higher and higher until it was the roar of a tempest. It spread from end to end of the city, for all were of one mind. No man living could have stood that excitement." Fort Moultrie's Capt. Crawford was there, too, and in his calmer witness experienced the scene much as the reverend did. "The whole heart of the people had spoken. Men in elegant life, who had never known labor for a day, stood side by side with the 'poor white.'"

The Secession Gun roared its approval as cannon blasts reverberated throughout town. A rider stationed at St. Andrew's dug spurs into horse and galloped one mile away to the camp of the First Regiment of Rifles, South Carolina Militia. His news was greeted with "the loud acclamations of the men."

With a draft copy of the ordinance in hand, supplied in advance by Rhett, Sr., the *Mercury* already had printed thousands of copies of a special edition declaring "THE UNION IS DISSOLVED!" By 1:20 p.m., five minutes after the ordinance's passage, the "extra" was on the streets. Small groups gathered to hear it read out loud. Perry O'Bryan's telegraph office wired the news to the nation.

Elderly men dressed in the uniforms of their volunteer regiments passed through the streets shouting the news. A militia man in a golden helmet paraded by St. Michael's on horseback with the ordinance held aloft. Young men gathered around the grave of Calhoun in St. Philip's cemetery and vowed to devote "their lives, their fortunes, and their sacred honor, to the cause of South Carolina independence." A lady placed evergreens on the tomb. Small palmetto flags were waved outside of windows, and a young Charleston poet felt inspired to compose "A Song of Deliverance":

Unnumbered fading hopes rebloom, and faltering hearts grow brave,
And a consentaneous shout
To the answering heavens rings out—
'Off with the livery of disgrace, the baldric of the Slave!'

Amid the chiming of church bells, with St. Michael's tolling "Auld Lang Syne," Petigru encountered one of his former law students. "Where's the fire?" Petigru quipped. The student replied, "Mr. Petigru, there is no fire. Those are the joy bells ringing in honor of the passage of the Ordinance of Secession." In the law student's telling, his old professor responded, "I tell you there is a fire. They have this day set a blazing torch to the temple of constitutional liberty and, please God, we shall have no more peace forever."

Petigru had managed to withstand the contagion when virtually all of his friends had succumbed. In part, his immunity owed to fixed character: he seemed to have been born a contrarian. More important was his un-faltering devotion to his ideal of reason: he could never be persuaded that secession made sense. He was also fearless, even on this most dangerous day, to affirm an allegiance to the Union. "If there were any like Mr. Peti-gru," Rev. Porter noted, "they hid themselves." One such closet Unionist, Jacob Schirmer, confined his feelings to his diary. "This is the commence-ment of the dissolution of the Union that has been the pride and glory of the whole world," he wrote in an entry on the 20th, and "after a few years," Schirmer predicted, "we will find the beautiful structure broke up into as many pieces as there are now States, and jealousy and discord will be all over the land." Doubtless others scribbled such notes to themselves. "So many were proud of our beautiful mother," a Charleston lady said of the Union, "but they are hidden by the mass who think themselves aggrieved."

Alone in his room at the Charleston Hotel, a glum captive to the tumult, sat Caleb Cushing of Massachusetts. Fondly regarded by Charles-ton for his sympathetic handling of the grievances of Southern delegates in his role as president of the Democratic National Convention, Cushing had arrived on a train just that morning as a special envoy from President James Buchanan. His task was to see if some sort of deal could be reached to stay South Carolina's hand on secession. But in a meeting at City Hall with Governor Pickens, who was temporarily operating out of Charleston,

Cushing was bluntly told, "There is no hope for the Union." Now that the ordinance had been passed, his mission was moot. He declined to attend a formal signing ceremony "as the envoy of a foreign state" that evening at Secession Hall and booked passage on the next train out of the city.

"To us it sounded like the *death-knell* of a nation's glory," wrote Reverend James W. Hunnicutt of the celebration in Charleston. A native of South Carolina, he now worked as the editor of the *Christian Banner*, a Unionist newspaper based in Virginia. He went on to say, "The cheering and dancing of wicked, ungrateful children over the grave of a kind and affectionate mother would have seemed no more unnatural to us than did the great cheering of the citizens of Charleston over the downfall of their State and country."

It can only be wondered how Charleston's slaves greeted the news of secession—that is, outside of the surveilling eye of white Charleston. It seems no remembrances were recorded. According to one Charleston lady, the slaves shared in the joy, "leaping and clapping their hands." A second lady recalled slave children reciting a ditty from a Minute Man song on the streets, "Wid a blue cockade and a rusty gun/We'll make dem Yankees run like fun." Perhaps this was a sly bit of mockery: Did the slaves really believe the Yankees would run at the sight of the rebels? As for the community of free blacks, tailor James M. Johnson said in his terse way of the street revelries, "It is very diverting, especially to children, who do not look to consequences."

Robert Gourdin returned home from St. Andrew's and wrote a note updating North Carolina governor Ellis on the convention's action and expressing his hopes that "we may, if possible, avoid collision with the general government, while we negotiate the dissolution of our situation with the Union." He apologized for the brevity of the letter: "It is written at the dinner table amid conversation, wine and rejoicing."

Chapter Thirty-Two

"BLOOD MUST BE SHED!"

Darkness came early to Charleston on this long-remembered Thursday, one day before the winter solstice. At 6:30 p.m., by the soft orange glow of the gas lamps, the delegates lined up outside St. Andrew's. The men faced east on Broad Street toward the Cooper River with their backs to Petigru's house. The procession began: past T. G. Trott's druggist shop, across King Street, left on Meeting Street at St. Michael's, past City Hall, past Chalmers Street, past Hibernian Hall and Mills House, and then across Queen Street to halt at the entrance to Institute Hall. There they were met by the members of the South Carolina Senate and House, and all together the men filed into the building with the delegates leading the way.

Inside the hall were three thousand ecstatic Charlestonians, a roiling sea of blue cockades and waving white silk handkerchiefs. "The people": only twelve months before, some advocates of secession had thought them all but asleep. They had since passed from the role of spectators to participants in this drama. They could now be seen as the main actors and perhaps even the authors. On the stage was a lone table above which hung a cotton canvas the size of a bedsheet flanked by a pair of potted palmetto trees. The banner was titled "Built from the Ruins" and had been displayed for the first time that afternoon, hanging from a line stretched from the Guard House to City Hall at Broad and Meeting. It depicted an arch made up of fifteen white marble blocks, one for each slave state. At the apex—the keystone—was South Carolina, topped by the image of Calhoun. To one side of him stood a male figure representing faith, to the other a female icon representing hope. Beneath the arch was a palmetto. Its trunk was encircled by the familiar rattlesnake, fangs exposed. At its base was a pair of cannon pointed outward. In front of the cannon lay the stones of the Northern states, broken into fragments. And above the arch, stretching the length of the banner, shone fifteen blue stars. Tied to the palmetto, a white ribbon fluttered in the wind bearing the words "Southern Republic."

The delegates made their way to their seats, and the legislators lined themselves along the side walls. An old man with snowy white hair raised his hands to quiet the assemblage and ask them to stand in prayer. This was Rev. Bachman, who begged for "wisdom from on high" to guide the leaders of the secession movement, forced by "fanaticism, injustice, and oppression" to take South Carolina out of the Union. He implored God to "enable us to protect and bless the humble race that had been entrusted to our care," and in the sad event of war, to deliver triumph and "prosperity to our Southern land."

Jamison advanced with the ordinance—or as the *Mercury* called the document, the "consecrated parchment." It displayed the "great seal of South Carolina," stamped in wax by silver matrices fashioned by a Charleston smith in 1776. It was read aloud, and on the last word—"dissolved"— those assembled "could contain themselves no longer. and a shout that shook the very building, reverberating, long-continued, rose to Heaven, and ceased only with the loss of breath," the Rhetts' paper said.

The ordinance was placed on the table on the stage, and one by one the delegates stepped forward to sign it. Ninety minutes into the ritual, the Charleston delegation took its turn. The men were called out in the order of their number of votes: Magrath was first, followed by Miles, Townsend, and Robert Gourdin. Rhett, Sr., the seventh to be named, sank to his knees before the parchment with his hands uplifted and his head bowed in seeming prayer. Behind him was Memminger, the man he had been quarreling with over secession for nearly thirty years. There were re-sounding cheers for all—and loudest, the *Mercury* insisted in its account, for Barnwell Rhett.

For more than two hours the ceremony continued, "yet no one was weary, and no one left," Edmund Ruffin noted. Finally, the signatures were all affixed, and Jamison held the document aloft: "I proclaim the State of South Carolina an Independent Commonwealth." The crowd rushed the stage, tearing the palmetto trees into souvenir scraps. Augustine Smyth, the eighteen-year-old son of Reverend Thomas Smyth and a future min-ister himself, sprang from his seat in the gallery, slid down a pillar onto the floor, and made off with a palmetto relic along with a pen and a blotter displaying the signature of Memminger. The banner managed to survive the scrum.

Nighttime Charleston blazed with bonfires lit from tar barrels. Mili-tias paraded. Roman candles were launched into the air. Colored lanterns adorned an East Battery Street home. The bands played on and on, "as if there were no thought of ceasing," Ruffin wrote. At 2:00 a.m., British consul Bunch, who had witnessed the signing ceremony from a spot be-side a pillar, was at home finishing off his reports to London on the day's events. Earlier he had sent a copy of the *Mercury*'s "The Union Is Dis-solved!" edition. "Everyone wears a pleased expression, as if he or others had done something very clever without knowing exactly what it was," he now wrote. "But I much fear it will be 'he who laughs on Friday will cry on Sunday.' I am somewhat sorry for the old Union, although he was a noisy old braggart."

The celebration spilled over to the next day with yet another nighttime parade through the streets. "I carried a lantern with the legend, 'There is a point beyond which endurance ceases to be a virtue,'" Simon Baruch, a Jewish immigrant from Prussia, recalled years later. At the time he was a twenty-year-old student at the Medical College of South Carolina in Charleston. He had lived in America for five years.

The procession of brass bands and militia, along with the German Fire Company, moved along to the tune of Thomas Caulfield's "Secession March" and stopped at the Mills House, where Governor Pickens, from the balcony, assured the throng that all would be well: "Allow me to say to you that I hope and trust I am in possession of information that, perhaps, there may be no appeal to force on the part of the Federal authorities." Rewarded with cheers, he allowed, "If I am mistaken in this, at least as far as I am concerned, we are prepared to meet any and every issue." But at the moment "I desire coolness and calmness." The always-popular General Schnierle addressed the populace, followed by the appearance on the balcony of George Christy's Minstrels, in town from Broadway, New York, for an engagement at Institute Hall. The popular troupe, beloved by Southern audiences for its blackface rendition of "Dixie," now treated the public to a performance of *La Marseillaise.*

———

Forty-five days had passed since Charleston had received the news of Lincoln's election—forty-five days of a sustained, wild excitement. Ordinary time seemed to have stopped. Supplies of adrenaline had proved inexhaustible. Life had been lived more intensely, more expressively, than ever before. With secession accomplished, there could be no more anxiety that the leaders would fail at this task. Whether other states would follow, and when, was a worry for another moment—and no matter if some thought, as a North Carolina planter wrote a friend in the city, that in Charleston, "everybody is drunk or crazy."

With Christmas just a few days away, a quieter and more sober mood took hold, although it was understood to be no more than a pause. Caroline Howard Gilman wrote to her children, "What a volcano we stand over!" She had moved to Charleston from her native Boston as a new bride forty-one years earlier. Her husband had died two years previously, and, although Gilman's sympathies lay with her adopted city, she could not identify with its wilder sentiments, as she told her children while writing from her home one evening:

> In the stillness of the house (for I am alone on this floor) and of the city (for not a sound breaks the quiet) it seems hard to think that we are on the eve of a revolution; indeed through the whole day you would see no

difference in old Charleston, were it not for the Palmetto trees that are being planted in the streets, and the flags that float everywhere, waving their silent story. But what a current is rushing on in the souls of men. . . .

It seems to me no time for vituperation and passion. Our destiny, whatever it is, has a muffled tread, but it is solemn and fixed. . . .

The great broken moon is just rising, and looks larger than her wont. What will she see on her next monthly visit!

Charleston and the world beyond now could read the "Declaration of the Immediate Causes which Induce and Justify the Secession of South Carolina from the Federal Union," a manifesto written by Memminger and printed as a short pamphlet by Evans & Cogswell. The stated "immediate causes" amounted to one: the failure of the federal government to enforce the clause of the Constitution, Article IV, Section 2, requiring the return of fugitive slaves to their owners. No mention was made of the federal tariff, the first galvanizer of the secession movement in South Carolina that Memminger had earlier ridiculed as a cause for "disunion." Nor was there any mention of his failed mission to Virginia at the start of the year to try to find a path for united action by the slave states. The declaration was a bloodless document.

Petigru paid a visit to the federal soldiers at Fort Moultrie. It was a good-bye call, his friend Doubleday perceived, "to express the deep sorrow and sympathy he felt for us in our trying position. As he knew that arrangements were being made to drive us out, he bade us farewell with much feeling. The tears rolled down his cheeks as he deplored the folly and the madness of the times." His friend Mary Boykin Chesnut later wrote in her diary, with a gentle touch, "Mr. Petigru alone in South Carolina has not seceded."

The old man reserved a measure of his sorrow for himself. "I made a great mistake in 1832, when I might have quit the country myself, with the prospect of doing something," he wrote Jane on Christmas Eve. "Here I have stayed until the active period of life is over." He closed by telling her to disregard the papers, which might "make you think that the poor fellows in the fort here are likely to be killed or captured. You need not grieve for them but for the fools that make the attempt. All Charleston and all the volunteers cannot take Fort Moultrie by assault."

Major Anderson, though, was not convinced of that—and neither was his devoted former pupil at West Point, Colonel William Tecumseh Sherman, who was well acquainted with Moultrie from his posting there years before. From Louisiana, Col. Sherman wrote to a friend in the military a letter brimming with indignation at Charleston's unremitting threats toward the men at the fort. "We are in the midst of sad times—It is not slavery—It is a tendency to anarchy everywhere," Sherman said. "Let them hurt a hair of his head in the execution of his duty," he said of Anderson, "and I say Charleston must be blotted from existence."

Charleston's surface calm lasted all of six days—shattered when the town woke up on the 27th to the flag of the federal soldiers waving over Fort Sumter and dense black smoke billowing out of Moultrie. Just after sundown on the 26th, under the light of a full moon, Anderson managed to move his entire command, the band included, by rowboat to Sumter. The fort, the only structure on this otherwise bare spot, offered relief from the prying eyes and sharpshooters on Sullivan's Island and occupied a commanding position in the middle of Charleston Harbor. At his orders, his men drove spikes into the vents of Moultrie's guns and set fire to the wooden carriages. The sudden departure had come as a surprise to the soldiers, including the officers, and the unsuspecting Mrs. Rippitt was left behind to prepare tea for men who would never return. "My Dear Sir," Anderson wrote to Robert Gourdin from Sumter, "I only have time to say that the movement of my command to this place was made on my own responsibility and not in obedience to orders from Washington. I did it because in my opinion it was the best way of preventing the shedding of blood." Gourdin read the letter aloud to the secession delegates, still in session. At Sumter, the band struck up the *Star Spangled Banner.*

Charleston was enraged—with their frayed nerves and turf-mindedness, the people seemed to think that the federal soldiers needed their permission to take leave of Moultrie. And it was true enough that

Anderson, to keep from being stopped, had taken great care to leave the city guessing as to his plans. "The wildest rumors were started," Rev. Porter recalled. "Everyone supposed that Fort Sumter was full of shells, and that Major Anderson had trained his guns on the city, and we would soon be bombarded." The federal soldiers were apt to sneak into the arsenal on Bee Street and blow it up, some said. Crowds gathered to denounce Anderson, the Kentuckian, as a traitor to the South. "Major Anderson has achieved the unenviable distinction of opening civil war between American citizens by an act of gross breach of faith," the *Courier* declared. Charleston militiamen threatened that "they would be heard from before twenty-four hours." The "Independent Commonwealth" of South Carolina took possession of the arsenal as well as Fort Moultrie and Castle Pinkney, raised the palmetto flag over all three, and also dispatched a contingent of Citadel cadets, most of them teenagers, to the tip of Morris Island to staff a battery of cannon. Their orders were to prevent any federal ship from reinforcing Sumter with men or supplies. Rev. Porter visited "the boys" encamped at Castle Pinckney and preached a sermon on the theme of Second Timothy 2:3: "Suffer hardship with me, as a good soldier of Jesus Christ."

Fighting was sure to come, Rev. Porter felt, and he was not dissuaded by a chance encounter with former senator James Chesnut the day after Charleston learned of Anderson's move to Sumter. They spoke by the Battery, from which the fort's guns could be glimpsed. "There will be no war, it will be all arranged. I will drink all the blood shed in the war," Chesnut said. Henry Gourdin, like Rev. Porter, was of a much gloomier mind. He was convinced that "nothing now but a miracle can arrest the onward course towards destruction and war."

With Charleston "in a blaze of excitement" over Anderson's gambit, suspicions even fastened on George Christy's Minstrels. The city was exercised by a report that some of its members had marched in New York in sympathy with the Wide Awakes, a kind of Northern Republican version of Minute Men bands that included black participants. The troupe was left unharmed, and the show, at Institute Hall, allowed to go on only after the manager assured townspeople that the report "was a falsehood, and done for the purpose of injuring us" and that "we had never engaged in any political demonstration."

Some in Charleston tried to act as if everything was normal. On the 29th, a friend wrote to Mary Amarinthia Snowden, still hard at work raising funds for the Calhoun monument project, to thank her, "at this festive season of the year, in your tasteful present of the china . . . as we toil on in the everyday duties of life." Of course, nothing was normal. Charleston's longing for catharsis was nowhere near complete. On the very last day of the year, Rev. Smyth picked up his pen to write old friend M. W. Jacobus, a professor at Allegheny Seminary in Pennsylvania. Smyth had before him a letter from Jacobus, dated December 21, asking him to use his "great influence" to try to halt a spiral into violence. "I know it may be said that South Carolina has fixed her policy of Secession immovably," Jacobus said in the letter. "But my dear brother, will nothing answer but a rupture of such sacred bonds—nothing but a rolling back of civilization and Christianity in the land and in the world, by the most awful and interminable of Civil Wars?"

It was hopeless, Smyth wrote in reply. The South required "a new birth," a "new life and character," he explained. "Blood must be shed! In an awful sense, without the shedding of blood there can be no peace, no atonement. Madness rules the hour, and the dogs of war are let loose, and howl and raven for their prey."

AFTERMATH

"City of Desolation"

Ruin—ruin—ruin—above and below; on the right hand and the left; ruin, ruin, ruin, everywhere and always." So said *Harper's Weekly* of Charleston, 1865, after the war. The *Boston Advertiser's* man wrote "of rotting wharves, of deserted warehouses, of weed-wild gardens, of miles of grass-grown streets, of acres of pitiful and voiceful barrenness." A *Tribune* reporter, in a visit to the *Mercury's* offices on Broad Street, found a bust of Calhoun in fragments and a black family using the newsroom as a makeshift residence. The city's remaining population suffered from smallpox, whooping cough, and the measles. It suffered, too, from starvation as a result of the widespread failure of crops. The corpses piled up.

In December of 1861, a great fire had ravaged a large swath of downtown, from East Bay Street by the Cooper River all the way down Broad Street to the Ashley. Institute Hall, St. Andrew's Hall, and the theater were destroyed, as was Petigru's home. The authorities suspected arson by slaves, but the fire appeared to be the result of a riverside campfire that got out of control and exploded the gasworks. Strong winds accounted for the rest of the damage.

President Lincoln had authorized the bombardment of the city, which began in August 1863, after Confederate general P. G. T. Beauregard refused a demand for the immediate surrender of the city. "It would appear," Beauregard told a Union general, that "you now resort to the novel measure of turning your guns against the old men, the women and children, and the hospitals of a sleeping city, an act of inexcusable barbarity." Charleston was shelled daily for 587 days—nearly twenty months. The lower section of the peninsula was hardest hit. Residents were forced to relocate to north of Calhoun, where the shells generally could not reach. The City Council permitted free blacks to join depleted firefighting outfits. Jefferson Davis, president of the Confederacy, visited Charleston that November. Speaking from the balcony at City Hall, he suggested it was better that Charleston be reduced to "a heap of ruins" than left "prey for Yankee spoils." Yes, his listeners replied, "Ruins! Ruins!"

Union guns complied. Over a span of nine days in January 1864, some 1,500 shells rained on Charleston. It was the first sustained bombardment of a civilian population during the war. "If there is any city deserving of holocaustic infamy, it is Charleston," the *Tribune* declared. "When the army leaves it," a Union soldier said of Charleston in a letter sent home to Pennsylvania, "the soldiers will shake its ashes from their feet, fearful to bear even such a vestige of its foul existence to any of the territory of the country."

In "The Swamp Angel," his ode to the "great Parrott gun, planted in the marshes of James Island" and employed in the shelling of the city, Herman Melville spoke of "the pale fright of the faces" and asked:

> *Is this the proud City? the scorner*
> *Which never would yield the ground?*

The first federal soldier to enter defeated Charleston was a black US Army man. He rode a mule up Meeting Street with a "Liberty" banner attached to the animal. Men from the 21st Infantry Regiment of the US Colored Troops arrived in the city, along with members of the black 55th Massachusetts. "Remember Denmark Vesey of Charleston" was a rallying cry for African American men under Union command. Charleston's slaves, deemed "forever free" by Lincoln's Emancipation Proclamation of

September 1862, were now so in fact—beyond the lash of their masters and unafraid to express their feelings in public. "I'se waited for you, and prayed for you," an elderly black woman tearfully exclaimed to federal soldiers, "and you done come at last." A delegation of thirteen black women, one for each of the original thirteen states, presented a Union commander an American flag, flowers, and "a fan for Mrs. Lincoln."

Black Charleston paraded in the streets with a "Slavery Is Dead" coffin. "No caste, no color," children proclaimed. A school on Morris Street opened its doors to 1,000 black students—a project of a northern abolitionist appointed as Charleston's new superintendent of schools. On a separate floor of the building, two hundred white students had their own classrooms. On April 14, 1865, five days after General Robert E. Lee's surrender at Appomattox, a son of Denmark Vesey stood with others gathered at Fort Sumter to watch Major General Robert Anderson raise the same Union garrison flag he had hauled down in his surrender of the fort after Confederate bombardment four years earlier. A brother of Harriet Beecher Stowe delivered a sermon calling for the punishment of the "remorseless traitors" who had "shed this ocean of blood." William Lloyd Garrison, burned in effigy in Charleston a quarter-century before, was there, too.

When word of Lincoln's murder reached Charleston, on a weekday morning, "weeping" older black schoolgirls asked to be allowed to go home. "Sobs and loud lamentations" reverberated in the black community, and children returned to school in rosettes and bows of black mourning crepe. White Charleston mostly kept off the streets.

———

Soon Northerners became eager to gaze upon the wonder with their own eyes, and a visit to the "City of Desolation," as Charleston was now called, became a tourist excursion. The ruins were "picturesque," one sightseer decided, suggestive of the rubble of ancient Rome or Athens. Not long after the war ended, Sherman himself paid a visit. He came by sea, passing by Forts Moultrie and Sumter without landing. On embarking in town, he walked through "the old familiar streets—Broad, Meeting, King, etc.," as he later wrote in his memoirs. He had not set foot in the city since his posting at Moultrie in the 1840s as a young lieutenant. "I inquired for many of my old friends, but they were dead or gone," he recounted. "I doubt whether any city was ever more terribly punished than Charleston, but as her people had for years been agitating for war and discord, and had finally inaugurated the Civil War," Sherman said, "the judgment of the world will be, that Charleston deserved the fate that befell her." He saw, too, a larger lesson in the city's destruction: "Anyone who is not satisfied with war should go and see Charleston, and he will pray louder and deeper than ever that the country may, in the long future, be spared any more war."

Charleston sent forty-two companies of one hundred to two hundred men each into the war, amounting to more than 5,000 officers and enlisted soldiers altogether. Many companies suffered the deaths of 30 percent or more of their ranks. It was more blood than James Chesnut could drink.

Petigru died nearly two years into the war, at the age of seventy-three. He was buried at St. Michael's. Rhett, Sr., eulogized "my tutor in boyhood, my friend in early manhood, my better friend in advanced life." As for Petigru's support for the Union, "as long as it lasted," the senior Rhett offered this gloss: "His generous and noble nature could not realize the dangers others thought they saw hanging over the destinies of the South from our Northern associates." It could be held as surprising that Petigru did not leap out of his grave to protest this fraudulent account of his unflagging opposition to secession.

Andrew Gordon Magrath served as a Confederate district court judge for three years and in December of 1864, with Charleston's fall only months away, was made governor of South Carolina. He urged the citizens to fight on. "Fear not to die," he declared in a message to the people. "All who desert us are as false as the foes which assail us." Union troops captured him and put him in prison at Fort Pulaski, in Georgia, where he was given the rations of a common inmate. "I am wearied and worn out," he wrote a sibling from jail. "My time, my spirit, my hope, are all wasting away." As he pondered the "motive power of the revolution," he came to the conclusion that the root cause of secession was "the idea that the right in property in slaves was about to be questioned and denied by the power of the political party which had then obtained its ascendancy." And the "right of property we must remember is the central and is regarded as the most sacred of all rights," declared the former judge and Harvard Law School graduate. He could not have felt comforted to learn that his Bee Street home in Charleston had been commandeered to house Northern teachers for new black schools in town.

In the midst of the war, John Townsend, with the rest of the planters and their families, evacuated indefensible Edisto Island on orders of the Confederate military. A "black republic" briefly reigned. When Union troops arrived, they took possession of Bleak Hall and employed its tall cupola to send signals to federal ships on the water. After the war, a visitor found Townsend and his family living in a shed. The mansion was burned to the ground, the prized gardens uprooted. The star pamphleteer of the secession movement, determined to begin anew, took an oath: "I, John Townsend . . . do solemnly swear in the presence of Almighty God, that I will henceforth faithfully support and defend the Constitution of the United States and the Union of the States thereunder."

The Gourdin brothers stuck out the war in Charleston. On the eve of the siege, consumed with anxiety that the remains of Calhoun, buried at St. Philip's, might be violated by Union soldiers, they supervised a secret nighttime mission to dig up the metal coffin, transfer it to "a strong pine case," and reinter the corpse under an unmarked spot in the rear of the church. The work was "accomplished with considerable difficulty, owing to the solidity of the masonry," but "the remains of your venerated father" are safe, Robert informed Calhoun's son, Andrew P. Calhoun, in a letter that meticulously recounted the operation.

The brothers were broke at war's end. Their savings had been invested in worthless Confederate bonds and their valuable stock of vintage Madeira destroyed. They were able to hold on to 2 Meeting Street— although the furniture was confiscated by Union soldiers—only with sister Anna's financial help. "Southern Independence," Henry soberly reflected, was a "dream" never to be realized. "God has not prospered us. Have we been mistaken in it? If so, may he turn our hearts to accept the destiny that he has prepared for us. . . . But we must suffer deep humiliation and all the pains of poverty and ruin. It stares us in the face and cannot be avoided. How happy they who have not lived to see it."

Few white Charlestonians were as philosophical as that. The gentry fumed—at the sight of blacks dressing as they pleased, no longer getting out of the way on sidewalks, and keeping their own guns; at the sound of "John Brown's Body" merrily sung on the downtown streets by black children. "You treat us well enough," a Charleston lady told a Union officer, "but the niggers are dreadful sassy. They don't turn out now when you meet them; they even smoke cigars, and go right up to a gentleman and ask him for a light!"

For the terrors and indignities of liberated Charleston, Robert Gourdin attached blame to "the Yankees, the authors of all this demoralization of a once happy and contented race and of all this frightful mortality and business." He labored with Henry to reestablish their brokerage business. By life's end he would be reduced to asking his nephew Louis for money to pay the laundress.

William Porcher Miles, once a beloved and respected mayor and legislator, renounced politics. "When we see the most ardent secessionists and 'Fire eaters' now eagerly denying that they ever did more than 'yield their convictions to the voice of their State,'" the former Congressman said with disgust, "it is evident that politics must be more a trade and less a pursuit for honorable men than it ever was before." He became president of South Carolina College.

Rev. Bachman's church was also destroyed in the siege, and he took refuge in an Upcountry plantation owned by a rich friend wanted by the Union. When Sherman's troops arrived at the property, the owner was away, and Bachman was apparently mistaken for him. An officer beat him with the dull edge of a sword, "permanently disfiguring his left arm and shoulder." Bachman's vast collection of scientific papers, stored in Columbia, was burned by Union soldiers. He returned to St. John's and railed against war profiteers. His friend Edmund Ruffin chose a different path. Shortly after the South surrendered, Ruffin propped the muzzle of his musket in his mouth and squeezed the trigger. His last words for the world: "I cannot survive the liberties of my country."

The industrious Christopher Memminger served the Confederacy in Richmond as its treasury secretary and won the acclaim of Robert E. Lee. This prodigy of the Charleston Orphan House returned from the war to find his home, on Wentworth and Smith Streets, used as an orphanage— for black children. He retook possession of it on application to the War Department and gained a pardon from President Andrew Johnson on pledging "to discharge the duties of a citizen of the United States." He reestablished his law practice, returned to Columbia as a state legislator in charge of the Ways and Means Committee, assumed direction of the Blue Ridge railroad and presided as chairman of the city board of school commissioners. The Memminger School, a high school for girls on Beaufain Street, honored his role as the father of Charleston's system of public education. In his way, he was still a man of vision.

In want of subscribers and advertisers and mired in debt, the *Mercury* expired. "I have faith to believe in the future independence and prosperity of the South," Barny declared, defiant to the last. "I take my place among her ruined children." His destitute father, who spent the war bitterly criticizing the policies of the Confederate administration, from which he had been excluded, found not a single banker willing to lend him as much as a dime. "Most humiliating," Barnwell Rhett told his wife. The stubborn pimple on his nose—the blemish the doctor in Paris told him not to worry about back in 1855—turned out to be cancerous. Surgery removed a chunk of his face, but the tumor killed him anyway.

In 1896, Confederate veterans of the "War of Secession" met in Charleston for a reunion. "Poor fellows—many of these men did not understand in the least what they were fighting about," a local realtor, Henry Schulz Holmes, wrote in his diary. "Our war was brought about by ambitious politicians who hoped," Holmes continued, "to get the places of profit and power. They used the prejudices of the day, slavery, and sectional interest, to stir up the ignorant masses and then took their chances, with much to gain for themselves if the war was successful or glory and notoriety if it were not successful. The masses always suffer."

———

In 1898, at the age of seventy, Reverend A. Toomer Porter published a memoir. He called it *Led On!* In his book, he returned to the afternoon of Thursday, December 20, 1860, when the throng gathered outside St. Andrew's Hall exulted at the passage of the Ordinance of Secession. The "deed was done, which cost millions and millions of money, tens of thousands of lives, destruction of cities and villages, plantations and farms. . . which made the North rich and the South poor, and has made Southern life one great struggle from this day to this." He recounted how, many years after that December day, he called on Memminger in Charleston, "and I said to him: 'Mr. Memminger, I am now as old as you were when this city and State went wild; why did not you older men take all of us young enthusiasts and hold us down?' 'Oh!,' he replied, 'It was a whirlwind, and all we could do was to try to guide it.'"

The mania for war had been expunged by war. It died with the men and boys who went off to battle and came back to Charleston shorn of limb or not at all. What remained was a flickering, sometimes more than flickering, spirit of defiance. States' rights endured as a political creed, signifying adamant opposition to Washington, often on matters relating to race and civil rights. That spirit was embodied in the bronze statue of Calhoun, cast-iron palmettos at the base, which finally took its place, a few years before the twentieth century began, on the spot once known as Citadel Square. From his lofty perch, feet planted on granite columns, a cloak draped over his shoulders, Calhoun towered over the city. There he stands today.

Acknowledgments

My agent, Andrew Stuart, was the first to suggest that there might be a book to be done about Charleston on the brink of the war—and so began my exploration of this idea. Many people in Charleston contributed to the project, starting with Jesse Bustos-Nelson for all-purpose research. At Special Collections at the College of Charleston's Addlestone Library, I received help from Harlan Greene, Anne Bennett, Sam Stewart, Sharon Bennett, Mary Jo Fairchild, Deb Kingsbury, Myrna Barkoot, Dale Rosengarten, Alyssa Neely, and Rick Zender. At the college's History Department, Robert P. Stockton and Bernard Powers graciously gave of their time.

Also in Charleston, Virginia Ellison, Karen Stokes, Celeste Wiley, Molly Inabinett, and Rick Fulton, all of the South Carolina Historical Society, were of assistance. At the South Carolina Room of Charleston County Public Library, I received help from Marianne Cawley, Lish Thompson, Molly French, Dot Glover, and Linda C. Bennett. Lish also welcomed me to her home to share materials on her distant ancestor, John Townsend. Katie Gray helped out at the Charleston Archive at Charleston County Library, Nicholas M. Butler at that library's Charleston Time Machine (blog), and Jennifer McCormick at the Charleston Museum Archives. Jean R. Hutchinson shared her thoughts, and Cathy Bennington and Joseph Jenrette let me prowl through their home—many years before inhabited by Robert Barnwell Rhett, Sr., and his family. The plates at Jestine's provided sustenance and the pillows at the King Charles Inn rest.

In Columbia, Beth Bilderback at the South Caroliniana Library at the University of South Carolina was of help, as was Steve Tuttle at the South Carolina Department of Archives and History.

Clive Priddle and Jane Robbins Mize at PublicAffairs Books championed this project from the start and provided wise guidance throughout. Also at PublicAffairs, Katie Haigler, Chris Juby, and Shena Redmond were of help. Thanks to Melanie Stafford for her copy editing of the manuscript.

My friends Jon Englund and John Judis offered useful advice on an early draft chapter of the manuscript. My family accompanied me on a visit to Charleston and patiently put up with "Dad" as he holed up in his office to get the job done—thanks to Nargiza, Sam, Deora, and Babula. Jolly was my constant companion. Any mistakes in the book are mine and mine alone.

Notes

Target: Charleston

2   *"that is the problem"*: Stephen W. Sears, ed., *The Civil War Papers of George B. McClellan: Selected Correspondence, 1860–1865* (New York: Da Capo Press, 1992), 178–179.

Chapter One: "Stomach for the Fight"

3   *"Rumors reached this city"*: *Mercury,* October 18, 1859.

3   *"As we anticipated"*: *Mercury,* October 21, 1859.

4   *"The great source of the evil"*: *Mercury,* November 1, 1859.

4   *"The press—the mightiest instrument"*: Robert Barnwell Rhett, Sr., speech, January 30, 1838, quoted in the *Mercury,* August 1, 1860.

5   *"my channel of communication"*: Edmund Ruffin, diary entry, cited in Eric H. Walther, *The Fire-Eaters* (Baton Rouge: Louisiana State University Press, 1992), 253.

5   *took a subscription:* David Herbert Donald, *Lincoln* (New York: Touchstone, 1996), 187.

5   *"all this talk"*: Abraham Lincoln, speech, Galena, Illinois, July 23, 1856, quoted in Glenn M. Linden, *Voices from the Gathering Storm: The Coming of the American Civil War* (Wilmington, DE: Scholarly Resources, 2001), 128.

5   *"red pepperish in head"*: *New York Herald,* reprinted in *Mercury,* August 1, 1860.

6   *"My belief is"*: Robert Barnwell Rhett, Jr., to William Porcher Miles, letter, January 29, 1860, quoted in Harold S. Schultz, *Nationalism and Sectionalism in South Carolina, 1852–1860* (Durham: University of North Carolina Press, 1950), 213.

Chapter Two: "Men, Women, and Rhetts"

8   *"The history of the Negro Race"*: Robert Barnwell Rhett, Sr., "Essay on Slavery," cited in William K. Scarborough, "Propagandists for Secession," *South Carolina Historical Magazine* 112, nos. 3–4 (July–October 2011): 135.

8   *"We are two peoples"*: Robert Barnwell Rhett, Sr., speech, Institute Hall, November 12, 1860, quoted in *Mercury,* November 20, 1860.

8   *"nervous and mercurial"*: Laura A. White, *Robert Barnwell Rhett: Father of Secession* (Gloucester, UK: Peter Smith, 1965), 6.

9   *"The day of open opposition"*: Ibid., 15.

9   *"Robert, the Disunionist"*: Christopher Memminger, pamphlet, quoted in appendix to Henry Dickson Capers, *The Life and Times of C. G. Memminger* (Richmond, VA: Everett Waddey, 1893), 586.

9   *"a vast quantity of cranks"*: Quote in William C. Davis, ed., *A Fire-Eater Remembers: The Confederate Memoir of Robert Barnwell Rhett* (Columbia: University of South Carolina Press, 2000), 133.

9   *"vain, self-conceited"*: US senator George McDuffie of South Carolina to John C. Calhoun, letter, March 10, 1844, cited in White, *Robert Barnwell Rhett,* 70.

10   *"Sir, if a Confederacy"*: Quoted in White, *Robert Barnwell Rhett,* 27.

11   *"My Dear Husband"*: Elizabeth Barnwell Rhett to Robert Barnwell Rhett, Sr., letter, October 17, 1851, quoted in Scarborough, "Propagandists for Secession," 136.

11   *"My heart actually sickens"*: Quoted in Davis, *Fire-Eater Remembers,* 145.

11   *"Too much pleasure"*: Quoted in William C. Davis, *Rhett: The Turbulent Life and Times of a Fire-Eater* (Columbia: University of South Carolina Press, 2001), 146.

12   *"one of you loafers"*: Walther, *Fire-Eaters,* 146.

12   *"Write for the papers"*: Quoted in Davis, *Rhett,* 336.

12   *"gone chicken"*: Quoted in Carl R. Oshaus, *Partisans of the Southern Press: Editorial Spokesmen of the Nineteenth Century* (Lexington: University Press of Kentucky, 1994), 80.

13   *"a thoroughpaced blackguard"*: Account of duel in *Nation* 410 (July 10, 1873).

14   *"We doubt not"*: Ogre sketch of Barny from Tampa, Florida, *Peninsular,* reprinted in *Mercury,* March 27, 1860.

15   *"picturesque development"*: *Mercury,* October 3, 1860.

15   *"the gloom of Destiny"*: *New York Tribune,* reprinted in *Mercury,* January 5, 1860.

16   "*We thus starve*": *Mercury,* March 6, 1860.

16   "*little, antique commercial metropolis*": *Mercury,* March 27, 1860.

16   "*So long as the Union lasts*": Henry Laurens Pinckney, 1858, quoted in Frederic Cople Jaher, *The Urban Establishment* (Urbana: University of Illinois Press, 1982), 342.

17   "*The world, you know*": Quoted in Davis, *Rhett,* 349–350.

Chapter Three: "I Mistrust Our Own People"

19   "*measures for united action*": Resolutions of the South Carolina legislature for Christopher Gustavus Memminger's mission to Virginia, quoted in Capers, *Life and Times of Memminger,* 248.

21   "*I mistrust our own people*": D. H. Hamilton to William Porcher Miles, letter, February 2, 1860, quoted in Steven A. Channing, *Crisis of Fear: Secession in South Carolina* (New York: Norton, 1974), 256.

22   "*personal violence*": *Mercury,* March 15, 1860.

23   "*Buzzard!*": Game described in Edward G. Mason, "A Visit to South Carolina in 1860," *Atlantic Monthly* 53 (February 1884): 243.

23   "*cries and shrieks*": Ibid., 244.

23   "*keeping down the niggers*": Quoted in Ivan D. Steen, "Charleston in the 1850s: As Described by British Travelers," *South Carolina Historical Magazine* 71 (January 1970): 42.

Chapter Four: "Prowling About Us"

24   "*concert of action*": Report on the January 3, 1860, Black Oak meeting in *Mercury,* January 20, 1860.

25   "*our negroes are constantly tempted*": *Mercury,* November 11, 1859.

26   "*ferret out*": *Mercury,* December 13, 1859.

26   "*irresponsible and disorganized*": *Mercury,* December 5, 1859.

26   "*as to whether strangers*": Quoted in Channing, *Crisis of Fear,* 51.

26   "*Negroes are to this country*": Quoted in Hugh Thomas, *The Slave Trade* (New York: Simon and Schuster, 1997), 502.

26   "*some provision should be included*": Quoted in "The Heritage Guide to the Constitution," Fugitive Slave Clause, http://www.heritage.org/constitution/#!/articles/4/essays/124/fugitive-slave-clause.

27   "*solely a black settlement*": Quoted in Maurie D. McInnis, *The Politics of Taste in Antebellum Charleston* (Chapel Hill: University of North Carolina Press, 2005), 21.

27 *the Vesey rebellion*: Documentary history in Robert S. Starobin, ed., *Denmark Vesey: The Slave Conspiracy of 1822* (Englewood Cliffs, NJ: Prentice-Hall, 1970).

27 *"There can be no harm"*: Quoted in David Robertson, *Denmark Vesey* (New York: Vintage Books, 2000), 100.

27 *"Ah! Slavery is a"*: Quoted in Robertson, *Denmark Vesey*, 100.

28 *"rob and plunder"*: John Bachman to Edmund Ruffin, letter, January 18, 1860, quoted in Lester D. Stephens, *Science, Race, and Religion in the American South* (Chapel Hill: University of North Carolina Press, 2000), 216.

28 *"My religion bids me forgive"*: Ibid., 216.

28 *"You are aware"*: Quoted in Schultz, *Nationalism and Sectionalism*, 209.

Chapter Five: "The Charleston Boy"

29 *"at perfect rest"*: Quoted in Capers, *Life and Times of Memminger*, 24.

31 *"you would have thought him"*: Ibid., 24.

31 *"There were others"*: Ibid., 26.

31 *"So accustomed"*: Ibid., 500–501.

31 *"the public mind"*: Quoted in Starobin, *Denmark Vesey*, 170–171.

32 *"social systems"*: Quoted in Laylon W. Jordan, "Schemes of Usefulness: Christopher Gustavus Memminger," in Michael O'Brien and David Moltke-Hansen, eds., *Intellectual Life in Antebellum Charleston* (Knoxville: University of Tennessee Press, 1986), 213.

32 *"patronage and power"*: Jordan, "Schemes of Usefulness," 222.

33 *"guest of the State"*: *Richmond Dispatch,* quoted in Capers, *Life and Times of Memminger,* 245.

33 *"many fire-eaters"*: Petersburg (Virginia) *Express,* quoted in Schultz, *Nationalism and Sectionalism*, 201–202.

33 *"peace and security"*: William Porcher Miles to Christopher Gustavus Memminger, letter, January 10, 1860, quoted in William J. Cooper, *We Have the War upon Us: The Onset of the Civil War, November 1860–April 1861* (New York: Vintage Books, 2013), 20.

33 *"new terms"*: Christopher Gustavus Memminger to William Porcher Miles, letter, January 3, 1860, quoted in Schultz, *Nationalism and Sectionalism*, 201.

34 *"would go on"*: quote and Christopher Gustavus Memminger response in Craig M. Simpson, *A Good Southerner: The Life of Henry A. Wise of Virginia* (Chapel Hill: University of North Carolina Press, 1985), 227.

34 *"attempt to involve her"*: Christopher Gustavus Memminger, speech, Richmond, Virginia, January 19, 1860, quoted in Capers, *Life and Times of Memminger*, 247.

34 *"Dear Sir"*: Quoted in Capers, *Life and Times of Memminger*, 279.

35 *"What a farce"*: D. H. Hamilton to William Porcher Miles, letter, January 23, 1860, quoted in Ollinger Crenshaw, "Christopher G. Memminger's Mission to Virginia, 1860," *Journal of Southern History* 8, no. 3 (August 1942): 347.

35 *"The election of"*: Robert Barnwell Rhett, Jr., to William Porcher Miles, letter, January 29, 1860, quoted in Schultz, *Nationalism and Sectionalism*, 203.

35 *"we further South"*: Christopher Gustavus Memminger to William Porcher Miles, letter, January 30, 1860, cited in William W. Freehling, *The Road to Disunion*, vol. 2: *Secessionists Triumphant, 1854–1861* (New York: Oxford University Press, 2007), 263.

Chapter Six: "Build High the Shaft!"

36 *"It seems to me"*: Marguerite J. Preston, letter, Mary Amarinthia Snowden Papers, South Caroliniana Library, University of South Carolina.

37 *"quite fresh and charming"*: *Mercury*, February 4, 1860.

37 *"There is no"*: *Mercury*, September 10, 1860.

37 *"Somebody says"*: *Mercury*, May 9, 1860.

37 *"intemperance and debaucheries"*: John C. Calhoun, 1807, quoted in Richard Hofstadter, *The American Political Tradition* (New York: Vintage Books, 1974), 92.

38 *"The entire design"*: *Mercury*, June 30, 1860.

38 *"Build high the shaft!"*: Lewis C. Levin lyrics, in Mary Amarinthia Snowden Papers.

38 *"a positive good"*: John C. Calhoun, speech to US Senate, February 6, 1837, quoted on TeachingAmericanHistory.org, http://teachingamericanhistory.org/library/document/slavery-a-positive-good/.

39 *"fetch us a cup"*: Quoted in Idella Bodie, *South Carolina Women: They Dared to Lead* (Orangeburg, SC: Sandlapper, 1978), 72.

39 *"faithful" slaves*: Caroline Howard Gilman, *Recollections of a Southern Matron* (New York: Harper and Brothers, 1838), 81.

39 *"the religious privileges"*: Ibid., 269.

39 *"Those who make"*: Quote in Hofstadter, *American Political Tradition*, 89.

Chapter Seven: To Charleston, "with Three Hundred Kegs of Beer"

41 *"demolition of the party"*: Freehling, *Road to Disunion*, vol. 2, 295.

42   *"enough liquor"*: *Philadelphia Bulletin,* quoted in *Mercury,* April 23, 1860.

42   *"a number of"*: *New York Herald,* quoted in *Mercury,* April 23, 1860.

42   *"rising, like another Venice"*: Douglas W. Bostick, *The Union Is Dissolved! Charleston and Fort Sumter in the Civil War* (Charleston, SC: History Press, 2009), chap. 3.

42   *"The negroes here"*: *New Albany* (Iowa) *Ledger,* May 2, 1860, reprinted in *Mercury,* June 11, 1860.

43   *"miserable affair"*: *Milledgeville* (Georgia) *Union,* April 28, 1860, reprinted in *Mercury,* May 12, 1860.

43   *"ferocious-looking policemen"*: Quoted in Bruce Catton, *The Coming Fury* (New York: Doubleday, 1961), 4.

44   *"great portly fellows"*: Murat Halstead, *Caucuses of 1860: A History of the National Political Conventions of the Current Presidential Campaigns* (Columbus, OH: Follett, Foster, 1860), 6.

45   *"all shades"*: F. C. Adams, *Manuel Pereira; or, the Sovereign Rule of South Carolina* (Washington, DC: Buell and Blanchard, 1853), 32.

46   *"at which slavery"*: Mason, "Visit to South Carolina," 243.

46   *"Play any music"*: Ibid., 244.

47   *"If the South sustains"*: Robert Gourdin to William Porcher Miles, letter, April 4, 1860, quoted in Philip N. Racine, ed., *Gentlemen Merchants: A Charleston Family's Odyssey, 1828–1870* (Knoxville: University of Tennessee Press, 2008), 386.

Chapter Eight: "Screaming Like Panthers"

49   *"Col. Richardson only smiled"*: Davis, *Fire-Eater Remembers,* 11.

50   *"Allowance must be made"*: James M. Johnson to Henry Ellison, letter, April 28, 1860, in Michael P. Johnson and James L. Roark, eds., *No Chariot Let Down: Charleston's Free People of Color on the Eve of the Civil War* (Chapel Hill: University of North Carolina Press, 1984), 57.

50   *"the empire city"*: Fernando Wood, remarks, quoted in *Mercury,* April 25, 1860.

51   *"sweet voice"*: Quoted in Walther, *Fire-Eaters,* 49.

51   *"twenty-seven feet high"*: Ibid., 48.

51   *"The godlike Rhett"*: Quoted in Eric H. Walther, *William Lowndes Yancey and the Coming of the Civil War* (Chapel Hill: University of North Carolina Press, 2006), 126.

52   *"the country's greatest"*: William Lowndes Yancey, speech, quoted in *Mercury,* April 30, 1860.

52 *"This great government"*: George E. Pugh, speech, quoted in *Mercury*, April 30, 1860.

52 *"In an instant"*: Halstead, *Caucuses of 1860*, 50–51.

Chapter Nine: "Fourth of July"

55 *"No man"*: Schultz, *Nationalism and Sectionalism*, 22.

55 *"You are a South"*: Quoted in Freehling, *Road to Disunion*, vol. 2, 306.

55 *"the power, the grandeur"*: James Simons to the *Mercury*, letter, February 27, 1860.

55 *"unwise and impolitic"*: James Lawrence Orr, letter, July 23, 1860, quoted in Schultz, *Nationalism and Sectionalism*, 215.

56 *"stir up the bitter"*: National Democratic Executive Committee, *Proceedings of the Conventions at Charleston and Baltimore* (Washington, DC: Maryland Institute, 1860), 118.

56 *"Mr. President"*: Ibid., 118–120.

56 *"nods and glances"*: Halstead, *Caucuses of 1860*, 73.

56 *"It is right"*: National Democratic Executive Committee, *Proceedings of the Conventions*, 122.

56 *"We wish to meet"*: Ibid., 120–121.

57 *"Mr. President and gentlemen"*: Ibid., 126.

57 *"Down many a manly"*: W.M.B., Editorial Correspondence of the *Washington Constitution*, Charleston, April 30, 1860, quoted in *Mercury*, May 10, 1860.

57 *"three cheers for Yancey"*: St. Andrew's meeting, reported in the *Mercury*, May 1, 1860.

58 *"some want of"*: Robert Barnwell Rhett, Jr., to William Porcher Miles, letter, May 10, 1860, quoted in Walther, *Fire-Eaters*, 75.

58 *"The night was beautiful"*: Halstead, *Caucuses of 1860*, 75.

58 *"The events of yesterday"*: *Mercury*, May 1, 1860.

58 *"There was a Fourth of July"*: Halstead, *Caucuses of 1860*, 76.

59 *"making arrests"*: James M. Johnson to Henry Ellison, letter, April 24, 1860, in Johnson and Roark, *No Chariot Let Down*, 55.

59 *"There seems to be a disturbance"*: Henry William Ravenel, diary entry, May 14, 1860, in Arney Robinson Childs, ed., *The Private Journal of Henry William Ravenel, 1859–1887* (Columbia: University of South Carolina Press, 1947), 17.

Chapter Ten: "I Foresee Nothing but Disaster"

61 *"You know how much"*: James Louis Petigru to Susan Petigru King, letter, November 28, 1856, in James Petigru Carson, *Life, Letters, and Speeches of James Louis Petigru, the Union Man of South Carolina* (Washington, DC: H. L. and J. B. McQueen, 1920), 318.

61 *"nullification has done its work"*: James Louis Petigru to Hugh S. Legaré, letter, July 15, 1833, in Carson, *Life, Letters, and Speeches of Petigru*, 125.

62 *"nigger church"*: Walter J. Fraser, Jr., *Charleston! Charleston! The History of a Southern City* (Columbia: University of South Carolina Press, 1989), 228.

62 *"How can you be such"*: Carson, *Life, Letters, and Speeches of Petigru*, 280.

62 *"bitterness of civil strife"*: James Louis Petigru, "Oration, Delivered on the Third Anniversary of the South Carolina Historical Society," May 27, 1858, Hibernian Hall, quoted in Carson, *Life, Letters, and Speeches of Petigru*, 326–337.

62 *"My unhappy fellow-citizens"*: Mason, "Visit to South Carolina," 245.

62 *"A venerable figure"*: Ibid., 245.

Chapter Eleven: "They Would Have Been Mobbed"

64 *"longed to pull"*: James Louis Petigru to Benjamin Franklin Perry, letter, December 8, 1860, in William H. Pease and Jane H. Pease, *James Louis Petigru: Southern Conservative, Southern Dissenter* (Columbia: University of South Carolina Press, 2002), 155.

64 *"Let them remain"*: Benjamin Franklin Perry, speech, in Perry, *In Memoriam: Benjamin Franklin Perry, Ex-Governor of South Carolina* (Greenville, SC: Greenville Daily News Presses, 1887), 9.

65 *"By nature I am passionate"*: Benjamin Franklin Perry, journal entry, July 9, 1837, in Lillian Adele Kibler, *Benjamin F. Perry: South Carolina Unionist* (Durham, NC: Duke University Press, 1946), 182.

65 *"I stand before you"*: Kibler, *Benjamin F. Perry*, 6.

65 *"I love to think"*: Ibid., 4–5.

65 *"The President will be nominated"*: Halstead, *Caucuses of 1860*, 61.

66 *"The People of the South"*: *Mercury*, May 2, 1860.

66 *"propriety"*: *Mercury*, May 2, 1860.

67 *"a poisonous reptile"*: Quoted in John M. Belohlavek, *Broken Glass: Caleb Cushing and the Shattering of the Union Storm* (Kent, OH: Kent State University Press, 2005), 309.

67 *"the calls for baggage"*: Halstead, *Caucuses of 1860*, 96.

67 *"There were many"*: Ibid., 101.

68 *"Will Old Virginia nestle"*: John Bachman to Edmund Ruffin, letter, May 23, 1860, quoted in Peter McCandless, "The Political Evolution of John Bachman from New York Yankee to South Carolina Secessionist," *South Carolina Historical Magazine* 108, no. 1 (January 2007): 29.

68 *"outside pressure in Charleston"*: Benjamin Franklin Perry, letter, May 15, 1860, printed in *Mercury*, May 19, 1860.

68 *"Their spirit rose"*: Robert Barnwell Rhett, Jr., to William Porcher Miles, letter, May 12, 1860, quoted in Channing, *Crisis of Fear*, 207.

68 *"perfect order"*: *Mercury*, May 1, 1860.

Chapter Twelve: "Black as a Charcoal"

70 *"It is reported that"*: *Mercury*, May 19, 1860.

71 *"It is an irrepressible conflict"*: William Henry Seward, speech, Rochester, New York, October 25, 1958, quoted on New York History Net, http://www.nyhistory.com/central/conflict.htm.

71 *"Then welcome be it"*: *Mercury*, May 19, 1860.

71 *"the power of"*: *Mercury*, April 18, 1860.

71 *"a little Illinois lawyer"*: Quoted in Dorothy Wickenden, "Union Man," *New Yorker*, October 1, 2012.

72 *"lull us asleep"*: John Bachman to Edmund Ruffin, letter, May 23, 1860, quoted in Channing, *Crisis of Fear*, 230.

72 *"Mr. Lincoln is a native"*: *Mercury*, May 19, 1860.

72 *"a refined, intelligent"*: *Mercury*, May 31, 1860.

73 *"He is a Northern man"*: *Mercury*, January 10, 1860.

73 *"He was not a pretty man"*: Billy Herndon, quoted in Donald, *Lincoln*, 115.

73 *"lighting up every homely feature"*: Charles Carleton Coffin, quoted in Allen Thorndike Rice, ed., *Reminiscences of Abraham Lincoln by Distinguished Men of His Time* (New York: Harper and Brothers, 1909), 173.

73 *"and a horrid-looking wretch"*: *Mercury*, June 7, 1860.

73 *"notorious buccaneer"*: Anonymous, letter, June 28, 1860, printed in *Mercury*, July 3, 1860.

74 *"Old Abe on the Battle Field"*: (Toledo, Ohio) *Times*, reprinted in the *Mercury*, June 26, 1860.

74 *"I had a good many"*: Roy B. Basler, ed., *The Collected Works of Abraham Lincoln*, vol. 1 (New Brunswick, NJ: Rutgers University Press, 1953), 510.

75   *"given him as"*: (New Hampshire) *Patriot*, reprinted in *Mercury*, June 26, 1860.

75   *"A. Lincoln appears to be"*: *Washington Constitution*, reprinted in *Mercury*, May 31, 1860.

76   *"the soul of a tarantula"*: *Mercury*, June 7, 1860.

76   *"We have as a candidate"*: (Springfield, Massachusetts) *Republican*, reprinted in *Mercury*, June 2, 1860.

76   *"to circulate W. L. Garrison's"*: Abraham Lincoln to John J. Crittenden, letter, December 22, 1859, in Gilbert A. Tracy, ed., *Uncollected Letters of Abraham Lincoln* (Boston: Houghton Mifflin, 1917), 121.

76   *"a few words"*: Abraham Lincoln, speech, February 27, 1860, Cooper Union, Brooklyn, New York, quoted in John G. Nicolay and John Hay, *Abraham Lincoln Complete Works*, vol. 1 (New York: Century, 1920), 605–611.

77   *"my beau ideal"*: Quoted in Carl Sandburg, *Abraham Lincoln: The Prairie Years and the War Years* (New York: Harcourt, 1939), 105.

77   *"slave hound"*: Donald, *Lincoln*, 137.

78   *"Charleston hangs fire"*: Abraham Lincoln to Lyman Trumbull, letter, April 29, 1860, quoted in Basler, *Collected Works of Abraham Lincoln*, vol. 4, 45.

Chapter Thirteen: "Do Not Blink"

79   *"our grand old man"*: I. Jenkins Mikell, *Rumblings of the Chariot Wheels* (Columbia, SC: State Company, 1923), 169.

80   *"That stars might fall"*: R. I. Breckinridge, quoted in Harriette Kershaw Leiding, *Historic Houses of South Carolina* (Philadelphia, PA: J. B. Lippincott, 1921), 223.

81   *"Knight of the Golden Crest"*: Leiding, *Historic Houses of South Carolina*, 223.

81   *"a dozen little picaninnies"*: Mikell, *Rumblings*, 169–177.

81   *"taste and skill"*: "Editorial Miscellany," *De Bow's Review* 28 (1860): 123.

82   *"We go out"*: Quote and depiction of Oqui's garden in Nell S. Graydon, *Tales of Edisto* (Orangeburg, SC: Sandlapper, 2000), 17.

82   *The first census*: Cited in Charles Spencer, *Edisto Island 1663 to 1860: Wild Eden to Cotton Aristocracy* (Charleston, SC: History Press, 2008), 78.

82   *The annual growing cycle*: Ibid., 73.

83   *brought to market*: Ibid., 94.

83   *$1 per pound*: Clara Childs Puckette, *Edisto: A Sea Island Principality* (Barnsley, UK: Seaforth, 1997), 189.

83   *A Reply:* John Townsend, *What Is the Character of the Late Tariff Law? . . . A Reply* (Charleston, SC: A. E. Miller, 1828).

84   *"painful anxiety":* John Townsend, to John C. Calhoun, letter, December 22, 1845, quoted in Clyde N. Wilson, *The Papers of John C. Calhoun,* vol. 22 (Columbia: University of South Carolina Press, 1995), 353–359.

84   *"Venice is":* Quoted in William W. Freehling, *The Road to Disunion,* vol. 1, *Secessionists at Bay, 1776–1854* (New York: Oxford University Press, 1990), 530.

84   *"defunct":* John Townsend, *Reply of Mr. Townsend in Defense of His Public Conduct* (Charleston, SC: Walker, Evans, 1858), 22.

85   *"can hope for distinction":* Ibid., appendix, 30, first published in *Charleston Standard,* September 22, 1854.

86   *"The causes which led":* John Townsend, speech, reprinted in *Mercury* (in two installments), June 13 and June 14, 1860.

Chapter Fourteen: "To Set Us Free"

90   *"How uncertain our future":* Mercury, July 6, 1860.

91   *"Southern people":* Mercury, July 10, 1860.

92   *"Everything that a man eats":* Robert Barnwell Rhett, Sr., speech, printed in *Mercury,* July 13, 1860.

93   *"Mr. Rhett I hold":* Childs, diary entry, June 1, 1860, quoted in *Private Journal of Ravenel,* 20.

93   *"so bloody, so terrible":* Quoted in Walther, *Fire-Eaters,* 287.

93   *"Lincoln and his 'irrepressible conflict'":* William Porcher Miles, speech, printed in *Mercury,* July 14, 1860.

94   *"damned Lincoln spy":* Quoted in J. Cutler Andrews, *The North Reports the Civil War* (Pittsburgh, PA: University of Pittsburgh Press, 1955), 16.

95   *"far from being":* Abner Doubleday, *Reminiscences of Forts Sumter and Moultrie in 1860–1861* (Charleston, SC: Nautical and Aviation Publishing Company of America, 1998), 14.

95   *"The contingency":* Ibid., 15.

95   *"violent speeches to the mob":* Ibid., 16.

95   *"I shall never have":* JoAnne Smith Bartlett, *Abner Doubleday: His Life and Times* (Bloomington, IL: Xlibris, 2009), 92.

96   *"were enjoying the sweets":* Doubleday, *Reminiscences,* 16.

96   *"The negroes overheard":* Ibid., 26.

Chapter Fifteen: "Hunted Down"

97   *tailor James M. Johnson:* Johnson and Roark, *No Chariot Let Down*; Michael
      P. Johnson and James L. Roark, *Black Masters: A Free Family of Color in the
      Old South* (New York: Norton, 1984).

98   *"free colored man":* Christopher Gustavus Memminger, speech, South Caro-
      lina legislature, printed in (Charleston) *Courier,* December 16, 1859, quoted
      in Johnson and Roark, *No Chariot Let Down,* 43–44.

99   *"good character":* Johnson and Roark, *No Chariot Let Down,* 87.

99   *"a good credit risk":* Jeffrey G. Strickland, "Ethnicity and Race in the Urban
      South: German Immigrants and African Americans in Charleston South
      Carolina During Reconstruction," PhD diss., Florida State University Col-
      lege of Arts and Sciences, 2003, 62.

99   *"They have not":* James M. Johnson to Henry Ellison, letter, August 20, 1860,
      quoted in Johnson and Roark, *No Chariot Let Down,* 85–86.

101   *"friend of the laboring":* Mercury, October 8, 1860.

101   *"higher class":* Johnson to Ellison, letter, August 20, 1860, 85.

101   *"and defied":* James M. Johnson to Henry Ellison, letter, August 28, 1860, in
      Johnson and Roark, *No Chariot Let Down,* 101.

102   *"In some parts":* "Constitution and Bylaws of the American Republican As-
      sociation of Charleston and the Address to All American Citizens, of the
      Parishes of St. Philip's and St. Michael's" (Charleston, SC: Miller and Browne,
      1844), 10.

102   *"to build up":* (Charleston) *Courier,* August 25, 1860, quoted in Johnson and
      Roark, *Black Masters,* 267.

103   *"It is vain":* Johnson to Ellison, letter, August 28, 1860, 101.

103   *"There are cases":* Johnson to Ellison, letter, August 20, 1860, 85.

104   *"Those who are now hunted":* Johnson and Roark, *No Chariot Let Down,*
      85.

104   *"Charleston, 1860":* Cited in Harlan Greene and Harry S. Hutchins, Jr., with
      Brian E. Hutchins, *Slave Badges and the Slave-Hire System in Charleston,
      South Carolina, 1783–1865* (Jefferson, NC: McFarland, 2004), 153.

104   *"I have seen":* Charley Johnson to Henry Ellison, letter, September 16, 1860,
      in Johnson and Roark, *No Chariot Let Down,* 119.

104   *"Pride of race":* James Redpath, *A Guide to Hayti,* quoted in Johnson and
      Roark, *No Chariot Let Down,* 144.

Chapter Sixteen: The Gentleman Revolutionary

106 *"I am in despair"*: Robert Gourdin to William Porcher Miles, letter, August 20, 1860, quoted in Racine, *Gentlemen Merchants*, 390.

107 *"May the smoke"*: *Boston Gazette*, June 9, 1860, reprinted in *Mercury*, June 15, 1860.

107 *"accessory liquids"*: *Mercury*, June 25, 1860.

108 *"I don't think"*: Carson, *Life, Letters, and Speeches of Petigru*, 356.

109 *"all of us Huguenots"*: Charles Izard Manigault to Alfred Huger, in Michael O'Brien, *Intellectual Life and the American South* (Chapel Hill: University of North Carolina Press, 2010), 290.

110 *"He advises me"*: Robert Gourdin to Anna Gourdin Young, letter, August 30, 1835, quoted in Racine, *Gentlemen Merchants*, 19.

110 *"My situation"*: Robert Gourdin to Henry Gourdin, letter, August 31, 1835, quoted in Racine, *Gentlemen Merchants*, 20.

110 *"to sacrifice the South"*: Thomas Cooper, speech, July 2, 1827, quoted in Songho Ha, *The Rise and Fall of the American System: Nationalism and the Development of the American Economy, 1790–1837* (London: Routledge, 2016), 103.

110 *"I was a nullifier"*: *Mercury*, December 8, 1860.

110 *"Under what evil stars"*: Robert Gourdin to Henry Gourdin, letter, September 23, 1835, quoted in Racine, *Gentlemen Merchants*, 21–22.

111 *"Il faut coupe"*: Charles Green to Robert Gourdin, letter, December 10, 1860, quoted in Racine, *Gentlemen Merchants*, 409, reminding Gourdin he had said this "many years ago."

111 *"You have always"*: D. H. Hamilton to Robert Gourdin, letter, November 26, 1860, quoted in Racine, *Gentlemen Merchants*, 401.

111 *"I am indeed sorry"*: Robert Gourdin to Henry Gourdin, letter, August 31, 1835, 20.

112 *"regret of his friends"*: Louis Gourdin Young to Robert Gourdin, letter, September 23, 1856, quoted in Racine, *Gentlemen Merchants*, 300.

112 *"to sweep away"*: Quoted in Jordan, "Schemes of Usefulness," 226.

112 *"as though it were situated"*: Anna Gourdin Young to Robert Gourdin, letter, October 12, 1860, quoted in Racine, *Gentlemen Merchants*, 395.

113 *"It will produce divisions"*: Robert Gourdin to William Porcher Miles, letter, November 28, 1856, quoted in Racine, *Gentlemen Merchants*, 304.

Chapter Seventeen: Secession Inc.

114 *"The Society"*: *Mercury,* September 20, 1860.

114 *"informal meeting"*: November 19, 1860, letter from Robert Gourdin to Langdon Cheves, Jr., in Racine, *Gentlemen Merchants,* 400.

115 *"an association"*: William Hammond, Jr., to James Henry Hammond, letter, October 19, 1860, quoted in May Spencer Ringold, "Robert Newman Gourdin and the '1860 Association,'" *Georgia Historical Quarterly* 55, no. 4 (Winter 1971): 502.

117 *"the only man"*: William Aikens, Jr., comment mentioned in William Henry Trescot to William Porcher Miles, letter, February 22, 1860, quoted in Channing, *Crisis of Fear,* 187.

118 *"in the hands"*: Tennent to M. L. Bonham, letter, October 1860, quoted in Freehling, *Road to Disunion,* vol. 2, 391, and Channing, *Crisis of Fear,* 262.

119 *"leading men"*: Robert Gourdin to Langdon Cheves, Jr., letter, November 19, 1860, quoted in Racine, *Gentlemen Merchants,* 400.

119 *"I question very much"*: E. C. Anderson to Robert Gourdin, letter, September 30, 1860, quoted in Racine, *Gentlemen Merchants,* 392–393.

120 *"In Charleston, S.C."*: (Atlanta) *American,* reprinted in *Mercury,* October 6, 1860, along with the response.

Chapter Eighteen: "A Large and Coarse Man"

121 *"Anney . . . small"*: *Mercury,* June 11, 1860.

122 *"rather dogmatic clerk"*: Samuel Wylie Crawford, *The Genesis of the Civil War: The Story of Sumter, 1860–1861* (New York: Charles L. Webster, 1887), vi.

122 *"I was alone"*: Caroline Bottsford, "A Woman's Story," *New York Tribune,* March 22, 1861.

124 *"profound indignation"*: Doubleday, *Reminiscences,* 26.

Chapter Nineteen: "Our Lives, Our Fortunes . . . "

127 *"solemnly pledge"*: David C. Keehn, *Knights of the Golden Circle: Secret Empire, Southern Secession, Civil War* (Baton Rouge: Louisiana State University Press, 2013), 78.

127 *"Let every son"*: *Mercury,* October 15, 1860.

127 *"There's many"*: Adam Goodheart, "Female Partisans," *New York Times, Disunion* series no. 18, April 18, 2011.

127 *"A gentleman"*: Doubleday, *Reminiscences,* 27–28.

127   *"The South knows"*: "Cockades," *New York Tribune*, reprinted in *Mercury*, October 22, 1860.

128   *"from their very nature"*: Doubleday, *Reminiscences*, 27.

128   *"mongrel tyrants"*: Channing, *Crisis of Fear*, 270.

128   *"to march"*: Keehn, *Knights of the Golden Circle*, 78.

128   *"It was easy to raise"*: Doubleday, *Reminiscences*, 27.

128   *"Strike the Blow"*: *Mercury*, October 4, 1860.

128   *"vote for an immediate"*: *Mercury*, September 27, 1860.

129   *"as a good omen"*: *Mercury*, October 12, 1860.

129   *"My surprise"*: Anna Gourdin Young to Robert Gourdin, letter, October 12, 1860, quoted in Racine, *Gentlemen Merchants*, 395.

129   *"I regret that"*: Allan MacFarlan to Robert Gourdin, letter, October 18, 1860, quoted in Racine, *Gentlemen Merchants*, 396–397.

Chapter Twenty: "Is It for Manly Resistance?"

131   *"MEN OF THE SOUTH"*: John Townsend and the 1860 Association, *The South Alone, Should Govern the South* (Charleston, SC: Evans and Cogswell, 1860).

132   *"The people take it"*: *Montgomery Mail*, reprinted in *Mercury*, October 29, 1860.

132   *"his cultivated intellect"*: *Mercury*, November 1, 1860.

132   *"undefined dread"*: John Townsend, Jr., to M. L. Bonham, letter, October 16, 1860, quoted in Freehling, *Road to Disunion*, vol. 2, 389.

132   *"Unmanly fears"*: John Townsend, Jr., address to Edisto Island Vigilant Association, October 29, 1860, published by the 1860 Association as *The Doom of Slavery in the Union: Its Safety out of It* (Charleston, SC: Evans and Cogswell, 1860).

133   *"the enormous expenses"*: Doubleday, *Reminiscences*, 26–27.

134   *"The enthusiasm"*: Ibid., 26.

134   *"obliterated forever"*: *Mercury*, October 25, 1860.

134   *"Why do you wish"*: *New York Tribune*, November 7, 1860, reprinted in *Mercury*, November 10, 1860.

134   *"our banks"*: *Mercury*, October 27, 1860.

135   *"Cotton is specie"*: *Mercury*, October 25, 1860.

135   *"Great jobbing houses"*: *Mercury*, October 27, 1860.

Chapter Twenty-One: "God Have Mercy on My Country"

137   *"the threatening aspect"*: Crawford, *Genesis of the Civil War*, 19.

137   *"If he is elected"*: William Lee Trenholm to Julian Mitchell, letter, October 29, 1860, Mitchell Family Papers, South Carolina Historical Society.

138   *"renowned"*: *Mercury,* October 30, 1860.

138   *"It is well known"*: Anonymous, letter, *Courier,* October 29, 1860, quoted in David Detzer, *Allegiance: Fort Sumter, Charleston, and the Beginning of the Civil War* (New York: Harcourt Brace, 2001), 10.

138   *"We are rejoiced"*: *Mercury,* November 1, 1860.

138   *"the beau ideal"*: *Mercury,* October 15, 1860.

139   *"The issue before"*: *Mercury,* November 3, 1860.

139   *"there will be"*: *Mercury,* October 17, 1860.

140   *"November had arrived"*: Doubleday, *Reminiscences,* 28.

140   *"I would like to hear"*: *Mercury,* November 5, 1860.

140   *"I hope Lincoln"*: *Mercury,* November 6, 1860.

140   *"If Lincoln Is Elected"*: *Courier,* cited in Marshall W. Fishwick, *Illustrious Americans: Clara Barton* (New York: Silver, Burdett, 1967), 26.

141   *"My own countrymen"*: James Louis Petigru to Edward Everett, letter, October 28, 1860, quoted in Carson, *Life, Letters, and Speeches of Petigru,* 360.

141   *"I don't think"*: James Louis Petigru to Jane Petigru North, letter, November 5, 1860, quoted in Carson, *Life, Letters, and Speeches of Petigru,* 361.

Chapter Twenty-Two: "Hurra for Lincoln"

142   *"anxious expectants"*: *Mercury,* November 8, 1860.

143   *"hush the sound"*: Quoted in Walther, *Fire-Eaters,* 213.

143   *"Hurra for Lincoln!"*: Doubleday, *Reminiscences,* 33.

144   *"the Disunionists were wild"*: Ibid., 32.

145   *"but the events"*: *Mercury,* November 8, 1860.

145   *"The business"*: Ibid.

Chapter Twenty-Three: The Judge

146   *"The elevation"*: Henry Edward Young to Robert Gourdin, letter, September 18, 1856, quoted in Racine, *Gentlemen Merchants,* 297.

148   *"Those wounds"*: A. G. Magrath, "An Address Delivered in the Cathedral of St. Finbar, Before the Hibernian Society, the St. Patrick Benevolent Society, and the Irish Volunteers," March 17, 1837 (Charleston, SC: Thomas J. Eccles), 18.

149   *"Many Citizens"*: A. G. Magrath, cited as the anonymous letter writer in Erskine Clarke, *Wrestlin' Jacob: A Portrait of Religion in Antebellum Georgia and the Carolina Low Country* (Tuscaloosa: University of Alabama Press, 1999), 146.

149   *"They will owe"*: *Mercury,* July 23, 1847.

150   *"In the political history"*: A. G. Magrath, speech, printed in *Mercury,* November 8, 1860.

150   *"few dry eyes"*: *Courier,* November 12, 1860, quoted in Freehling, *Road to Disunion,* vol. 2, 399.

151   *"protection"*: Alfred Huger to Joseph Holt, letter, November 12, 1860, quoted in Freehling, *Road to Disunion,* vol. 2, 400.

151   *"the interests"*: *Mercury,* November 8, 1860.

151   *"Tremendous cheers"*: *New York Tribune,* November 10, 1860.

151   *"its rattle sprung"*: *Mercury,* November 8, 1860.

152   *profound shock*: In an interview in 1883, Black said of A. G. Magrath's abrupt resignation, "The act of that man caused more anxiety to Mr. Buchanan than any other event that occurred" in the months before the war "except Anderson's movement from Moultrie to Sumter." Crawford, *Genesis of the Civil War,* 16.

152   *demanding a halt*: Doubleday, *Reminiscences,* 30.

152   *"the mob"*: Ibid., 31.

153   *"All the stars"*: *Mercury,* November 8, 1860.

153   *"Mercury stands vindicated"*: Ibid.

153   *"their late ex-Judge"*: Ibid.

153   *"a citizen of South Carolina"*: Ibid.

Chapter Twenty-Four: "Will Not Delay Cool the Ardor?"

155   *"The tea has been thrown overboard"*: *Mercury,* November 8, 1860.

156   *"boys of the city"*: Edmund Ruffin, diary entry, November 9, 1860, 488.

156   *"to add a star"*: *Mercury,* November 9, 1860.

156   *"'Brown' us all"*: Mary Boykin Miller Chesnut, *A Diary from Dixie* (New York: Appleton, 1906), 1.

156   *"fear that the people"*: Ruffin, November 9, 1860, 488.

157   *"to prevent any irregular"*: Doubleday, *Reminiscences,* 43.

157   *"very tired"*: Anthony Toomer Porter, *Led On! Step by Step, Scenes from Clerical, Military, Educational, and Plantation Life in the South, 1828–1898* (New York: G. P. Putnam's Sons, 1898), 73.

158   *"a second nullification madness"*: Porter, *Led On!,* 115–116.

158   *"The time for deliberation"*: Ibid., 119.

158   *"await the action"*: *Mercury,* November 12, 1860.

158   *"The city which is most exposed"*: Anthony Toomer Porter to James Henry Hammond, letter, November 11, 1860, quoted in Channing, *Crisis of Fear,* 251.

159 *"the proposition to secede"*: Jefferson Davis to Robert Barnwell Rhett, Jr., letter, November 10, 1860, in Jefferson Davis Papers, Rice University, https://jeffersondavis.rice.edu/Content.aspx?id=85.

159 *"time for re-action"*: Robert Barnwell Rhett, Sr., to the editor of the *Mercury*, draft letter, November 10, 1860, quoted in Channing, *Crisis of Fear*, 248–249.

159 *"the consummation"*: *Mercury*, November 10, 1860.

160 *"I am tired"*: Francis Stebbins Bartow, speech, in Lucian Lamar Knight, *Reminiscences of Famous Georgians*, vol. 2 (Atlanta, GA: Franklin-Turner, 1908), 587.

160 *"The greatest meeting"*: *Courier*, November 10, 1860, quoted in Charles Edward Cauthen, *South Carolina Goes to War, 1860–1865* (Columbia: University of South Carolina Press, 2005), 58.

160 *"The gentlemen from Savannah"*: C. W. Howard to Robert Gourdin, letter, December 3, 1860, quoted in Racine, *Gentlemen Merchants*, 404–405.

Chapter Twenty-Five: "To Arms, Citizens!"

162 *"Up, up!"*: *Mercury*, November 10, 1860.

162 *"First President"*: Abraham Lincoln, diary entry, November 10, 1860, quoted in Stephen A. Wynalda, ed., *366 Days in Abraham Lincoln's Presidency: The Private, Political, and Military Decisions of America's Greatest President* (New York: Skyhorse, 2010).

163 *suspicious fires*: Detzer, *Allegiance*, 10.

163 *"For distribution amongst"*: Boston Athenaeum Digital Collections, http://cdm.bostonathenaeum.org/cdm/ref/collection/p16057coll14/id/91274.

163 *"We have fallen"*: James Louis Petigru to Jane Petigru North, letter, November 13, 1860, quoted in Carson, *Life, Letters, and Speeches of Petigru*, 361.

164 *"Disunionists, per se"*: Lincoln prepared these remarks for Lyman Trumbell to deliver on November 20, 1860, in Springfield, Illinois. Tracy, *Uncollected Letters of Abraham Lincoln*, 168.

164 *"We shall be envied"*: James Louis Petigru to Susan Petigru King, letter, November 10, 1860, quoted in Carson, *Life, Letters, and Speeches of Petigru*, 361.

164 *"My old friend"*: James Louis Petigru to Jane Petigru North, letter, December 6, 1860, quoted in Carson, *Life, Letters, and Speeches of Petigru*, 363.

165 *"in this land"*: Myer Moses, speech, Hebrew Orphan Society, Charleston, October 15, 1806, quoted in Theodore Rosengarten and Dale Rosengarten, eds., *A Portion of the People: Three Hundred Years of Southern Jewish Life* (Columbia: University of South Carolina Press, 2002), 59.

165 *"nine vociferous cheers"*: Henry T. Peake, letter, *Mercury,* November 17, 1860.

166 *"I thought Magrath"*: James Henry Hammond to Marcus C. Hammond, letter, November 12, 1860, quoted in Detzer, *Allegiance,* 14–15.

166 *"We shall soon"*: James Henry Hammond, quoted in Goodheart, "Female Partisans."

166 *"Southern Rights"*: *Courier,* November 12, 1860.

166 *"The long weary night"*: Robert Barnwell Rhett, Sr., speech, quoted in Benson J. Lossing, *Pictorial History of the Civil War,* vol. 1 (Mansfield, OH: Estill, 1866), 96.

167 *"They painted the future"*: Doubleday, *Reminiscences,* 45–46.

167 *"numbers of men"*: Mrs. C. L. Pettigrew to C. L. Pettigrew, letter, November 26, 1860, Pettigrew Family Papers, Southern Historical Collection, University of North Carolina Libraries.

167 *"I am happy to say"*: William Lee Trenholm to Julian Mitchell, letter, November 15, 1860, Mitchell Family Papers, South Carolina Historical Society.

168 *"I am myself"*: Anonymous, letter, *Mercury,* November 17, 1860.

Chapter Twenty-Six: The Gospel of Secession

170 *"to implore the direction"*: Thomas Smyth, *The Sin and the Curse* (Charleston, SC: Evans and Cogswell, 1860), title page.

170 *"has warned us"*: William Owen Prentiss, sermon, quoted in Mitchell Snay, *Gospel of Disunion: Religion and Separatism in the Antebellum South* (Chapel Hill: University of North Carolina Press, 1993), 170–171.

171 *"History assures us"*: William Owen Prentiss, sermon, quoted in Johnson and Roark, *No Chariot Let Down,* 141.

171 *"One of its distinguishing"*: Ibid., 133.

171 *"the infidel, atheistic"*: Smyth, "The Sin and the Curse," 13.

171 *"perfect stranger"*: Thomas Smyth, *Autobiographical Notes, Letters, and Reflections* (Charleston, SC: Walker, Evans, and Cogswell, 1914), 61.

171 *"I find that a few years"*: Unidentified to Thomas Smyth, letter, n.d., in David T. Gleeson and Brendan J. Buttimer, "'We Are Irish Everywhere': Irish Immigrant Networks in Charleston, South Carolina, and Savannah, Georgia," in Enda Delaney and Donald M. MacRaild, eds., *Irish Migration, Networks, and Ethnic Identities Since 1750* (London: Routledge, 2007), 46.

172 *"Is it a fact"*: David Magie to Thomas Smyth, letter, December 19, 1860, in Smyth, *Autobiographical Notes,* 562.

172 *"It is permitted us"*: William C. Dana, sermon, printed in *Mercury,* December 1, 1860.

172 "*I will not disgrace*": Quoted in McCandless, "Political Evolution of John Bachman," 24.

172 "*our cause is just*": Ibid., 29.

173 "*My mind is not*": *Courier*, obituary, February 25, 1874.

173 "*as a great turnout*": Jacob Schirmer, diary entry, November 22, 1860, Alfred Schirmer Papers, South Carolina Historical Society, quoted in Detzer, *Allegiance*, 13.

173 "*awful foreboding*": James Louis Petigru to Jane Petigru North, letter, November 20, 1860, quoted in Carson, *Life, Letters, and Speeches of Petigru*, 362.

173 "*noisy demonstrations*": Doubleday, *Reminiscences*, 19.

173 "*prominent citizens*": Crawford, *Genesis of the Civil War*, 64.

173 "*The approaching battle*": Doubleday, *Reminiscences*, 42.

174 "*took turns in*": Ibid., 50.

174 "*The spattering of*": Ibid., 40.

174 "*Good-bye, Yankee Doodle*": November 29, 1860, entry, "Fort Moultrie 1809–1898: A General Timeline," Battlefields in Motion, http://moultrie.battlefields inmotion.com/General-Timeline.html.

175 "*all who are true*": *Courier* advertisement, November 20, 1860, reprinted in Andrea Mehrlander, *The Germans of Charleston, Richmond, and New Orleans During the Civil War Period, 1850–1870* (Berlin: de Gruyter, 2011), 172.

175 "*private and confidential*": D. H. Hamilton to Robert Gourdin, letter, November 26, 1860, quoted in Racine, *Gentlemen Merchants*, 401.

175 "*temporizing ticket*": Ibid., 401.

Chapter Twenty-Seven: Catch Me If You Can

176 "*tarred and feathered*": *New York Tribune*, March 22, 1861.

177 "*to ensure a more natural*": George Ripley, letter on Brook Farm, 1840, American Transcendentalism Web, http://transcendentalism-legacy.tamu.edu/ideas/letter.html#ripley2.

177 "*a man of rough*": Walt Whitman, cited in Louis M. Starr, *Bohemian Brigade: Civil War Newsmen in Action* (New York: Knopf, 1954), 15.

177 "*a being to whom*": Starr, *Bohemian Brigade*, 15.

177 "*it wouldn't surprise me*": Ibid., 13.

177 "*a subtle and utterly*": Ibid., 21.

178 "*There is much financial*": Charles D. Brigham, letter, *New York Tribune*, December 3, 1860.

178 "*All kinds of property*": Charles D. Brigham, letter, December 7, 1860, printed in *New York Tribune*, December 13, 1860.

178 *"flags and banners"*: New York Tribune, December 3, 1860.

178 *"or indeed almost"*: New York Tribune, December 13, 1860.

178 *"The supposed or real"*: Ibid.

179 *"an abolition correspondent"*: Doubleday, Reminiscences, 25–26.

180 *"he would come"*: Starr, Bohemian Brigade, 1.

180 *"Lincoln sheet"*: Andrews, North Reports the Civil War, 14–15.

180 *"Mr. Gunn brings"*: Courier, January 1861.

180 *"a square-set man"*: Thomas Butler Gunn diaries, vol. 17, Missouri History Museum, 2.

181 *"to offer his services"*: Ibid., 18–23.

181 *"administer tar and feathers"*: Starr, Bohemian Brigade, 22.

181 *"If the Mercury is still"*: New York Tribune, December 13, 1860.

Chapter Twenty-Eight: "I Have, Doubtless, Many Faults"

182 *"All are galloping"*: James Louis Petigru to Jane Petigru North, December 6, 1860, quoted in Carson, Life, Letters, and Speeches of Petigru, 363.

182 *"I saw a melee"*: James M. Johnson to Henry Ellison, letter, December 7, 1860, in Johnson and Roark, No Chariot Let Down, 132.

183 *"Shall we kneel"*: (Greenville) Southern Enterprise, December 6, 1860, quoted in Kibler, Benjamin F. Perry, 342.

183 *"The time for action"*: November 22, 1860, gathering, quoted on Signs of History, http://www.waymarking.com/waymarks/WMMD3D_Site_of_Speeches_Secession_Hill_Abbeville_SC.

183 *"I am unalterably opposed"*: John Townsend, statement, December 4, 1860, printed in Mercury, December 8, 1860.

184 *"should leave this Union"*: Robert Gourdin, statement, December 4, 1860, printed in Mercury, December 8, 1860.

184 *"It is a fit"*: William Porcher Miles to Robert Gourdin, letter, December 10, 1860, quoted in Racine, Gentlemen Merchants, 410.

184 *"Upon your election"*: Charles Green to Robert Gourdin, letter, December 10, 1860, quoted in Racine, Gentlemen Merchants, 409.

184 *"immediate and permanent"*: Cauthen, South Carolina Goes to War, 65–66.

184 *"nothing more"*: Mercury, December 1, 1860.

185 *"I have, doubtless"*: Mercury, December 8, 1860.

185 *"Elect Robert Barnwell Rhett"*: Mercury, October 26, 1860.

185 *"For God's sake"*: J. J. Wardlaw to Samuel McGowan, letter, December 3, 1860, quoted in Davis, Rhett, 404.

186 *"spavined old horse"*: Davis, Rhett, 392.

246   NOTES

186   *"It is undoubtedly"*: Ibid., 392.

186   *"the gross injustice"*: *New York Tribune,* December 13, 1860.

186   *"The Union is dissolved"*: *Mercury,* December 1, 1860.

Chapter Twenty-Nine: The Flight of Reason

187   *"The air smells strongly"*: Edward Laight Wells to John Wells, letter, December 4, 1860, Papers of the Smith and Wells Families, 1856–1914, South Caroliniana Library.

187   *"The all-absorbing"*: Edward Laight Wells to Thomas L. Wells, letter, December 6, 1860, Papers of the Smith and Wells Families, 1856–1914, South Caroliniana Library.

187   *"became warmly imbued"*: *Mercury,* November 30, 1860.

188   *"three rousing cheers"*: Signed SORREL of the Charleston Light Dragoons, *Mercury,* December 15, 1860.

188   *"is too small for a Republic"*: James Louis Petigru to Benjamin Franklin Perry, letter, December 8, 1860, quoted in James M. McPherson, *Drawn with the Sword: Reflections on the American Civil War* (New York: Oxford University Press, 1996), 37.

189   *"Men, it has been"*: Charles Mackay, *Extraordinary Popular Delusions and the Madness of Crowds* (London: Office of the National Illustrated Library, 1852), xv–xvi.

189   *"I dare say"*: William Woodcock to Henry Gourdin, letter, December 10, 1860, quoted in Racine, *Gentlemen Merchants,* 408.

190   *"my old fellow-citizens"*: Richard Lathers to Henry Gourdin, Christopher Gustavus Memminger, A. G. Magrath, Nelson Mitchell, and George A. Trenholm, letter, November 28, 1860, quoted in Alvin F. Sanborn, ed., *Reminiscences of Richard Lathers* (New York: Grafton, 1907), 74–80.

190   *"There is no"*: Henry Gourdin and A. G. Magrath to Richard Lathers, letter, December 8, 1860, in Sanborn, *Reminiscences of Richard Lathers,* 83–91.

190   *"If war is"*: Henry Gourdin to Richard Lathers, letter, December 12, 1860, in Sanborn, *Reminiscences of Richard Lathers,* 81–82.

190   *"fears expressed"*: James Mercer Green to Robert Gourdin, letter, December 15, 1860, quoted in Racine, *Gentlemen Merchants,* 414.

190   *"Pray heaven that"*: John M. Richardson to Robert Gourdin, letter, December 14, 1860, quoted in Racine, *Gentleman Merchants,* 412–413.

191   *"Sir, if Alabama"*: John W. Pratt to Robert Gourdin, letter, December 10, 1860, quoted in Racine, *Gentleman Merchants,* 411.

191 *"as you must understand"*: New York Tribune, dispatch, December 13, 1860, published December 18, 1860.

191 *"I will state"*: New York Tribune, quoted in *Prairie Farmer,* vol. 22, 410.

191 *"Thus there exists"*: New York Tribune, December 18, 1860.

191 *"South Carolina May Well"*: Mercury, December 15, 1860.

192 *"which Great Britain views with horror"*: Robert Bunch and Robert Barnwell Rhett, Sr., quoted in Christopher Dickey, *Our Man in Charleston: Britain's Secret Agent in the Civil War* (New York: Crown, 2015), 183.

192 *"indulges in an abundance"*: Robert Bunch, note, January 8, 1861, British Foreign Office, 5, vol. 781, reprinted in White, *Rhett,* 190.

192 *"You need no"*: E. C. Anderson to Robert Gourdin, letter, December 11, 1860, quoted in Crawford, *Genesis of the Civil War,* 69.

192 *"Your sentiments"*: Robert Gourdin to E. C. Anderson, letter, December 16, 1860, quoted in Racine, *Gentlemen Merchants,* 415.

193 *"It seems strange"*: Meta Morris Grimball, entry December 15, 1860, Journal of Meta Morris Grimball, of South Carolina: December, 1860–February 1866, Southern Historical Collection, University of North Carolina.

Chapter Thirty: "To Dare"

194 *"the gravest, ablest"*: Quoted in Henry Alexander White, *The Making of South Carolina* (New York: Silver, Burdett, 1906), 219.

195 *"To dare!"*: Full text of "Journal of the Convention of the People of South Carolina, Held in 1860, 1861, and 1862" (Columbia, SC: R.W. Gibbes, 1862), 4.

195 *"To a New Yorker"*: New York World, quoted in S. L. Kotar and J. E. Gessler, *Smallpox: A History* (Jefferson, NC: McFarland, 2013), 143.

195 *"Is there any spot"*: John A. Inglis, transcript, Mercury, December 19, 1860.

196 *"We would be sneered at"*: William Porcher Miles, transcript, Mercury December 19, 1860.

196 *"Our brave secessionists"*: Benjamin Franklin Perry Papers, quoted in Freehling, *Road to Disunion,* vol. 2, 422.

196 *"Charleston Police"*: (Columbia) South Carolinian, quoted in Kotar and Gessler, *Smallpox,* 143.

197 *"permanent institution"*: Mercury, December 18, 1860.

197 *"composed for"*: Mercury, December 19, 1860.

198 *"I only want"*: James M. Johnson to Henry Ellison, letter, December 19, 1860, quoted in Johnson and Roark, *No Chariot Let Down,* 143.

198 *"It is now"*: James M. Johnson to Henry Ellison, letter, December 23, 1860, quoted in Johnson and Roark, *No Chariot Let Down,* 147.

198   *"We are by birth"*: Petition presented to Thomas J. Gantt, n.d., South Carolina Historical Society.

198   *"We ask to be heard"*: *Mercury* transcript, December 19, 1860.

198   *"to prepare an address"*: Ibid.

199   *"to debate intelligently"*: James Lawrence Orr, *Mercury* transcript, December 19, 1860.

199   accosted as a *"Yankee"*: Gunn diaries, vol. 17, 7–12.

Chapter Thirty-One: "Wine and Rejoicing"

200   *"some crowd on any night"*: *Mercury* transcript, December 20, 1860.

200   *"The excitement here"*: *Mercury,* December 19, 1860.

200   *"may be said"*: *Mercury,* December 20, 1860.

200   *"we are not"*: *Mercury,* December 19, 1860.

201   *"It seems that"*: *Mercury* transcript, December 20, 1860.

201   *"The Union is being"*: Nina Glover to Mrs. C. J. Bowen, letter, December 21, 1860, Caroline Howard Gilman Papers, South Carolina Historical Society.

201   *"The feeling exhibited"*: Crawford, *Genesis of the Civil War,* 52.

201   *"by a number"*: *Mercury,* December 20, 1860.

202   *"Before the sun sets"*: Robert Gourdin to John W. Ellis, letter, December 20, 1860, quoted in Racine, *Gentlemen Merchants,* 417.

203   *"And then a mighty"*: Porter, *Led On!,* 118.

203   *"The whole heart"*: Crawford, *Genesis of the Civil War,* 55.

203   *"the loud acclamations"*: Ibid., 55.

203   *"their lives"*: Lossing, *Pictorial History,* 104.

203   *"Unnumbered fading"*: Ibid., 104.

204   *"Where's the fire?"*: Carson, *Life, Letters, and Speeches of Petigru,* 364.

204   *"If there were any"*: Porter, *Led On!,* 118.

204   *"This is the commencement"*: Jacob Schirmer, diary entry, December 20, 1860, Alfred Schirmer Papers, South Carolina Historical Society, quoted in W. A. Swanberg, *First Blood: The Story of Fort Sumter* (New York: Charles Scribner's Sons, 1984), 81.

204   *"So many were proud"*: Caroline Howard Gilman, letter, n.d., Caroline Howard Gilman Papers, South Carolina Historical Society.

205   *"there is no hope"*: Quoted in Swanberg, *First Blood,* 81.

205   *"as the envoy"*: Ibid.

205   *"To us it sounded"*: James W. Hunnicutt, *The Conspiracy Revealed: The South Sacrificed; or, the Horrors of Secession* (Philadelphia, PA: J. B. Lippincott, 1863), 93.

205 *"leaping and clapping"*: Glover to Bowen, December 21, 1860.

205 *"Wid a blue cockade"*: Rhett Family Papers, Claudine Rhett's Writings of the Civil War, the Charleston Museum.

205 *"It is very diverting"*: James M. Johnson to Henry Ellison, letter, December 23, 1860, quoted in Johnson and Roark, *No Chariot Let Down*, 147.

205 *"we may, if possible"*: Robert Gourdin to John W. Ellis, letter, December 20, 1860, quoted in Racine, *Gentlemen Merchants*, 418.

Chapter Thirty-Two: "Blood Must Be Shed!"

207 *"wisdom from on high"*: Charles H. Lesser, *Relic of the Lost Cause: The Story of South Carolina's Ordinance of Secession* (Columbia: South Carolina Department of Archives and History, 1990), 9.

207 *"consecrated parchment"*: *Mercury*, December 21, 1860.

208 *"I proclaim the State"*: "Journal of the Convention of the People of South Carolina," 49.

208 *"as if there"*: Edmund Ruffin, diary entry, December 21, 1860, 513.

208 *"Everyone wears a pleased"*: Robert Bunch, quoted in Dickey, *Our Man in Charleston*, 195.

208 *"I carried a lantern"*: Simon Baruch, quoted in *Confederate Veteran* 23 (August 1915): 343. Baruch's father, Bernard Baruch—born in Camden, South Carolina, in 1870—became a famous Wall Street financier and adviser to presidents.

209 *"Allow me to say"*: Francis W. Pickens, quoted in *Mercury*, December 22, 1860.

209 *"everybody is drunk"*: James C. Johnston to J. Johnston Pettigrew, letter, January 2, 1861, Pettigrew Family Papers, South Carolina Historical Society, quoted in William Kauffman Scarborough, *Masters of the Big House: Elite Slaveholders of the Mid-Nineteenth-Century South* (Baton Rouge: Louisiana State University Press, 2003), 292.

209 *"What a volcano"*: Caroline Howard Gilman to her children, letter, December 24, 1860, Caroline Howard Gilman Papers, South Carolina Historical Society.

209 *"In the stillness"*: Caroline Howard Gilman to her children, n.d., Caroline Howard Gilman Papers, South Carolina Historical Society.

210 *"Declaration of the Immediate"*: pamphlet printed by Evans and Cogswell, Charleston.

210 *"to express the deep"*: Doubleday, *Reminiscences*, 56.

210 *"Mr. Petigru alone"*: Chesnut, *Diary from Dixie*, June 12, 1861, 63.

210 *"I made a great mistake"*: James Louis Petigru to Jane Petigru North, letter, December 24, 1860, quoted in Carson, *Life, Letters, and Speeches of Petigru,* 363–364.

211 *"We are in the midst"*: W. T. Sherman to George Mason Graham, letter, December 25, 1860, in Brooks D. Simpson and Jean V. Berlin, *Sherman's Civil War: Selected Correspondence of William T. Sherman, 1860–1865* (Chapel Hill: University of North Carolina Press, 1999), 27.

211 *"I only have time"*: Robert Anderson to Robert Gourdin, December 27, 1860, note, quoted in Crawford, *Genesis of the Civil War,* 128.

212 *"The wildest rumors"*: Porter, *Led On!,* 120.

212 *"Major Anderson has achieved"*: *Courier,* December 28, 1860, quoted in *New York Times,* December 30, 1860.

212 *"they would be heard"*: Crawford, *Genesis of the Civil War,* 108–109.

212 *"as a good soldier"*: Porter, *Led On!,* 121.

212 *"There will be no war"*: Ibid., 122.

212 *"in a blaze of excitement"*: Business agent of Christy's Minstrels, letter, March 16, 1861, printed in "Charleston in a Blaze of Excitement," *New York Clipper,* quoted in Joanne Martell, ed., *Firsthand Accounts of Holiday Happenings from Early Days to Modern Times* (Winston-Salem, NC: John F. Blair, 2005).

213 *"at this festive season"*: John Boone DeSaussare to Mary Amarinthia Snowden, letter, December 29, 1960, Mary Amarinthia Snowden Papers.

Aftermath: "City of Desolation"

214 *"Ruin—ruin—ruin"*: *Harper's Weekly,* March 25, 1865, quoted in Maurie D. McInnis, *The Politics of Taste in Antebellum Charleston* (Chapel Hill: University of North Carolina Press, 2005), 1.

214 *"of rotting wharves"*: Sidney Andrews, reporter for *Boston Advertiser* and *Chicago Tribune,* on visit to Charleston in September 1865, quoted in Robert N. Rosen, *Confederate Charleston: An Illustrated History of the City and the People During the Civil War* (Columbia: University of South Carolina Press, 1994), 2.

215 *"It would appear"*: P. G. T. Beauregard to General Quincy Gilmore, August 21, 1863, quoted in Clint Johnson, *A Vast and Fiendish Plot: The Confederate Attack on New York City* (New York: Citadel Press, 2010), 92.

215 *"a heap of ruins"*: November 1863 visit by Jefferson Davis to Charleston, cited in Robert N. Rosen, *A Short History of Charleston* (Columbia: University of South Carolina Press, 1982), 118.

215   *"If there is any city"*: New York Tribune, June 9, 1862, quoted in Douglas W. Bostick, *Charleston Under Siege: The Impregnable City* (Charleston, SC: History Press, 2010), 34.

215   *"When the army"*: Soldiers from Harrisburg, Pennsylvania, marching with General William T. Sherman, correspondence to *Harrisburg Telegraph,* reprinted in Andrew S. Coopersmith, *Fighting Words: An Illustrated History of Newspaper Accounts of the Civil War* (New York: New Press, 2004), 222.

215   *"great Parrott gun"*: Herman Melville's note on the poem, quoted in Robert Penn Warren, ed., *Selected Poems of Herman Melville* (New York: Random House, 1967), 370.

216   *"I'se waited for you"*: Quoted in W. Scott Poole, *South Carolina's Civil War: A Narrative History* (Macon, GA: Mercer University Press, 2005), 156.

216   *"a fan for"*: Rosen, *Short History of Charleston,* 122.

216   *"No caste, no color"*: Poole, *South Carolina's Civil War,* 158.

216   *"remorseless traitors"*: Ibid., 159.

216   *"Sobs and loud"*: Esther Hawks (director of a Charleston school for black pupils), diary entry, April 22, 1865, quoted in Carolyn L. Harrell, *When the Bells Tolled for Lincoln: Southern Reaction to the Assassination* (Macon, GA: Mercer University Press, 1997), 57.

216   *"picturesque"*: Unidentified Northern visitor, quoted in Don Harrison Doyle, *New Men, New Cities, New South: Atlanta, Nashville, Charleston, Mobile, 1860–1910* (Chapel Hill: University of North Carolina Press, 1990), 56.

216   *"the old familiar streets"*: William T. Sherman, *Memoirs of General William T. Sherman* (New York: Da Capo, 1984), 369.

217   *"Anyone who is not"*: William T. Sherman, *General Sherman's Official Account of His Great March Through Georgia and the Carolinas* (New York: Bunce and Huntington, 1865), 130.

217   *"my tutor in boyhood"*: Robert Barnwell Rhett, Sr., in *Memorial of the Late James L. Petigru,* March 25, 1863 (Charleston, SC: Walker, Evans, and Cogswell), 25–33.

217   *"Fear not to die"*: A. G. Magrath, appeal to people of South Carolina, printed in *Philadelphia Inquirer,* February 17, 1865.

217   *"I am wearied"*: A. G. Magrath, letter, November 15, 1865, Magrath Papers, South Caroliniana Library, University of South Carolina.

217   *"motive power"*: A. G. Magrath, letter, November 20, 1865, Magrath Papers, South Caroliniana Library, University of South Carolina, quoted in Cauthen, *South Carolina Goes to War,* 71–72.

218   *"I, John Townsend"*: Quoted in Graydon, *Tales of Edisto,* 19.

218 *"a strong pine case"*: Robert Gourdin to Andrew P. Calhoun, letter, April 6, 1863, quoted in Racine, *Gentlemen Merchants,* 580.

218 *"Southern independence"*: Henry Gourdin to F. C. Matthiessen, letter, February 23, 1865, quoted in Racine, *Gentlemen Merchants,* 750.

219 *"You treat us"*: William A. Spicer, *The Flag Replaced on Sumter: A Personal Narrative* (Providence, RI: Providence Press, 1885), 29.

219 *"the Yankees, the authors"*: Robert Gourdin to Louis Gourdin Young, letter, July 15, 1865, quoted in Racine, *Gentlemen Merchants,* 775.

219 *"When we see"*: William Porcher Miles to Robert Gourdin, letter, quoted in Walther, *Fire-Eaters,* 292.

219 *"permanently disfiguring"*: *Post and Courier,* May 22, 2014.

219 *"I cannot survive"*: Lossing, *Pictorial History,* 48.

220 *"to discharge the duties"*: Christopher Gustavus Memminger to Andrew Johnson, memorial, quoted in Capers, *Life and Times of Memminger,* 381.

220 *"I have faith"*: Robert Barnwell Rhett, Jr., "A Farewell to the Subscribers of the *Charleston Mercury,*" *Mercury,* n.d. (1868), Rhett, Jr., Papers, South Caroliniana Library, University of South Carolina.

220 *"Most humiliating"*: Robert Barnwell Rhett, Sr., to "My Dear Kate," letter, June 9, 1867, quoted in Scarborough, "Propagandists for Secession," 138.

220 *"Poor fellows"*: Henry Schulz Holmes, diary entry, n.d. (1896), Holmes Papers, South Caroliniana Library, University of South Carolina.

221 *"deed was done"*: Porter, *Led On!,* 119.

Index

253

Christians. *See* religion and faith

church(es). *See* African Church; Episcopal church(es)

Citadel Green, 27, 90, 138

civic unrest, 156–158, 166

Civil War, 1–3

blacks in, 215–216

Charleston fate during and after, 214–221

class prejudice, 101–102

Clay, Henry, 41, 61, 77, 110

clergy. *See* religion and faith

Cohen, Aaron Nathan, 66

Colcock, William Ferguson, 151, 153

Colt, A. H., 199

Columbia, 156, 176

Columbia, South Carolina

secession concerns from, 158–159

Secession Convention in, 194–195

smallpox in, 191, 195

Committee of Safety, 25–26

Common Sense (Paine), 131–132

Confederacy, 140, 215

Townsend on border states and, 87

veterans reunion, 220–221

See also "Southern Republic"

Congress, U.S.

slave trade banned by, 113

state representation in, 16, 40

Conner, James, 150, 151, 153

the Constitution, 164, 210

Constitutional Convention. *See* Seceding Convention

Cooper, Thomas, 110

Cooper Union speech, 76–77

Cooperationist(s), 118

Magrath as, 20, 147

Rhett, Sr., defeat by, 10–11, 54

cotton production, 82–83, 86, 88, 192

The Courier, 15, 88, 124, 138, 140

Courtenay, William Ashmead, 137

Crawford, Samuel Wylie, 121, 173, 201, 203

Crean, Mary Walsingham, 127

Cushing, Caleb, 48–49, 52, 53, 56, 67, 204–205

Dana, Charles Anderson, 177–178, 180

Dana, William C., 172

Darwin, Charles, 28, 172–173, 189

Davis, Jefferson, 158–159, 215

De Bow, James Dunwoody Brownson, 143, 153

De Bow's Review, 81, 143

debt. *See* financial system

Declaration of Independence, 90, 127

Democratic National Convention, 22, 54

commerce surrounding, 45

delegates and accommodations at, 43–44

delegates remaining after breakup of, 67–68

Douglas delegation at, 43–44, 51, 56, 64

Dred Scott case and, 51, 55, 56

hopes for, 46–47

journey to, 42–43

nomination failure at, 66

Perry speech at, 64–65, 107

preparation and supplies for, 42, 44

press at, 44–45, 48

setting for, 40–41, 48, 49–50

slavery debates at, 52

Paul Starobin has been a frequent contributor to the *Atlantic* and the *New Republic* and is a former Moscow bureau chief for *Business Week*. His writing on history, politics, and culture has appeared in the *Wall Street Journal*, the *New York Times*, and the *Washington Post*, among other publications. He is the author of *After America: Narratives for the Next Global Age*, and he lives with his family in Orleans, Massachusetts.

Photograph by Kim Reilly, Studio K Photography

PublicAffairs is a publishing house founded in 1997. It is a tribute to the standards, values, and flair of three persons who have served as mentors to countless reporters, writers, editors, and book people of all kinds, including me.

I. F. STONE, proprietor of *I. F. Stone's Weekly*, combined a commitment to the First Amendment with entrepreneurial zeal and reporting skill and became one of the great independent journalists in American history. At the age of eighty, Izzy published *The Trial of Socrates*, which was a national bestseller. He wrote the book after he taught himself ancient Greek.

BENJAMIN C. BRADLEE was for nearly thirty years the charismatic editorial leader of *The Washington Post*. It was Ben who gave the *Post* the range and courage to pursue such historic issues as Watergate. He supported his reporters with a tenacity that made them fearless and it is no accident that so many became authors of influential, best-selling books.

ROBERT L. BERNSTEIN, the chief executive of Random House for more than a quarter century, guided one of the nation's premier publishing houses. Bob was personally responsible for many books of political dissent and argument that challenged tyranny around the globe. He is also the founder and longtime chair of Human Rights Watch, one of the most respected human rights organizations in the world.

·   ·   ·

For fifty years, the banner of Public Affairs Press was carried by its owner Morris B. Schnapper, who published Gandhi, Nasser, Toynbee, Truman, and about 1,500 other authors. In 1983, Schnapper was described by *The Washington Post* as "a redoubtable gadfly." His legacy will endure in the books to come.

Peter Osnos, *Founder and Editor-at-Large*

21982318451428